LAUGH ON THE WAY TO HEAVEN

Laugh on the Way to Heaven

My Journey with the Spirit Agnos

for Jennifer,
It's all about love
and the courage to show it.

TOM CURTIS

Tom Curtis

SEABOARD PRESS

JAMES A. ROCK & COMPANY, PUBLISHERS

Laugh on the Way to Heaven:
My Journey with the Spirit Agnos by Tom Curtis
SEABOARD PRESS

is an imprint of JAMES A. ROCK & CO., PUBLISHERS

Laugh on the Way to Heaven:
My Journey with the Spirit Agnos copyright ©2007 by Tom Curtis

Address comments and inquiries to:
SEABOARD PRESS
9710 Traville Gateway Drive, #305
Rockville, MD 20850

E-mail:
jrock@rockpublishing.com   lrock@rockpublishing.com
Internet URL: www.rockpublishing.com

Trade Paperback ISBN: 978-1-59663-561-6

Library of Congress Control Number: 2007924149

Printed in the United States of America

First Edition: 2007

Table of Contents

Chapter 9

CHRISTMAS

Chapter 10

MYTHOLOGY

Chapter 11

DEMONS

Chapter 12

WAR

Acknowledgments
Prologue and Dedication

My gratitude is owed to Bridget Olson who taught a fourteen year old boy with wavering self esteem that he had an inquisitive voice and a talent for turning a phrase well enough to entertain others. Bridget, you transformed my life.

John Judson further encouraged me at university, informing me of my progression beyond just the mechanics of writing. I played the game. I remember your explanation of how literature informs us better than anything else that we are not alone. Thank you, John.

Lilda RockWiley, Lynne Rock and James Rock have been comfortably friendly and gracious, helping me take this next step to sharing my thoughts with a wider audience. Thank you Lilda, Lynne and Jim and all those at James A. Rock Publishing who have made this book happen. My experience with them has taught me that a book is not really done when an author passes it along to the publisher. Although I drew the cover illustration, it was Lynne's idea to focus attention on the beanie by itself as it is on the back cover. Thank you, Lynne. People to whom I've shown this have all said, "I love the beanie." Besides being cute, the beanie is a metaphor for attempting the seemingly impossible with little more than imagination and courage. If you want, it also can represent agape found even in small packages. Again thank you, Lynne.

Dan Kurtti and I met in 1980, as Navy medical officers caring for marines on the island of Okinawa. That was a year with time enough to exercise regularly and to talk about the meaningful questions of life that have no clear answers.

For orderliness, marines at Camp Hanson ran the three mile perimeter in counter-clockwise direction, everybody the same direction, but one night Dan and I ran it clockwise against the flow. It was late in the evening on a clear, starry night, and soon into the run we came across a young marine running the correct direction toward us. Dan said, "At least we're not alone."

Looking up into that beautiful sky I answered, "Yes, we know there's an Intelligence out there somewhere." That scene resembles the personality of this book.

Dan and I went our separate ways, communicating by holiday letters, and then in January of 2005, I visited him and his lovely wife, Yuko. Into the wee hours we again discussed the meaningful, unanswerable questions most people ask at some time or another.

Dan and I describe ourselves as spiritual agnostics, and that was part of the origin of this book. Dan's contributions have helped to shape this book into a more complex and interesting work than it would have been if only I had written it.

Thank you, Dan, for suffering some of the slings and arrows with me. Also, nice work!

Sven Conradi and I met in 1990, at Sunnaas Sykehus in Nesodden, Norway, a magnificent rehabilitation hospital just south of Oslo, nestled in the woods atop a peninsula in the fjord. When I worked there for a year and struggled with personal problems, Sven taught me that the person for whom I had been given greatest responsibility to nurture was myself. Sven, thank you for your friendship and contributions.

Tom Sproger is the friend who sat with me mornings before work in the European Deli, drinking coffee and laughing. That also was during a time of trouble for me, and Tom taught me how to forgive myself, a Jew teaching a Christian how to forgive! Go figure. My experience with Tom has prompted me to announce, "The next time you see Christ, he just may be a Jew." Thank you, Tom, for your friendship and contributions.

Ben Huddleston was the discussion professional aboard bus 941 who brought the rest of us out of our shy, personal caves into the light of hooting and hollering. Ben has been an idea factory for me. Thank you, Ben.

Ryan Curtis, my nephew, and Joshua Curtis, my son, have contributed laudable pieces to this book. Both of you have inspired me.

Marcia Wollam has instigated thought by sending clever articles and stories that remind me of the wonderful creativity of other writers. Marcia, thank you for that and for your eloquently presented challenge in the final chapter of this book.

My brother Stan, a Methodist minister, has been a critical mentor allowing me to find my own way, to arrive at conclusions different than his own, but he always has insisted that I measure up to standards of respectable theological discourse. He and I have had several arguments that increased our love for one another. Thank you, Stan for your contributions, but more for your generosity of spirit and guidance.

Beverly Kenyon is my sister who, when we were kids, protected me bodily from Stan. Thank you, Bev. Without you this book might never have been written.

Harold and Alberta more than anyone else made me who I am. Thank you, Mom and Dad.

Thank you to the approximately fifty people on my email distribution list, *The Willing*. I have written better because I had an audience.

Thank you to my patients who shared the intimacy of sometimes startling lives. You have enriched me.

My wife Barbara provided an environment that allowed me to write honestly, and she comforted me when my boldness took me beyond my own barriers into despair or anxiety. At those times when I leapt before looking, she caught me. Barb, thank you for all you have given to me and our children. We are so lucky that you are part of us.

Christoffer, Joshua and Stella; this book is yours, so that you will know who I am even after I no longer can cuddle you in my arms and laughter. I hope reading this book will help you understand how very much happiness you have given me. I'm never going to let you go; no, no, no!

Here is my heart and soul on paper, given to all you who read it. Thank you. It is fine with me if you merely enjoy it, but if it moves you to deeper thought or reverence for our universe, or love for our fellow beings, so much the better. I started out just wanting to write humor, and then something happened. This book is the result.

Father, you pushed me into this, and I hope you're satisfied. Thank you for giving me life.

ONE

Creation

1. IN THE BEGINNING

In the beginning was a void, and the void was with me, and the void was me. Oh yeah, there also was the page. There was the void that was me, and there was the page, but the page was blank.

A voice cried out to the cosmos, and it was my voice. It was an appeal to the muses of the spheres. I would dedicate myself to a muse.

Let me take just a moment here to let you in on a little something that I wish I knew before I started crying out to the muses. Listen now because this is good advice. If you ever decide to appeal to the muses be specific with your request.

My voice accosted the spirits of the universe, beyond the reaches of science into the potentialities of the quantum world. I cast forth my beseeching devotion for days, and finally a voice whispered back to me, "For what do you search little babe little babble? Is there more to you here than the sound of your prattle? Before you, behind you, it sings all around you, the rabble, the battle, little babe little babble?" Then it started chuckling, "I really don't know how much more of this mysterious act I can take. Stop me before I hurt myself. You want something?"

Like a child's rhyme it whispered to me, or was I whispering to myself? I asked, "Who is there?"

"Agnos."

"Agnos? Who are you, Agnos?"

"I am Agnos."

"What do you mean by Agnos?"

"I don't know."

This intrigued me. It was sort of like the answer given by God in the Old Testament, "I am who I am." Pretty lame.

1

I reassured the whispering spirit, "Okay, so you don't know what your name means. Big deal. Don't let it get you down."

"I do know what my name means."

"You do? So what does it mean?"

"I don't know."

It was time to change the subject. I didn't care to get caught in one of those Abbot and Costello routines. So I asked Agnos, "Would you like a cheese sandwich? I can make one that looks like the Virgin Mary."

Agnos said, "Spirits don't eat of the material world."

"That's cool," I said. "It's the same with us material people; we don't always eat either."

Agnos responded, "Man does not live by bread alone, but by every word uttered by the mouth of God."

"So you believe in God?" I asked.

"I don't know. I am Agnos."

"Why did you say that bit about man living by the words of God?"

"It's a nice line. I like to think about it."

My voice had called out to the muses of the spheres, and it was Agnos who showed up. He was an unassuming character, mysterious and even a bit charismatic. I asked him, "So how can you help me write?"

"My gift is that I do not know the answers to important questions."

"That's a gift?"

"Yes. If I do not know, and I know that I do not know, then I will continue to seek. If one seeks, then one finds."

"But if you find something, then you know it, right?"

"Not necessarily. Maybe I'll believe something, but knowing it? I am Agnos."

I decided to give it a shot. "Agnos, how would you like to help me write a book?"

He answered, "I don't know."

2. WHAT'S IT ALL ABOUT?

Agnos wanted to know why I'm writing this book.

A few years ago a group of us were talking about violence in the Middle East, and one of my friends, Mehran, said that in order for the violence to end, "We need to evolve." That stuck with me.

We fight each other because we perceive ourselves as being members of a group that's different from others. Long ago such a mind-set had protective value. A person belonging to a group derived protection from that group against wandering bands of thieves or cutthroats. In

Darwinian terms, a person who identified with a group had selective advantage, and so our minds and societies evolved along these lines.

But then groups fought against other groups, and later it became nation against nation, alliance against alliance. Ronald Reagan once commented that if the Earth were confronted by an external, alien assailant, nations of the world would unite in a common goal of defending ourselves. Of course he was right, but this again would be group against group of a grander, cosmic scale.

If we want peace we must stop perceiving ourselves as different. If each of us recognizes that we are of the same group, then there may be peace. For this to happen, Mehran said we need to evolve. Our minds, our societies, our religions need to evolve.

Agnos answered, "Seems you've already got this figured out."

"Not quite. People are not going to abandon ways they have believed and lived for centuries, even though they can see that things aren't working the way they are. Maybe there is some hope for some of them if a compelling argument can be made."

"I don't know about that," Agnos said, and of course that is the key to learning. Admit you don't know. Start out with a premise and go from there. "What's your premise?" He asked.

"If there is one God, then he is God of us all. What we believe must apply and fit for all people. That is a necessary test for wherever our wandering leads us."

"But what if there is not a God?"

"Then we all still are in the same boat. We are together in our aloneness. Or if maybe we are never to know, then we are united by our agnosticism."

"I can be useful there."

"Yes, I know. Welcome aboard."

"What if there are many gods, lots of them?"

"Then Agnos, my friend, we're screwed."

"Isn't that the way it is? The Jews say there is no other God but Yahweh, and the Christians say Jesus is God. Muslims say no God but Allah, and Hindus talk about the Brahman. There are lots of different gods."

"Agnos, even though what you say is true, each of these religions believes that their own God is God for all people. We just perceive him differently."

"And so differences of perception are what instigate and warrant war between factions? There even are wars of Muslim against Muslim and Catholic against Protestant. People are like unruly children fighting without parental guidance."

"Yes, and that will be our second premise. People will stop fighting only with appropriate parental guidance."

"Okay. What was the first premise again?"

"If there is a God who created this world, then he is God of all that there is."

"What if God is a great big bastard who hates Children?"

"Agnos?"

"Well, you never know. All this 'God is Love' business is an assumption, isn't it? What if God is an ornery, junk yard dog with fleas, and he hasn't had his breakfast yet?"

"I hope in that case I would defy such a God."

"He'd eat you for breakfast. Do you know what a Buddhist would say? A Buddhist would tell you that the matter of God, heaven or hell; these things are not pertinent questions to ask because they cannot be answered on this plane of existence."

"So Buddhists are agnostic?"

"No, they just meditate their way to another plane, and then when they come back they tell us that their experience can't be explained with words."

"Everything can be explained with words if the writer is talented enough."

"You're not Buddhist, are you?"

"You don't think I'm Buddhist?"

"I don't know. Maybe you are. Maybe we all are Buddhists, and most of us just don't know it yet. I'll have to meditate on that. O-o-o-o-o-o-o-o-m. Nope we're not."

"How do you know?"

"Can't be put into words."

3. SPLOG

Splog is short for spam log. It's what I do. It's a lot like blogging except it gets delivered right to the doorstep of its lucky recipients. My mailing list is called *The Willing*.

At a dinner party I asked a gentleman sitting on my right what he liked to do in his free time, and I listened awhile to his bicycling stories. Then he asked me what I do. I told him about splogging, and suddenly he became sullen, quiet, and turned to talk to the person on his other side. Later when he turned back to me he held his fork and knife like a cross between himself and me.

That's the effect I can have on people. Sometimes they hold crosses between themselves and me. Get back Spam Demon.

Actually receiving a short splog isn't such a bad thing every now and then, especially mine. I specialize in quality splog. Enjoy.

4. BIG BANG

Dan Kurtti, DK from the heartland, wrote to me, and here is what he said. I worry about the big things, things too big to worry about. What happened before the Big Bang? Probably a lot. This may have been the 46th Big Bang. Here on Earth we are grandiose. It probably wasn't very big at all. Our Bang probably was a mediocre Bang.

Using the Big Bang-o-meter scientists have determined our Big Bang measured only a four on the UCS (Universal Creation Scale). While it disappointed the research team on Mount Palomar that our Bang was so small, they were quick to point out the last three Big Bangs before this were only 2.7, 3.8 and 3.3. There was a real whopper ten universes ago when the participants experienced a 7.7.

Actually in the story of the Universe, the Big Bang is chapter eleven. Here's an excerpt from chapter one: When God woke up from her deep slumber, she realized something was amiss. Space? … gone! Time? … gone! Her Timex watch? … missing! It was obvious she had a tremendous amount of work to do. "I am going to think this one out very carefully," she said. "It's going to be extra special."

The Pagan (Earth) religions give equal time to the feminine goddess and the masculine god. I have my own names for God: MOM (Mystical Oriental Mother) and POP (Paternalistic Occidental Person).

My brother died in 1991 at the age of 48. In my grief I turned to POP and asked, "Couldn't there have been some other way?"

POP can be quite tight lipped. He just said, "No."

I asked him, "Why did this have to happen?"

He said, "Because." He certainly is a god of few words.

Then I approached MOM and asked, "I'm hurting deep down, MOM. Can't we bring my brother back?"

She replied, "No dear. That is impossible in this physical realm. The laws of the universe can't be broken by such a deed."

Then I asked her the same question I had asked POP. "Why did this happen?"

She said, "You are so young, Sweetie, and there are many things you just don't understand yet. You're a babe, only in year 42 of the 12th life-time in the Earth phase of your physical universe educational program. Just remember this: Bad things do happen to good people. She then gave me a warm hug. I didn't understand any more by her reply, but I felt comforted by her action.

I have thought long and hard about why this universe was created and have come up with two theories.

In the psychic realm God was going psychotic. In dreams and in after-death experiences thought can instantly manifest into a situation. God's thoughts were going much too fast. In fact they were racing. Many experiences were manifesting too quickly. The psychic realm, Heaven, was accelerating at a faster and faster pace. "Stop the World; I want to get off!" God shouted. He needed a rock solid realm with very strict rules, (time, space, gravity, mass, etc.) in order to stabilize his thoughts. Secret exposed: God has a bipolar affective disorder.

The second theory is that God needed a warm hug, something not done in a psychic world. The hug is God's most satisfying creation. If you would like to give God a warm embrace, and he could use one right now, hug your children or your spouse or your parents, or the filthy, stinking bum asking you for a buck so he can buy a beer. God will appreciate that.

5. HAVE YOUR CAKE AND EAT IT TOO

In response to DK's letter I splogged the following.

Most people are more comfortable with a concept of time reaching eternally backward into the past rather than yielding to the scientifi-cally espoused idea of the Big (or mediocre) Bang, before which, well before which there was no before. That is to say, time did not exist.

We have trouble understanding or believing there was a time when there was no time, and so we resort to the Hindu concept that this Big (or mediocre) Bang is just one of many. This is why charlatans have been able to sell us on these Bang-o-meters. It is simply a money mak-ing market scheme, much like therapeutic magnets. I used to say, "Go ahead and buy that crap. At least it's not going to hurt you." Then I found out how much these things cost. Magneto-therapy has come down a bit mainly because of the shear volume of sales, but how many people do you know who own their own Bang-o-meter? You should see the budget request NASA has made to purchase theirs. You'd throw a fit.

I'm not so much a believer in multiple Big (or mediocre) Bangs, and it's not just because I never know how to pronounce it. Is it bang-AHH-meter? Or is it BANG-oh-MEET-her?

If God is as great as the marquis would have us believe, then the world could have been created so we could have it both ways. We can have a very clear beginning of the universe, and we can have time that stretches eternally into the past. God is talented. We can have our cake and eat it too.

Now comes the hard part, explaining it to you. Actually this should be an expected result of Einstein's theory of relativity. If we were to take a time-travel machine far, far toward The Beginning, something like 13.7 billion years ago, we would see remarkable things.

By the way, I asked one of my time-traveling operatives if he would do this; take us all on such a trip. He growled at me and threatened to bite. You see, he admires and sometimes pretends to be Mr. Peabody from the Rocky and Bullwinkle show. His name is Peter, but he calls himself *P theBrain*, and he barks and calls me Sherman. Where do I find these guys? He actually had me fooled for awhile. I really thought he was Mr. Peabody, and I went around telling people that I had been bit by Mr. Peabody, but I hadn't. Mr. Peabody is not that kind of dog. I was bit by an imposter.

P the Brain calls his own time-traveling device his *Back Again Machine*, because things always are changed when he goes away and comes back again. He says menacingly, "When I get back again, Sherman, things will be different." Then poof, he's gone. Then poof, he's back again and my clothes smell faintly like urine.

If we did go back toward The Beginning we would see all the matter of the universe coming together toward a single point, and as this matter got closer and closer, it would travel faster and faster until it would be going damned near the speed of light. What that would mean is that time would nearly stop. As the universe continued to come together, faster and faster, gradually approaching the speed of light, time also would get slower and slower. So we'd never get there. We would approach The Beginning like the asymptotic curves you used to have to draw on graphs in algebra class.

Looking backward from the twenty-first century, the universe looks like it's about 13.7 billion years old, but if we were on Mr. P Brain's back again machine near The Beginning and approaching the speed of light, it would seem as though The Beginning continued to stretch backward say, 13.7 billion years. It also would be pretty tight with all that matter squeezing together. We'd be squashed like potato-bugs, forever.

My own mom used to tell me God always was and always will be. No beginning and no end. She was surprisingly on target.

Personally I don't think of God as a She or a He. Can you imagine the social mess it must have made when He had that affair with Mary, mother of Jesus? Whew! We won't even go there, not now. I think of God as an IT. IT is a wonderful, abstract and glorious IT, nicely fitting in with other ITs such as LOVE and TOLERANCE, APPRECIATION and ICE CREAM. There are a lot of ITS. They're all over the place.

6. I'M A BOOB

I got a telephone call. "Is this T the splogger?"

I was flattered. "Why, yes it is." I smiled.

"One moment please."

Then a robotic voice came on the line, and I know that sometimes I have a hard time hearing things correctly, but it sounded like the voice introduced itself as Thievin' Hawk King. Who would name their kid Thieving Hawk?

The robotic voice asked, "Are you the splogger who wrote that bit about the asymptotic curve at the beginning of time?"

"Yes."

"You're a boob."

"I'm a what?"

"A boob."

"A boob?"

"Yes."

"Curious way to start a conversation." I was perturbed.

"Look, may I call you T?"

"Certainly, if I may call you Thieving Hawk."

There was a long pause, and then he went on. "What if the curve isn't asymptotic? What if it's parabolic?"

"Parabolic?"

"Yes, you know, time would get slower and slower and then would suddenly get faster and faster again."

"How would that happen?"

Thieving Hawk continued patiently, "If all the matter of the universe came together toward a point, a singularity, it's quite possible that before it reached that singularity it would attain a critical status at which it would explode outward again."

"You mean another Big Bang."

"I mean another Big Bang."

"So you're telling me it wouldn't be right to put away the Hindu idea of multiple Big Bangs."

"I'm also telling you I'd like you not to make fun of my Big Bang-o-meter."

"You have a Big Bang-o-meter?" I was wondering because the cost would be prohibitive for most people.

"The university has one."

"So you like your bang-o-meter."

"I love my bang-o-meter."

"What do you do with it? I mean do you just measure Big Bang after Big Bang?"

"I also like to wax and polish it."

"You polish your bang-o-meter?"

"Every day."

"If there have been many Big Bangs, then there's still no answer to how this all began. How did the first Big Bang happen?"

Thieving Hawk didn't need any time at all to answer this one. "Chance," he said.

"Chance?" I asked.

"Yes, you see we now know that it is possible for matter to be created out of a void. It happens all the time at the borders of black holes. As long as there is an equal amount of matter and anti-matter created at the same time, matter can be created out of nothing at all."

"So God does that?"

"No need for a God."

"No need for a God?" I asked.

"Chance."

"Chance?"

"Chance. It just happens. Probability mathematics tells us such a thing can just plain happen, and as I've already said, it is happening all the time around the borders of black holes."

"Wow! So I guess we really don't know all the answers, do we?"

"Particularly you don't know the answers."

"Oh, well, uh … thank you, Thieving Hawk."

"Don't mention it."

7. ANVIL

Soon after DK's letter I splogged a colossal error. "In support of his MOM and POP perspective, DK from the heartland may point out that Jesus referred to God as 'Abba,' a term small children called their father, equivalent to 'Poppa.' Jesus wanted to dissuade us from the jealous, wrathful impression people had of God before that. So to the extent you are a Jesus addict, Jesus is the one who gave us a loving God." Oops!

I got another telephone call. This time the voice sounded familiar.

"Are you T the splogger?"

"Speaking."

"You're a boob."

"Hey, I've already done that routine."

"Not with me you haven't." It was my brother, Stan the Rev. "Don't quit your day job. When you and your friend, DK from the heartland, discuss theology you need to get some facts straight. The Hebrew people never considered God to be jealous or wrathful. That is a construct created by the church early on to keep people under control. For example, the Hebrew word that was translated as *fear,* such as in *The fear of God is the beginning of wisdom,* is more correctly translated as the *awe of God."*

As Stan went on I was beginning to feel sheepishly apologetic. "That was me who wrote that. You can leave DK out of this."

The Rev continued. "Jesus was not the one who gave us a loving God. The Jewish people already understood that God was loving. *But you are a God ready to forgive, gracious and merciful, slow to anger and abounding in steadfast love, and you did not forsake us.* Nehemiah 9:17."

Stan was bringing out the verses. I knew he'd cream me with the verses. It was about at that point I started wondering if any of you gentle readers might think I'm anti-Semitic. Sometimes we are blind to our own hidden racism. In medical school, two of my three roommates were Jewish, and it seemed we got along alright.

In fact, let me tell you a story about a Catholic girl I dated for awhile at Marquette University. I hadn't asked her out for awhile, and so she called me for a date to renew our relationship. She came over to my apartment, and while she waited for me to get ready she talked with my friend, Steve. He asked her what she wanted to do with her life. She told him clothing design.

Steve asked, "Do you ever plan on going to New York? Isn't that where the real action is in fashion?"

She answered, "Yes it is, but I'm not sure that's where I'd want to go. The industry there is pretty much controlled by Jews. There are a lot of Jews in New York."

Without hesitation Steve remarked, "Yes I know. My mother is from New York."

Later over drinks this pretty young lady asked me, "Steve's Jewish, isn't he?" She had already figured out that would be our last date.

Back to Stan. "The Jewish people of Jesus' day thought that God was removed from the people. Jesus was reminding them that the scriptures never intended to convey the idea that God was remote. On the contrary, God was intimate with them, and as a way of bringing that point home, Jesus used an intimate name that children used in the home, Abba. The idea of wrath never entered into it."

Stan the Rev said some more interesting things, and I appreciated them, but let me conclude here with just his final remark. "One last thought," he said. "I'm sure glad that God has a sense of humor because I wouldn't want to hear that she dropped an anvil on your head."

8. ELOHIM

The Bible gives two stories of God's creation of the world, and each one puzzles me, but before getting into that let's savor the awesome image in Genesis, first chapter, first verse. *The earth was a formless void. There was darkness over the deep, and God's spirit hovered over the water.*

It is not until verses twenty-six and twenty-seven that God got around to making humankind. *God said, "Let us make man in our own image, in the likeness of ourselves."*

That's the puzzle. God said, "Let us make man in our own image, in the likeness of ourselves." God spoke as though he were one of a group. Some biblical scholars have suggested that this was perhaps the plural of majesty. The common name for God was Elohim, a pleural form. Others have thought this plural expression implied a discussion between God and his heavenly court. So angels, like humankind, would resemble God. That's as much as I know of what biblical scholars have had to say about this.

Enter the science fiction weirdoes. What if God were a race of alien beings who found earth to be an uninhabited but habitable world? They would have been capable of interstellar travel, certainly also of robotics and genetic engineering. They made us like them. We are Elohim look-alikes, copycats. Maybe that's why we never quite have found the missing link between ancient apes and modern man. Maybe instead of evolving from a common ancestor, we evolved parallel to the apes. Of course that wouldn't explain why chimpanzees are genetically closer to humans than to gorillas, but still it's a nice story.

There is another way to explain the plural designation. Maybe the writer just made a mistake. Maybe the writer was a grammatical tenderfoot, a novice. "Hey ma," he shouted. "Is there one or two esses in the word *caress?*"

And his mother answered, "Who cares?"

We all make mistakes at grammar, but there are some that drive me nuts. My name ends with s, and it bugs me when someone writes something like, *Curtis' pet peeves*. That's just plain wrong. I know some of you will disagree with me on this, but from the very first page of *Strunk and White, The Elements of Style*, we learn that to form the possessive singular of nouns, a person is to add *'s*, no matter what the final consonant is. So it would be *Burns's sideburns, Mays's amazing catch* and

Curtis's pet peeves. A notable exception to this is the name of Jesus. You would write *Jesus' mother*. To tell you the truth it bugs me not to lump that lovable guy in with the rest of us.

To make a plural of a noun ending in s, it is done the same as with any other word. As an example: *If what quantum mechanics holds is true, and there may be a multitude of parallel universes, then there must also be a multitude of parallel Jesuses.* Way cool!

One final pet peeve. I don't like split infinitives when people write. You can do what you like talking, but you ought to take time to do it right when you put words on paper. As soon as I say that I know that somewhere in this book I'll slip up. I'm going to obviously split an infinitive, and a number of you observant readers will write to me, "Hey Mr. Un-split Infinitive Geek. You're a boob."

Just as I finished writing this I noticed Agnos was watching me and he looked amused. I thought it was because I had been so clever, but he said, "Actually I was curious why you didn't go ahead and say the truly blasphemous possibility."

"What's that?"

"There's God making all these animals, and then he says, 'Let's make man in our own image.' Doesn't that imply that he's saying the animals resemble him, and that he decided to make man to resemble animals and himself? Maybe this is the Bible's endorsement of the theory of evolution. Now that is a concept to set off some tempers."

"Hmmmm. It's also quite a stretch. I wonder what biblical scholars would say about it."

"Your whole book is a stretch, and you already know what biblical scholars are going to say. You're a boob. Get used to it."

9. ADAM AND EVE

The second story of creation found in Genesis is the one about the Garden of Eden, or as Iron Butterfly called it, *Inna Godda Davida* (in the Garden of Eden). This is another story that puzzles me. It seems to puzzle me more than it puzzles other people.

It is clear that Adam was created well in advance of Eve. Adam appeared in the second chapter, verse seven. *Yahweh God fashioned a man of dust from the soil. Then he breathed into his nostrils a breath of life, and thus man became a living being.* There wasn't mention of Eve until verses twenty-one through twenty-three. Eve was made really as an afterthought because Adam was lonely.

So here's my question. Since God made Adam originally without a plan for sexual reproduction, what came first, Eve or Adam's penis?

And if he already had a penis, say for directional target shooting, then what came first, Eve or Adam's erection?

In verse twenty-one, *Yahweh God made the man fall into a deep sleep, and while he slept he took one of his ribs and enclosed it in flesh. Yahweh God built the rib he had taken from the man into a woman.* The man exclaimed, "Wow!" Some years later a poet revised this exclamation to make it more literary. *This at last is bone from my bones and flesh from my flesh! This is to be called woman* (wow man), *for this was taken from man.*

At first Adam and Eve were quite happy because they were ignorant. They behaved as the animals behaved, and everyone was okay with that. God forbade them from eating fruit from the tree of knowledge, and for awhile all was peachy.

Let's be fair with Adam and Eve. At the time they were stupid as two blocks of wood. God told them what not to do; they nodded, and later they asked each other, "Do you know what he was talking about?"

"No, do you?"

Genesis tells us that Satan came to Eve as a snake and lured her into eating the forbidden fruit. The Bible tells us that it was only afterward that snakes became repulsive to women, but I suspect even before this all happened Eve did not include snakes among her favorite animals. Also, even as stupid as she was she would have been suspicious of a talking snake.

Satan was cunning. Maybe he started out as a snake, but he knew better. Women like horses, so Satan decided he would come to her as a horse, and not just any horse either. He approached her as the famous Mr. Ed. Music please: A snake is the horse, of course, of course; and no one can talk to a snake of course. That is of course, unless the snake is the famous Mr. Ed. People go yackety-yak a streak, and waste the time of day, but Mr. Ed will never speak unless he has something to say. A snake is the horse, of course, of course; and no one can talk to a snake of course. That is of course, unless the snake is the famous Mr. Ed. Then Satan finished with his beautiful baritone voice, "I am not a snake."

Eve liked Mr. Ed a lot. Hell, I like Mr. Ed a lot. So when Mr. Ed told Eve, "Wilbur loves this fruit. It's his favorite," Eve gave in and ate it. Immediately she became intelligent. She also instantly became compulsively neurotic. She looked at herself and declared, "Oh, I'm so fat!"

Then it was Eve's turn to be lonely. Adam bored her. He couldn't participate in a decent conversation. He'd say stuff like, "Football good. Beer good. Broccoli bad." She had to do something to make life livable.

She put a slice of forbidden fruit on a cracker and melted cheese over the top of it. Then she came to Adam and straddled his thigh. She licked his lips and slid the fruit into his mouth.

God hadn't prepared Adam for this. You're the jury. I ask you. Was Adam to blame, or was God negligent in his planning?

At any rate, Adam smiled, "This is sinfully delicious."

Eve purred, "I know." Then they made love and felt ashamed about it, but not ashamed enough, so God threw them out of the Garden of Eden, banished them and placed angelic guards at the entrance so they couldn't get back in. I've always thought that was rather harsh.

Eve remained bored with Adam. Adam developed a preference for micro-brewed ales and discussed the West Coast Offense.

Thereafter Adam and Eve had offspring that populated the earth, but we must ask ourselves how. Did their children cavort with each other? Incest? In their defense it is right to point out that incest did not become illegal until after humans ate from the tree of genetic understanding of congenital anomalies. So it wouldn't have been as shameful as it now seems looking back at it.

I've heard it suggested that the practice of incest in the original family might be a clue that the Garden of Eden was somewhere in Appalachia, but clearly that is not the case. Genesis puts the Garden of Eden near four rivers. They were the Pishon, the Gihon, the Tigris and the Euphrates. So maybe that's why throughout history there have been so many battles for the real estate around Baghdad. It is interesting that God placed the Garden of Eden smack dab in the middle of a gigantic oil field. Amazing really.

10. SINFUL FRUIT

Stan the Rev wrote to me simply, *You have a sinfully fruitful mind.*

Thanks Stan. I'm a bit afraid to send out my story on sarcasm. In it I have Jesus tell a dirty joke, a good one. Talk about sinful!

The real meaning of Adam and Eve is that we cannot return to Eden by ignorance. Yes, we can return by grace, but I believe God wants us to come nearer to him through knowledge, so that we may come to understand him better.

God loves me as he loves everyone. He thinks I'm funny, and I enjoy making him laugh. He has given me a message to share. In John 16:12-15, Jesus said, *I have much more to say to you, more than you can now bear. But when he, the Spirit of truth, comes, he will guide you into all truth. He will not speak on his own; he will speak only what he hears, and he will tell you what is yet to come. He will bring glory to me by taking from what is mine and making it known to you. All that belongs to the Father is mine. That is why I said the Spirit will take from what is mine and make it known to you."*

Do you ever hear God speaking out of other people's mouths? Do you remember Gandhi telling us we must be the change we wish to see in the world?

I enjoy writing these things; I really do, but it scares me.

TWO

Musings on the Universe

11. ABILITY TO BELIEVE

Once upon a splog I wrote about up quarks and down quarks, strange quarks and cultural quarks. When I got home that evening I was accosted by Brian Greene. He's one of the minds who live in my library. "There's no such thing as a cultural quark," he gently scolded. "What were you thinking? There are six kinds. They are up, down, strange, charm, top and bottom." Then he prattled on, and I'll spare you the details. He told me that if we could examine these particles, which we can't because they are way too small to see with our technological limitations, then we would find that each quark consists of a tiny, vibrating filament that physicists call a string.

"A string?" I asked.

"Yes, a string."

Brian Greene believes in strings. He believes that these strings are the smallest, most fundamental building blocks of our universe. According to him you can't get any smaller than a string.

I found myself wondering what the string is made of. I also thought how wonderful it is that acclaimed scientists are able to believe in something that is not proved, not provable. They are not so different from the rest of the world of believers.

Simply put this is faith, whether the faith is placed in philosophical concepts, the scientific method, theological instruction or the promises made by those we love and whom we believe love us. It is faith.

I'm convinced that the origin and continuation of society require that we have this quality about us. It gives us selective advantage for the survival of our species. It is the lynchpin of cooperative building of our social infrastructure.

Looking at history enlightens us on beliefs we once clutched tightly.

We did not let them go until they were pried out of our minds by proof. Even then we often relinquished our grasps reluctantly.

Long ago we believed the world was flat and that we could fall off the edge. We believed that the sun revolved around the earth. We believed that God required sacrifice of life to protect us from the thrashings of natural disasters. Now these things seem absurd.

Only a short while ago, during the time of the American Revolutionary War, our scientists believed there was an unseen substance in the air around us that was responsible for remarkable phenomena. They called it phlogiston. There really was phlogiston in the air, but now we call it hydrogen. In the days of phlogiston we believed its chemical properties to be something quite different from what today we believe are the properties of hydrogen. I point this out because scientists are just like the religiously faithful in their ability to believe in something that has not been proved.

During the years between 1774 and 1786, a scientist named Joseph Priestley published a six volume account of his research, *Experiments and Observations of Different Kinds of Air*. Priestly demonstrated persuasively that phlogiston could be absorbed by a substance called *minium* or *lead calx*, and that by its absorption the phlogiston would transform the lead calx into lead. Today lead calx is called *lead oxide*. It's instructive and fun to understand how Priestly did this.

If you were to take an open jar, turn it upside down and press it into a tub of water, the air within the jar would keep water from entering the jar. Priestly did precisely that with a glass jar of phlogiston. Floating on top of the water inside the bottled phlogiston he had a crucible of minium. He heated the minium using a magnifying glass and rays of sunlight. The minium turned into lead. The evidence that this had occurred as a result of phlogiston being absorbed was that the water level rose dramatically into the glass jar. This is pretty convincing if you ask me, but that's just because I'm a boob. You see, I'm coming to accept my position in life.

Let's be sensibly aware that in Priestley's experiment nobody actually saw the phlogiston being absorbed. They could not see things that small. Absorption was assumed from the circumstantial evidence of the rising water.

There was one problem. If the minium had turned into lead as a consequence of phlogiston being absorbed, then the resultant lead should have been heavier than the original minium. It wasn't. It was lighter. Oh-oh! Did phlogiston have negative weight? Well, that would be one explanation. Scientists said, "We'll answer that one later."

The point I want to make is that this conception of phlogiston's properties is what scientists believed. There was evidence both to support and to reject their belief, but they believed it.

Today we have a different understanding of what happened. Heating of the lead oxide caused oxygen to escape from it and to combine with the hydrogen in the jar to make water. This consumed the hydrogen in the jar and allowed the tub water to rise into the jar. Are we right? Still nobody has seen at microscopic enough levels actually to observe this. The modern concept fits the data better, but it still is a theory, improved from the phlogiston theory, but still a theory. And we believe it, at least for now.

Such theories are useful because they allow us to predict consequences of actions. They allow us to develop technologies.

Theologies are beliefs also based on faith and circumstantial evidence. In both science and religion there are conservatives who clasp tightly to the old concepts, and there are progressives who seek newer theories that are better at predicting results. Scientific psychology is a fascinating link between science and religion, and we ought to pay attention to it. I'm impressed particularly with cognitive theory behavioralism as a useful tool in psychological technology.

What are some of the things, unproved, that we believe today? We believe that missing socks have to be somewhere. We believe the Bible is holy. We believe there is a God. We believe there is unobservable dark matter in the cosmos. We believe there once existed a man named Jesus who was more than just a made up Paul Bunyan myth. We believe that at the end of a criminal trial we indeed have established guilt versus innocence. We believe there is a soul. We believe that life is a better existence than death. We believe that representative forms of democracy do in fact represent the desires of the people.

None of this has been proved or disproved, and the Spirit Agnos insisted I make that clear to you.

12. ABILITY TO BEE LEAVE

At the age of two years my daughter, Stella, began to show a peculiar and wondrous talent for a sport that may be called, "catch and release of flies." She was able to go to any fly in the house, even the still energetic ones, and she'd gently pick them up and put them outside. This had nothing to do with speed. It had everything to do with the insects just plain letting her do it. They didn't try to escape.

Often we have a lot of bees around our front yard, and we told Stella to leave those alone, but Stella is without question made out of the substance of curiosity, and she is much more likely to ask forgiveness afterward than to ask first and take the risk of being denied permission to do something she wants.

One Spring day when she was three years old, she came in for lunch with a serious face, and she gripped tightly with her left hand onto her right. She ate her peanut butter and jelly sandwich like that, squeezing her right hand with her left. She drank her milk like that. Stella's mother asked her about this, and Stella answered, "I don't want to talk about it." Stella knew she had been disobedient.

Finally it dawned on her mother. "Stella, did you get stung by a bee?"

Tears quietly appeared in Stella's eyes.

"Did you try to pick up a bee?"

Stella nodded.

"Bees are so small compared to people. People scare them. If you try to pick up a bee it will be frightened, and of course it will sting you."

Stella responded, "The first one didn't."

13. DARK MATTER

Wanting to point out the characteristic of all of us, scientific or religious, both or neither, that we are similar in our ability to believe things that are not proved, I sought more information on the dark matter that physicists believe must bind the universe together.

Here's a little background to help you understand the dark matter problem. The universe is expanding, but is it expanding in a reasonable fashion? Or is it just flying apart, repelled by the bad breath of the ascendant creatures on the fourth planet of the star, 55 Cancri? In order to balance the observed expansion of the universe, there has to be a certain amount of mass within the universe. The problem is that we don't see that much matter, and this has a lot of people a bit on edge.

It's not just the universe as a whole that doesn't seem to be balanced correctly. Scientists observe galaxies and galaxy clusters that hold together by means of some massive gravity that is not explainable by the matter they see.

The matter in the universe that can be seen, such as stars and galaxies, is referred to as *bright matter*. Bright matter accounts for only four percent of what the universe needs to balance its equations. Physicists account for another twenty-three percent by adding all the known dark matter in the universe. This is what they know is there even though it isn't shiny like stars. That means seventy-three percent of the needed mass of the universe just isn't there. But scientists believe it is there anyway because their mathematics tells them so. That's what the search for dark matter is all about.

Some scientists have said this is just an error of mathematical fudge factors. All the equations will work if you just use different fudge factors. That worked for us in high school, so certainly we could do it again. It's a tried and true remedy for lots of things.

One possible solution to the problem may simply be to apply Einstein's Theory of Relativity. The mass of heavenly bodies increases the faster they move. This is an argument for never allowing Christina Applegate to ride in a jet that can exceed mach 2. Christina, are you listening? I've managed to keep my wife from riding on space ships or spy planes, and it has worked. Her figure has remained beautiful, and yours can too. Maybe that book about French women not getting fat also can help.

As heavenly bodies approach the speed of light their mass approaches infinity. Infinity is significant and maybe could account for the missing mass.

In my search on the internet for other possible solutions, I came across articles that explore the possibility of subatomic particles that collectively can think. And although you may think this is silly, it's not. There are mathematicians who believe the universe itself is one humongous computer.

This idea of thinking subatomic particles excited me because long ago in the early eighties Dan Kurtti had informed me of his idea that there are tiny, as yet too small to identify, particles that he named spiritons, and these were responsible for our spiritual nature. This coincidence was too cosmic for me not to let DK know, so I gave him links to the websites and awaited his response. Here it is.

I have tried to read these articles a couple of times, but I daydream. The interesting thing about dark matter is that it seems to have come about as a fudge factor. Physicists needed to make the rate of the universe's expansion palatable, and the fudge factor appears to be ... well, a lot of fudge.

Even so, Michio Kaku would say evidence indicates that despite matter, the universe still is flying by leaps and bounds out of control. Hmmmm, I have trouble listening to the brilliant physicists. They are so far above me that it makes my head swim. They could say anything they want and the average person (me) would just have to believe it at face value. I take pride that I got As in advanced calculus and physical chemistry/quantum mechanics, but I know nothing about the level of mathematics these salient ones use. You have to study whole new levels of mathematics just to understand what they are saying when they get into superstring theory, etc.

So I guess God just may be a fudge factor, one gigantic scoop to make a delicious hot fudge sundae.

I'm in a mental block with the spiritons. Maybe inspiration is just around the corner. Maybe my search awaits studying the next level of mathematics in my "spare time." I think I'll watch *Revenge of the Sith* first. I'll take up the math study next week, or next decade, next lifetime.

I have believed for a long time that inspiration breeds even higher levels of inspiration. Momentum built by initial hard work and willpower leads to higher and higher levels of success. We all build from the inspirational moments of others.

I imagine you have seen the movie, *Contact*, with Jodie Foster. One of my favorite scenes is when she traveled unimaginable distances through worm holes inside *the machine* built from blueprints given by aliens who had contacted Earth. When she landed she found herself on a beach, and her deceased father walked up to her. After releasing her emotions and hugging him she realized things weren't right. "You're not real," she said. "None of this is real. When I was unconscious you downloaded my thoughts, my memories."

Her father replied, "We thought that this would make things easier for you."

Well, what if the after death experience is just talking to God in various forms, talking with parents, relatives, friends, soul mates, ascended masters, Jesus, the saints, Buddha. God may make things easier for us with comfortable settings, familiar persons. Heaven in the 16th century would be much different than heaven in the 21st century. So God in the after-death experience would be basically the same as the super advanced alien talking to Jodie Foster's character in the movie. In fact we will ultimately merge into God, all of us, and it will just appear that there are individual souls talking to each other. Actually it will just be God talking with God.

We might even think of this same scenario in our present lives. Then it would be just one life here on earth too. God talking with God, it's food for thought.

14. FABRIC OF THE UNIVERSE

Imagine the fabric of space-time is composed of energy and particles too small for us to see, even with the most powerful microscope.

Maybe they are strings, but maybe I can apply to them the name given by my friend, DK. They are spiritons. The void, the vacuum of space, is filled with them. This is the sink or reservoir out of which observable matter is produced at the edge of black holes. This is the potential world of quantum mechanics. When a particle is not a particle, its disappearance is into this world of spiritons.

For subatomic particles, quantum mechanics has explained and experiments have demonstrated that matter can be in more than one place at the same time. More than that, a particle sometimes is a wave. A particle may exist and then not exist. These remarkable phenomena have been observed only at the subatomic level.

Sir Roger Penrose has arrived at a theory that would explain why this weirdness happens with subatomic particles but not with macroscopic structures. His answer involves gravity, and so maybe Doctor Penrose is showing us one interaction that, even if only in a tiny way, helps us to envision a reconciliation of Einstein's theories of gravity with quantum mechanics. Only a structure of miniscule mass can occupy two places at once. The more massive the object, the more energy is required for it to occupy two places at once. A larger structure cannot climb out of its single gravitational depression in the fabric of space-time. His ideas are detailed more in the June 2005 issue of *Discover* magazine.

In that article is a little blurb talking about the question, what is consciousness? Penrose sees it as quantum mechanical processes operating within a nervous system. Some research supports a concept that microtubules within brain cells can operate as instruments of quantum phenomena.

It is not a matter of conjecture that quantum processes can occur at levels of matter larger than was earlier thought. Whole atoms, such as sodium and rubidium, can behave like waves and can have the same non-local characteristics as electrons and other subatomic things. If such particles are *entangled*, then what we observe by measuring the behavior of one of the particles will determine immediately what is happening with the other. This is not the speed of communication so much as it is the fact that these entangled particles are actually two different parts of the same entity, no matter how far apart they are. That this happens with whole atoms was verified scientifically in 1995, an accomplishment for which the physicists Eric A. Cornell, Wolfgang Ketterle and Carl E. Wieman were awarded the 2001 Nobel Prize.

Have you wondered about how a soul could interact with the material construct of a human mind? In his book, *The Self-Aware Universe*,

Amit Goswami, Ph.D. posits that consciousness occurs at microscopic or even subatomic levels, and the brain acts as a receiver, amplifier and transmitter, allowing this subatomic thinking to interact with our macroscopic world. The model he proposes is an attempt to answer what heretofore have been irresolvable problems in the study of consciousness. It explains how neuronal activity can initiate simultaneously at long distances within the brain because the quantum behavior of subatomic particles can have them in more than one place at the same time. It also explains why brain injury, including stroke, disturbs what we perceive as a person's thinking. On the quantum level thought processes and self awareness remain intact, but the brain's amplifying and communicating processes get broken.

Spiriton may indeed be an appropriate name for this imagined particle that forms the fabric of all that is. What if it or groupings of it think? What if this fabric of space is the creator's mind? What if it wants us to discover it because it craves our company? What if it is ourselves craving for us to realize who we really are, to recall memories lost when Adam and Eve first learned to think with their macroscopic brains? What if this thinking fabric is able to put into our minds the sudden epiphanies of discovery? What if?

Go ahead all you boob hunters out there. I've made you a nice target.

The Spirit Agnos was first in line. "You're a boob," he smiled, "but a likeable one. Actually your idea is not a new one. It's as old as the ages, now being reborn by physicists trying to find solutions to problems that cannot be answered by our current understanding of the universe. If your readers want to read more about this they should look at Ervin Laszlo's amazing book, *Science and the Akashic Field*. It is clear from the letter your friend Dan Kurtti sent you, the one called *I Make Stuff Up*, that he has read Laszlo's book. By the way, he will be sending a copy of it to you soon. Read it. You're not alone, Mr. T the splogger."

"Mr. Agnos, it sounds like even you may be a believer."

"Oh, I wouldn't go so far as to say that. No, I wouldn't want you to go away with that idea. I have trouble with the idea that the macroscopic brain acts predominantly as a transceiver. There has to be a significant amount of thought occurring in the brain itself. If you've ever talked with a demented person you recognize this. I know of a ninety year old woman who believes her mother dresses her in the mornings. And then later she asks if her mother has died. This is more than an impairment of just communication. The thinking process itself is involved."

Agnos continued, "I think the idea of quantum events participating in biological systems is intriguing, but the rest of it, eeeeeeeeh." He shrugged his shoulders.

15. THE DIVINE PROPORTION

On July 3, 2005, the Associated Press sent out an article about a Japanese psychiatric counselor, Akira Haraguchi, who had recited from memory the number pi out to 83,431 decimal places. It will take authorities awhile to confirm accuracy of his recitation before he will be put into the Guinness Book of Records as having bested his own previous record of 54,000 digits. That old record still is being reviewed.

Pi has an infinite number of decimal places. It goes on forever. It usefully is abbreviated to 3.14 and is the ratio of the circumference to the diameter of a circle.

I'm not much into memorizing numbers just for the challenge of it, but were I to do that the number I would choose is phi, another unending number with a Greek name. Phi is abbreviated 1.618, and it has been called the golden section, or ratio, because it shows up in our world over and over and seems to be connected with our concepts of what is right and beautiful. Throughout history the ratio of 1.618 has been used in design of architecture such as that of the pyramids and the Parthenon. Leonardo Da Vinci called it the Divine Proportion and used it when designing Notre Dame Cathedral in Paris.

The Ark of the Covenant is a Golden Rectangle. In Exodus 25:10, God told Moses, *"They shall make an ark of acacia wood: two cubits and a half shall be its length, a cubit and a half its height."* The ratio of 2.5 to 1.5 is 1.666, as close to phi as you can come with numbers as small as this. When God told Moses to make the arc according to phi, Moses asked him, "Do you mind, Lord, if we round the number up just a tad? Easier to measure, you know."

Noah and God had a similar conversation in Genesis 6:15, about the arc. *"This is how you are to make it: the length of the ark three hundred cubits, its breadth fifty cubits, and its height thirty cubits."* The end of the ark then would be 50 by 30 cubits, again a ratio of 1.666 ... .

The design of Stradivarius's violins conforms to the golden section. Sound studios often are designed with the golden section in mind, and some have said that the golden ratio directly relates to the western musical scale.

What aesthetes have considered as the ideal and most beautiful proportions of the human face and body, also have ratios of the divine proportion.

Soccer balls and the geodesic dome popularized by Buckminster Fuller are based on the golden ratio, and I think this next thing is deeply significant. Sixty atoms of pure carbon in its most spherical form would have the shape of a soccer ball, complying with the ratio of phi. Carbon is of course the prime building block of organic matter, of all living things on earth. Maybe at its most basic level, life is molded by this one number.

All of this I've mentioned mainly to let you know that through the ages the number phi has appealed to us. We are susceptible to its charm. Modern mathematicians and physicists tell us that such numerical co-incidences are not merely accidental. They occur because the structure of the universe makes them so.

During the twelfth century Leonardo Fibonacci discovered a simple numerical series that predicted the number phi. Starting with 0 and 1, each new number in the series is the sum of the two before it: 0, 1, 1, 2, 3, 5, 8, 13, 21, 34, 55, 89, 144 ... and so on forever.

The ratio of each successive pair of numbers in the series approximates phi (1.618). 5 divided by 3 equals 1.666. 8 divided by 5 equals 1.60. As it goes on, the ratios of successive numbers in the Fibonacci series more and more closely approach phi. It gets amazingly accurate at larger numbers. 987 divided by 610 equals 1.6180327.

Now we all should stop for ten seconds of quiet reverence for this accomplishment of Leonardo Fibonacci.

Now you know enough to enjoy the next entry in this book, *I Make Stuff Up*.

16. I MAKE STUFF UP

Dan Kurtti sent a picture of himself wearing a t-shirt on which was written *I MAKE STUFF UP*. Along with it he sent a copy of this article.

EVERYONE WON!

Something phenomenal occurred last night. Everybody who entered the Power Ball Lotto has a winning ticket. The odds of such an event have boggled mathematicians, and several university math departments are running super computers to figure this out. The winning numbers are 3, 5, 8, 13, 21, and the power ball is 34. These numbers instantly were recognized as part of the Fibonacci series.

Why did everyone select these numbers? Even the many participants who knew nothing about the series selected them. Those who selected multiple picks strangely happened to have chosen these numbers for every pick. Those who used the quick-pick, allowing the computer to choose, also had these numbers. Quite a few participants expressed skepticism when they first found their multiple quick-pick choices all had the same sequence of numbers, but when they complained they were reassured that nothing was wrong with the machines. Already, before the Saturday night drawing, there was widespread suspicion that something was amiss.

The bottom line is that everyone will get the amount of money they had put into the lotto plus a tiny bit more. As somebody had won the previous jackpot, the new one was reset at $10 million. There are a lot of disgruntled winners today because everybody will cash in on a meager prize.

Speculation runs high. UFO devotees are looking at the skies, and doomsayers are proclaiming that the end is near. Bible-belters are preaching that the rapture is upon us. So far government officials have remained silent. It's anyone's guess what this all means.

- - - - - - - - - - - - -

Then DK gave this explanation. What caused this? Well, it turns out there are problems with the Big Bang theory. One of the issues facing Big Bang scientists is the fine-tuning of the universal constants. In his book *Science and the Akashic Field*, 2004, Inner Traditions, Ervin Laszlo explains how amazingly finely tuned the universe is to have allowed emergence of the improbable conditions in which life could occur. Paul Davies also elaborates on this concept of our universe being amazingly and improbably tuned for the possibility of life to emerge, in his apply named book *Cosmic Jackpot; Why Our Universe is Just Right for Life.* Simple things are important, like the weight of a proton or a neutron or an electron. If these things were just slightly different than they are, life would not have happened, and in many scenarios there would not have been even stars or galaxies.

How could the universe have been so finely tuned that we came to exist? I can't find any calculation of the odds of this occurring, just phrases such as "extremely improbable," "highly unlikely," etc. Nobody says it's impossible, and how could they? Here we are right now speculating about the universe. So I thought, why not get the point of improbability across by using a scenario that people have some familiarity with, the Power Ball Lotto.

Big Bang theory number one: the space/time fluctuations prior to the Bang, those that set the parameters of the emerging universe, occurred randomly. This makes sense because nothing was there that could have influenced the occurrence.

But an alternative would be that traces of prior universes might have been present in the pre-Bang space/time from which our universe arose. Our universe could have been born in the womb of a Metaverse. Then how would the parameters have been set? By God? I don't know.

The prior universe wouldn't necessarily have to have ended for the new universe to be created. The bubble for the new universe might have been generated from a live, evolving and flowering, existing universe, or maybe from just part of that universe. What if the new universe were generated from the mind of a famous or infamous person? What if the new universe popped out of the mind of Jesus or Hitler, Mother Teresa, George W. Bush, Tom Curtis, Wow!

Just think how many different kinds of universes there could be. God forbid that Adolph Hitler's thinking will be the template for a new creation. Suppose it were Jesus Christ? Heaven on earth! Maybe a universe could be created by combination of two or more persons, or a relationship. What about a universe that is half Jesus and half Adolph? Hmmmmmm ... Good and Evil. Sounds something like our own confused world. What would such a world lead to? Certainly there would be different paths to choose from, paths to perdition and paths to heaven. We would have our choice.

Here is my response to DK. The point you make is that the universe, as we see it, is so improbable that it is beyond reason to believe it is entirely a random event. To explain this some scientists now suggest there have been successive, conscious universes, each one bringing with it the accumulated knowledge of previous universes, each one becoming more finely tuned. This does not answer how the series of universes started in the first place. Consistent with the history of modern science it avoids the simple answer. It declares that the simple answer is beyond the scope of science, even theoretical science.

Some scientists now, and likely more in the future, will accept that the universe was created with purpose, with dedication, with thoughtfulness, but they refuse to take the final step of assigning to it the signature of a creator. They say the universe itself is the conscious awareness, responsible for its own creation. With a smug little smile I answer, "Semantics," and I am comfortable with that.

Here's Agnos's response to me. "Semantics-schmantics. With a smug little smile I answer, what kind of booze have you been putting in that cup of coffee?"

17. TIME AND SPACE

This morning I awoke and noticed it was twenty minutes later. *How very interesting,* I thought to myself as I stumbled into the bathroom. I managed to get ready and was on the road five minutes earlier. *How very interesting*, I thought to myself as I stumbled into the local Seven and Eleven to get my newspaper and jolt of java.

This just goes to show that time is not what it used to be, and neither is space. You may ascribe my experience to normal psychological nuances of an amusing twit, and of course you know that, as an amusing twit, I'll attribute such happenings to a distortion of the time/ space continuum, specifically my very own spacetime continuum.

How can I get across to you my concerned amusement about recent developments in theoretical physics having to do with the way our space and our time are constructed? Maybe you say, "Yawn. Old stuff. Einstein got that all figured out in the last century. Time isn't constant, but the speed of light is, right? Got it. Now how about them Seahawks? Can you figure?" But now there are challenges to the very way my hero, Albert Einstein, thought about the structure of the universe. He himself was open to the possibility that his way of thinking was wrong, and that all of modern physics has developed along a path that fundamentally is mistaken.

This reminds me of what my mother used to tell me when I complained of not having enough of either time or space to clean my bedroom. She told me I was fundamentally mistaken. This is not the only way that I possibly may resemble Albert Einstein. I also try to wear my hair messy.

In 1954, about a year before his death, Einstein wrote to his close friend, Michele Besso, *I consider it quite possible that physics cannot be based on the field concept, that is, on continuous structures.* He added, *Then nothing remains of my entire castle in the air, including the theory of gravitation, but also nothing of the rest of modern physics.* How do I know Einstein wrote this? I read it in the December 2005 issue of *Scientific American*, the fascinating article written by Theodore A. Jacobson and Renaud Parentani. These authors wrote that the quest for unification of the theories of general relativity and quantum mechanics may force us to relinquish our concept that space and time are continuous from one point to another. We may have to accept that space and time are particulate. The fabric of space may consist of tiny separate packets of spacetime. This would collapse the foundation of twentieth century physics, and as of yet scientists have not come up with a replacement.

So how about this for a wake up call? If you think you or anyone else knows for sure what the physical laws are of the universe, then you are either naïve or full of crap. I'll be gracious; you're naïve.

Now it's my enjoyable task to attempt an explanation of an extraordinary emerging concept, as described in the article, *An Echo of Black Holes*, December 2005 issue of *Scientific American*.

Up until now we have conceived of time and space as being continuous. Space has been described as a field, present even in a vacuum, present when nothing else is there. One point in space has been thought to blend imperceptibly with another. There is no break or interruption of space between one point and another. We think of time the same way, continuous without interruption. With this concept of space and time, Einstein built his theories on the basis of light being essentially different from sound. Sound requires a medium in which to travel, whether that medium is air or water or whatever. But we've thought that light can travel in a vacuum and does not require a medium.

Sound travels by jostling particles. They move and bump into others, setting the others in motion. This is just like waves in an ocean. The particles themselves move more or less in a circular pattern, up and down, side to side, but the wave continues on and on. Sound travels sensibly when it is mediated by the still water of a pond. However, in a stream or a whirlpool or waterfall, or in any situation in which particles of water are moving vigorously by a means other than the simple circular movements caused by a sound wave, sounds get distorted. Pitch of sound gets higher if the particles are rushing toward the listener and lower if the particles are rushing away.

We thought the travel of light waves was above all that. We thought light traveled in a vacuous field of space and time, independent of a particulate medium. As it turns out, around black holes light demonstrates distortions similar to the distortions of sound in a whirlpool of water. It is as though a black hole is a whirlpool of space and time. A mathematical model that can explain this in a way that is consistent with both relativity and quantum mechanics, conceives of light traveling via a medium of tiny particles that bump into each other and can flow in a whirlpool. If we extrapolate the physical rules of sound to waves of light, then the distance between these particles must be considerably smaller than the smallest wavelength of the electromagnetic spectrum, smaller than gamma waves.

So let's get a little scary. What are these tiny particles? They are tiny packets of space and time. Distortion of light occurs around black holes because these tiny packets of space-time flow in a whirlpool caused by gravity.

Let's get scarier still. What are these particles flowing in? What is between the particles? Is it still part of the universe? Maybe. All we know is that whatever lies between the particles of space and time, whatever it is that these particles flow in, is not space and it is not time. It is something else. Oh, we know one other thing. It is everywhere. It is inside each and every one of us, inside each and every item in the universe. Is it infinite? Is it eternity?

So let me say it again. If you think you or anyone else knows for sure what the physical laws are of the universe, then you are either naïve or full of crap. I'll be gracious; you're naïve. Believe what you will; in the quest by humankind for complete understanding of our world, we remain at the rudimentary beginnings, and much remains inexplicable. A thousand years from now people will look back upon our current knowledge much as we now look back upon the mystical imaginings of our ancient history.

To be smug is to show your ignorance. Humility is the means by which we must continue our search. Humility is what allows us to believe even the miraculous.

18. EACH AND EVERY MOMENT

You must want to know how the theory of special relativity explains that every moment is eternal. And you want to understand it without reading Brian Greene's 493 page book, *The Fabric of the Cosmos*, or the special edition of *Scientific American* entitled *A Matter of Time*. So I'll explain it to you in a few paragraphs just to show you how gifted a writer I arrogantly think I am.

I grew up on the banks of the Mississippi River and as a teenager became fascinated by something as simple as the reflection of light on the water. Let me put it to you with a similar but more pristine image.

Think of a large pond with still water and a surface as smooth as glass. There is a large and bright torch at its center, and looking across the water you see the torch reflected in a column of light on the surface of the water extending straight toward you. The rest of the pond is dark. As you walk around the pond, this column of light follows you. That part of the water which was dark from one vantage point becomes brilliant as you pass by, and soon it dawns on you that if you could stand at every location around the perimeter of the pond, you would see that all of it blazes golden with reflected light. But being able to see from only one vantage point at a time, you see only the column of light.

Keep this image in mind as I show you how in grander fashion, time works the same way.

At its core, the theory of special relativity states that time and space are not constant. The constant thing in our universe is the speed of light in a vacuum. When two observers are at rest with respect to each other, neither one moving, they will record time as passing at the same pace. However, if the observers are moving with respect to one another, they will record time as passing at different speeds, and each is as correct as the other.

The commonly used scenario to explain this involves two gunslingers in a showdown aboard a moving train. Billy the Bumpkin is on the leading end of the car, and Jessie Jancowicz is on the following end. Aboard the train car, it seems to these gunslingers that they are still, and the rest of the world is hurtling past them. And so it satisfies them to use a light signal at the very center of the train car to alert them to when they should draw their guns. This seems fair to them since they are equidistant from this signal.

However it looks not so fair when observed from a platform outside the train. Wyatt Whiskers, standing on the platform as the train speeds by, protests because it is clear to him that the movement of the train makes it so that Jessie will see the signal light earlier than Billy.

This is only a scenario used as a pictorial image to help novices like us understand. As a simple illustration it is not perfect, has its loopholes, so don't take the illustration as the actual theory. The theory states basically that movement through space causes time to change velocity. We don't notice this in every day life because the change of time velocity is miniscule at the speeds with which we are familiar.

Here is the key. The change of time speed becomes more significant with greater velocity difference between the observers, AND with greater distance between the observers. In other words, distance through space magnifies the effect.

On page 134 of his book, Brian Greene describes an extraterrestrial being, sitting in a playground ten billion light years from earth. Dr. Greene named the extraterrestrial, Chewie, but I'll name him Migraine, and you'll understand why in a minute. Imagine the improbable notion that you and Migraine, sitting right where the two of you are right now, are not moving at all with respect to one another. If both you and Migraine make a list of all the things you perceive happening at any precise moment, your lists would agree. The same things would be happening at the same time. Dr. Greene calls these, *now lists*. If Migraine the extraterrestrial stands up and runs ten miles an hour directly away from you, his perception of time changes. The change is miniscule perceived by anyone else on Migraine's planet, but magnified by ten billion light years of space this modest motion by Migraine would mean that his now list no longer even includes you. His now list would change to events that occurred roughly 150 years ago here on earth.

If Migraine decided to run ten miles an hour directly toward you his now list would include events 150 years in our future.

Magnified by the vast reaches of space, even modest movement can make it seem as though events pop into and out of existence, except we are too far away actually to see that happening. Thank God.

Now add to this the enormous speed of planets and galaxies, the influence of gravity, and the expansion of the universe itself. If you were capable of observing the universe from every possible vantage point at the same moment, you would see all of time from beginning to end. It is one whole and constant piece.

Since we can be at only one vantage point at any given moment, it seems like time is flowing forward into the future. But according to the theory of special relativity, time does not flow. It does not move. It just is. We ourselves move through time, just as we move through space, and we are aware of only one part of time at any one moment. We see only one column of light reflected in the water as we circle the pond.

What would be the omniscient, omnipresent vantage point from which we could see all of time and all of space at once? Would it be the eternity existing in the interstices between packets of time and space? Is it necessary for the universe to continue expanding so that the God Eternity can continue to have the vantage point necessary to see the very beginning of time?

A couple of years ago I sent out the following poem in honor of the passing of my friend Michael's mother in law. It wasn't just Hallmark sentiments.

19. EACH AND EVERY MOMENT

> Is each and every moment eternal
> as a few of us suppose?
> or is it fast as time, fleeting,
> as everybody knows?

20. LOVE AND RELATIVITY

I dedicated this to my friend Frank and his wife Barbara, as they awaited her passing into the next experience.

The thought came to me of how my love for my wife reminds me of Einstein's theory of relativity, the concept that the faster one moves through space, the slower one moves through time. Or conversely, the slower one moves through space, the faster one moves through time.

It seems that no matter how close I get to my wife, still there is too much space between us. It seems that no matter how long I spend with her, still it is not enough time.

When we pass from the confines of this existence limited by time and space, we enter the consummate closeness where there is no space that separates us, and there is not time that rushes us. There is just eternity.

THREE

Personality and Behavior

21. DETERMINANTS OF BEHAVIOR

Behavior is determined by two major contributors, genetic inheritance and environmental influence. Each of us inherited a package of genetic information, half our genes coming from Mother and half from Father. We didn't ask for the genes we got and neither did they. Our genome came to us more or less as a gift. Our parents would have liked to give us only their best genes and throw the rest away, but life doesn't work that way. We get what we get. Some of us are luckier than others. Some are pitifully unlucky. I for one will not blame you for the genes you got.

The other determinant is environment. What kind of reinforcement do we get for the things we do? What kind of physically or psychologically traumatic events have influenced us? This is extremely important during childhood, during which time the foundation of our personality is molded. During the first fifteen years of life we are not in control of how our surroundings nurture us. Our environment is provided by parents, siblings, teachers, doctors, friends, ministers, police officers, city councils, television, books and newspapers, etc. Some people are luckier than others. Some are pitifully unlucky. I for one will not blame you for the environment you got as a child.

The two major determinants of behavior are things over which we do not have much control. Each of us is a product of the genetic inheritance and the society from which we emerge. We tout our free will, but even the way we think has been shaped by others. I for one will not blame you for who you are.

We are responsible for our actions. As part of your environment I am responsible for providing you with an influence that will reinforce good behaviors and curb naughty ones. I can do that while still respecting the fact that you are who you are because of factors beyond your control. I don't have to hate you for the bad things you've done.

This does not mean you aren't responsible for your behavior. What you do to nurture your environment now that you are adult will reap you benefits or heartache in the future. Use what you have as well as you can. It matters.

Similarly I will not be conceited or self-righteous about my own accomplishments, having emerged from advantageous genetics and environment. It disturbs me when I witness arrogance in successful people. It disturbs me when I witness people punishing themselves mercilessly because of their failures.

Don't protect yourself from the realization of who you are. We all have frailties. Maturation of your personality depends on learning its strengths and weaknesses. Be fascinated with yourself as a three dimensional person, and learn what you can and cannot expect from yourself. If you want, share the information with others. Do not be afraid to allow your friends to see a glimpse of what you may be at your worst, and certainly don't shield yourself from that knowledge. You are not perfect, though you may pretend to be. Confront your demons.

Mark 4:3-8: *"Listen! A farmer went out to sow his seed. As we was scattering the seed, some fell along the path, and the birds came and ate it up. Some fell on rocky places, where it did not have much soil. It sprang up quickly because the soil was shallow. But when the sun came up, the plants were scorched, and they withered because they had no root. Other seed fell among thorns, which grew up and choked the plants so that they did not bear grain. Still other seed fell on good soil. It came up, grew and produced a crop, multiplying thirty, sixty, or even a hundred times."*

The point for the religious among you is that whether the seed grew or perished, it was sewn by God. Whether the seed fell beside the path, on rocky ground, into the thorns or into rich soil, wherever it landed was an environment created by God.

The point for the scientific among you is that whether or not it was God who distributed the seed or created the environment, one thing we know for sure. It wasn't the seed itself that did it.

The point for the atheists among you is that if you're still reading this it is a rather curious thing. By the way, you atheists and I have one thing very much in common. Our behavior is not driven by a desire to be saved. For you heaven is just a preposterous construction of mythology. For me it simply is for God to decide this fate for me.

I am driven by a conviction, bathed in love, that I am to share with you this same love called agape.

What bathes me in love and gives me that conviction? The scientific among you will say that it is my genetics and environment. I asked Agnos, and in his usual, quizzical way he answered, "God only knows."

22. UGLY THOUGHTS

Ben Huddleston is my friend whom I call Fearless Leader because on the back of the bus riding on our way to work, he has been the main instigator of conversation. In response to one of my not so splendid splogs Fearless Leader replied, "ZZZZZZZZzzzzzzzzZZZZZZZZZ zzzzzzzzZZZZZZZZZ."

Of course he was right. Even I couldn't read it a second time. Probably it was boring because I had run out of my medicine. Mental note: Don't write when hypothyroid. Hey, I'm hypothyroid again today! That's okay. I can handle it.

No goof-off; you're breaking your own rule.

I can handle it! Get off my case.

In the 2004 gubernatorial election for the state of Washington, they found out that dead people had voted. That's scary, but maybe they weren't really dead. Maybe they were just hypothyroid. Remember the zombies in the cult classic *Dawn of the Dead*. I think hypothyroid people get a bum rap.

When I run out of levo-thyroid I tend to drink more coffee for energy, but it's not the same. I become a wired zombie. Levo-thyroid gives me a sense of humor. It's better.

It took me awhile to think of how to approach the topic of Scott Peterson, the creepy guy who murdered his pregnant wife and then took her body out in a small boat and dumped it into the ocean. There are at least two differences between Scott and the rest of us. Are they that he is a thug and a pimp? No, but close.

Also I doubt he's hypothyroid. He couldn't have pulled it off if he were. Without levo-thyroid he wouldn't have had enough energy, and with it he would have been too nice a guy, chuckling all the time.

First of all, most of us have a healthy respect for rules, for orderly adherence to laws. We have a love for moral responsibility. We get nauseated by what is horrible. Scott doesn't. He's a sociopath.

The second thing, and maybe here is where you get upset with me, is that unlike many of us, at least Scott took personal responsibility for solving his own problem. He wanted out of his marriage, and he got out of his marriage.

This is not to say he had the right solution, of course not. That would have been divorce. But divorce is so messy, so expensive. A little fishing boat costs much less and can be cleaned up afterward without lingering alimony and child support. Little fishing boats aren't all that demanding.

When people feel trapped it is common for them to think UGLY. Instead of taking personal responsibility they pray. "God, please make her die in a car accident." "Please God, make him have a fatal heart attack." This is the UGLY extension of our more common prayer, "God, please let me win the Lotto."

The difference between Scott and the rest of us is that we don't act on our ugly thoughts.

Why doesn't God answer these prayers? Reading the Bible you can be sure God is capable of horror. Take the story about the time God told Abraham to sacrifice his son, Isaac, as an offering. Isaac was bound and placed on an altar. Abraham was about to stab him with a knife when, at the last moment, an angel of the Lord stopped Abraham's hand, and a ram was found in the thicket for sacrifice.

I hate this story. If you take this story away then I can like God. It is touted as a demonstration of Abraham's tremendous faith in God, but I regard it as a testament to Abraham's cowardice. He should have thumbed his nose at God and said, "Up yours Grandpa." I like the Don Quixote attitude, to be willing to march into hell for a heavenly cause. That's courage. Do the right thing.

The Genesis account of Abraham and Isaac doesn't tell the whole story. My secret operatives contracted Mr. P-Brain with his back-again-machine, and so I can tell you the rest.

Isaac grew up a very troubled boy. He became a cutter. He would sneak up on little kids with his knife and say, "Boo! Then he'd sneer, "You're not the Lamb of God. I am." Then he'd cut himself and run around cackling hysterically. Once he cut his left thigh a bit too deeply, and he limped around swearing sarcastically, "Shit; that's just frickin' beautiful." Isaac spent a lot of money on therapy.

God doesn't answer these kinds of prayers because he's smart enough to know that the key to spiritual learning is not whether one wins or loses in the game of life; it's how the game is played. This age-old wisdom was taught to us in grade school, revised by high school football coaches, and hopefully later in life we learn it again as old-age wisdom. One of my heroes, Vince Lombardi, said, "Winning isn't everything. It's the only thing." Well, football isn't a paradigm for life, and getting out of a marriage isn't a touchdown. Loss of life is not a fifteen yard penalty for roughing the kicker.

The difference between Scott and the rest of us is that we understand these things. He doesn't. Also he's a thug and, who knows, maybe a pimp.

It's not what you think. It's what you do. It's not what you believe. It's what you do with that belief.

23. TERROR ON BUS 941

In T2B2 (Think Tank on the Back of the Bus), the question was asked, who would you choose if you could invite anybody from all of history to a dinner party. The big calm man suggested that if it were a picnic on a beach, with this tsunami risk, you would be wise to invite Moses to protect you with his power over water. That got me thinking. I said, "What if Moses was the culprit? What if he started acting crazy, as though the Red Sea were small potatoes? So he decided to part the Indian Ocean, and that's what caused the tsunami."

That's when the bus started rocking violently back and forth. Later I learned from my psychic operatives that Moses got really peeved with me. "That irreverent little pinhead," he complained. "He makes fun of my parting the Red Sea, and he can't even make a decent part when combing his hair. I'll make short work of this ass-brain."

You're not used to hearing Moses talk like that, but you know the Bible doesn't tell every little detail. Remember when he had temper enough to break his first set of stone tablets over the heads of his followers, and that was just because they decided to make a cow statue out of gold. Don't forget the plagues he brought to Egypt. Don't mess with him.

So there we were in bus 941, rocking with our heads and torsos each going different ways. Our bodies resonated violently with the nauseating rhythm of the bus. Just as I was wondering if the bus driver's mother knew he drove that way, he pointed at me with both hands, and the bus swerved. "It's him!" He shouted, "He's a devil."

Then everybody pointed at me. Torches and ropes appeared out of nowhere. "Lynch him," the people cried. "No, burn him at the stake." Then they rushed me, picked me up and were about to throw me head first out of the bus.

An angel of the Lord appeared and stopped them. "Leave him alone. He's just a dumb animal."

Tell me, should I send the angel a thank you card?

24. SARCASM

On May 23, 2005, the Scripps Howard News Service distributed an article by Lee Bowman. It came with the headline: *Complex thinking required to understand sarcasm.* The first sentence was, *Sarcasm is lost on many people ... because they may be missing part of a complex set of cognitive skills based in specific parts of the brain.* You knew that all along, didn't you?

The article described research by a group of Israeli psychologists who mapped out the brain pathway by which a person may appreciate sarcasm. First the left half of the brain interprets the language to establish the literal meaning of what was said. Then the frontal lobes and right half of the brain process the intended meaning and the social and emotional context of what was said, identifying the contradiction between what's going on and what was said. Finally the rear part of the right prefrontal cortex must integrate the literal meaning with the social and emotional knowledge of the current and previous situations to empower the listener to appreciate the true meaning. Don't try to understand that sentence. It'll only slow you down.

This is my kind of information. In times past I've had occasion to chat with and about the right prefrontal cortex of the brain. In fact I have one of my own. It sits behind the right side of my forehead, and I like to believe mine is well developed.

A year or two ago I learned that the medial part of this right prefrontal cortex, the part closest to the midline of the body just behind the nose side of the eyebrow, is where we understand why something is funny. We may laugh at a joke without that part of the brain, but we'd never make it as a joke writer for Jay Leno. We'd laugh at something funny, but we'd have no idea why.

There is yet a third function I know for the prefrontal cortex of the brain. This is where we understand the implications of pain, what a given pain means to us. It's a good part of the brain to have, and to illustrate this I'd like to tell a story.

As kids, my friends and I rode our bikes to and from the municipal swimming pool, and on the way home it was customary to buy a snack from the stand across the street from the pool. One day I purchased a bag of popcorn, and of course I rode no-handed in order to eat it. A friend extolled the excitement of riding a bike no-handed with your eyes closed, so I tried it. The collision of my bike with a parked car was not as remarkable as the collision of my family jewels with the handlebar. Popcorn burst into the air in an explosion of popped cloud, lightly salted and with lots of butter. My friends laughed, and I laughed as well because I really could see the humor in it, even though I suspected I might need to go to the emergency room to have my scrotum sewn back on. As it turned out, my scrotum never left my body; it only felt that way.

In the midst of my pained laughter I asked my friend sarcastically, "I bet you had no idea something like that would happen, did you?" This expression of sarcastic humor in the face of pain is the value of the right prefrontal cortex.

If I hadn't had a right prefrontal cortex, I might still have laughed, but I would have been dumfounded as to why. "Stop laughing," I'd say to myself and my friends. "This ain't funny. And you, Shit-head, you did this to me on purpose. I'm going to rip you a new one, just as soon as I can stand up again." Nobody would have had fun with that.

Losing some functions of the prefrontal cortex may in some situations be beneficial. For example, consider a has-been boxer with brain injury from all the poundings he's had. During a fight he gets his face torn open one more time, but he hasn't a clue as to what it matters. "Aw, it's nothin.'"

It's hard to understand why people take up the sport of boxing. You train incessantly and painfully through grueling sessions of mind-over-common-sense to put yourself into peak condition, just so that some few months later you can climb into a ring and have somebody else pound you senseless. Then you do it all over again. This is existentialism for people without prefrontal portions of their brains.

I suspect that someone way back, making important decisions about the meaning of the Bible, did not have a sense of sarcasm. Back in biblical days, women were considered property. They were slaves to their husbands, and of course the good people like Paul exhorted husbands to be good to their slaves. That's the flavor of it all. There were women who escaped from abusive relationships, and while some of them just disappeared there were others who joined the group that surrounded Jesus. Even some of his disciples questioned the validity of women assuming a position of sharing in religious conversations. This was a role reserved for men. Jesus once said a curious thing about one such woman. He said, "Then let her walk with me, and I will make her a man. " Sarcastic guy, that one!

Well what about this biblical scholar without a sense of sarcasm, and probably also without a sense of humor. In the nineteenth chapter of Matthew, Pharisees came to complain to Jesus about the women who had left their husbands and had come to join his flock. *Some Pharisees came to him to test him. They asked, "Is it lawful for a man to divorce his wife for any and every reason?" "Haven't you read," he replied, "that at the beginning the Creator 'made them male and female,' and said, 'For this reason a man will leave his father and mother and be united to his wife, and the two will become one flesh.' So they are no longer two, but one. Therefore what God has joined together let man not separate." "Why then," they asked, "did Moses command that a man give his wife a certificate of divorce and send her away?" Jesus replied, "Moses permitted you to divorce your wives because your hearts were hard. But it was not this way from the beginning. I tell you that anyone who divorces his wife, except for marital unfaithfulness, and marries another woman commits adultery."*

Whew! Does anyone truly believe Jesus was so naïve as to suggest all marriages were inseparable no matter what? Except for adultery alone? Maybe Jesus simply was elevating women to the status of men. If women could not divorce their husbands, then men could not divorce their wives. What was good for the goose was good for the gander. Jesus turned the table on the Pharisees, spun the intellectual Lazy Susan on them so to speak. This was to put them in their place. It left them speechless.

Then later when the disciples were discussing among themselves how silly it would be for the Law to be so strict, several of them *said to him, "if this is the situation between a husband and wife, it is better not to marry." Jesus replied. "Not everyone can accept this word, but only those to whom it has been given. For some are eunuchs because they were born that way; others were made that way by men; and others have renounced marriage because of the kingdom of heaven."*

Okay, so some scholar without a sense of sarcasm interpreted this literally. He also must have had great faith in the trustworthiness of the authors and the interpreters of that suspiciously sacred text. That is why the Catholic Church decided to prohibit divorce and to keep its priests celibate. We all know how well that has worked.

However, these verses can be interpreted differently, with a sense of sarcasm. Please forgive me for suggesting that Jesus, the consummate humorist, might have said something like, "Yes gentlemen, marriage takes balls. Some men have them and some men don't."

God's spirit yearned to speak through a man with a sense of humor, a man with a super-sized right prefrontal cortex, and by God he found one in Jesus.

25. TRUST AND CONTROL

When somebody has broken your trust, how do you learn to trust that person again? You will not like my answer to this question, but you will gain strength and stability from it. Ultimately you cannot trust any other human being. You cannot trust even yourself fully. All people can be trusted in some ways and to certain extents, but not totally, and part of your fascination with others may be learning the ways and extents of their trustworthiness. We all are frail, one way or another.

Promises are good as strong statements of intent, goals to be accomplished or maintained, but only seldom are they completely reliable. For example when we marry we promise to be faithful, and we mean it. Yet look how often this promise gets broken. Sometimes the passions within us take control, and we lose it. This is normal human behavior. It is not admirable. It is painful. It is normal. What are some other promises that get broken? "I'll never take another drink." "I'll never hit you again." "I'll study next term; really I will. Just send money for tuition." Get the picture?

When somebody makes you a promise, appreciate the intent and strength of the statement, but care more about the person than the promise.

When establishing a healthy relationship, what you must be able to trust is that the other person ultimately will be responsible for her or his own happiness. If she or he is unhappy it is not automatically your fault. She or he also must be willing to accept consequences for her or his own behavior. You must trust yourself on the same points. To make this work requires that you be independently secure, comfortable alone. That may not be easy.

This doesn't mean you can't be interdependent with another, that wonderful state of affairs in which people find different and compatible roles, helping each other to enhance their lives. There is a fine but important line between healthful interdependence and manipulative codependency.

You cannot trust that any relationship will last forever, although hoping is normal and okay. Nurture the relationship, and it may last. Don't nurture it, and it may not. Good luck.

Do as much as you can to stay in control of your own behavior, and keep it consistent with the moral rules you have inside. Do as much as you can to avoid control of other people's behavior. Encourage them to be responsible for themselves, and let them make their own decisions. Of course you may express your opinions, but let them do for themselves. Many people strive to become important, indispensable. Happiness will be found more likely by empowering others so that you yourself can become expendable. Free yourself!

26. HAPPINESS

Buddhism offers that the path to happiness is acceptance. That may be, sort of, not that happiness is necessarily what everybody wants or needs. In the case of Buddhism the goal ultimately is not to be happy here on earth, but rather to escape the never ending cycle of rebirth, of reincarnation, and instead live indefinitely although not permanently in Nirvana. This means that if you want to change something, like the communist regime in China, you do something like stand in front of a military tank, and you can't expect to be really happy. Still there is a choice of whether or not to be happy, whether or not to accept things the way they are.

Happiness may not be all it's cracked up to be. Nevertheless there are a lot of people who want to be happy, and so on February 11, 2004, the *Seattle Times* ran a rather good article: *The How and Why of Happiness.* Here is the list of strategies given by experts.

1. Be grateful.
2. Forgive.
3. Make friends.
4. Challenge yourself.
5. Be good to others.
6. Let small things slide.
7. Don't sacrifice any of the above things in a pursuit of wealth.

There you have it, advice from the experts on the study of *subjective well-being.* There are a few more items I'd like to add.

8. Be oblivious to the world. Even though you really can be hurt by what you don't know, oblivion will numb you to the consequences. This can be obtained by drugs, but it's better gotten by meditation along the lines of that little known guru I discovered in *Mad Magazine,* Alfred E. Neuman. If you really want to be happy, read *Mad Magazine* because Guru Neuman is truly an unsung master. His mantra is "What, me worry?" But I wanted to be original, so I came up with my own. "It's okay to be a boob. People expect it of me."

9. A corollary to the technique of oblivion is the artificial construct method whereby you can achieve happiness by restructuring in your mind what constitutes success. For example if you worry about your health and longevity, and if you are religious, then once you pass the age of 33 years, about the age Jesus died, you can say to yourself, "Hey wow! I'm more successful than God." If you're not religious, but you are musical, a good choice is Mozart. Once you pass 29 years say, "Hey wow! I'm more successful than Mozart." When you pass 37 say, "Hey wow! I'm more successful than George Gershwin." If you worry about finances, maybe choose Gandhi or Mother Teresa. "Hey wow! I'm richer than Gandhi and Mother Teresa."

10. If all else fails, you need Stimpy's helmet. Awhile ago *Ren and Stimpy* was an outrageous animated television program that mothers everywhere dreaded. Adolescents loved it. I loved it. Ren was a mongrel dog that looked more like a rat, and he was grumpy, complained about everything. Stimpy was a cat with a never ending smile and a Pollyannaish

disposition that drove Ren crazy. In one episode Stimpy tried to help Ren by inventing a helmet that, once put on, clamped tightly and never let go. It forced Ren to smile and even laugh no matter what was going on. It worked, sort of, until Ren was so overwhelmed with his own seething underneath that smile, that he hit himself over the head repeatedly until the helmet was broken. Life is like that. Religion is like that. Ren was a cartoon heretic.

So you don't really have to be happy; that's my point. Don't let anybody pressure you into that way of thinking. But if you want to be happy, maybe these several tips will help.

27. D.C. COMICS

Sorting out details in my mind, often it's nice to categorize things according to how meaningful they have been in my life. For example I can remember exactly where I was the day my sixth grade teacher announced that President Kennedy had been shot. I remember being in the cardiac rehabilitation clinic on January 28, 1986, when Space Shuttle Challenger exploded. I recall sitting in my father's workshop reluctantly allowing him to give me a military haircut the time he assaulted my sense of polite demeanor with the secret of the birds and the bees.

But for the life of me I can't remember where I was when I first learned Dick Cheney had shot Harry Whittington. I didn't right away join in the hoopla, mainly because the jokes were way too easy, and there were plenty of them. My favorite was told by my friend Kyle who thought of making a t-shirt with a map of Texas and the proclamation, "Texas, shooting people in the face since 2006."

My friend Marcia got political and suggested maybe George Bush should go lame duck hunting with Dick. Of course that will never happen. Somewhere in the Constitution it says the vice president is prohibited from carrying a loaded shotgun within range of the president.

Doctors in T2D2 (Think Tank in the Doctors Dining room) wondered if Cheney's internal defibrillator suddenly went off, "Ah—h-h-h-h-h-h-gh." BLAM! The device's warning label should inform of this possibility. *Use of this contraption may cause irreparable harm to those around the recipient if it goes off while he's wielding a firearm.*

There are lessons here to be learned about quail hunting. Don't shoot low. Don't shoot uphill. Don't shoot into the blinding sun. And if you are unlucky enough to shoot someone anyway, whatever you do, don't be seen in public afterward for a good twenty-four hours or so.

Sleep it off. In fact mix yourself a stiff one. Whether deemed intentional or not, this will confound any blood alcohol tests that may be requested.

The Cheney team could have done a better job releasing this story to the press. When Katharine Armstrong reported it, she said something to the effect that hunting is inherently dangerous, and mistakes like this happen all the time. I remember my immediate response being, you mean this isn't the first time Dick Cheney has shot someone?

The vice president's social calendar changed a bit after that event. As an example of this, on February 27, 2006, Jay Leno asked Colin Powell what he would do if Mr. Cheney invited him to go hunting. "I've got an easy answer for that," replied Powell. "I don't hunt." Then he went on to say he would keep his eye on exactly where he was standing and where the Vice President was standing. It would sort of be like business as usual, guarding against the fat guy shooting from the hip, of course on a more personal rather than political level.

Mr. Cheney got suggestions from companions like, "Hey instead of bird hunting maybe we could just play laser tag."

And Dick, with his famous avuncular style answered, "Let's do paint ball. It's more like the real thing."

Shortly after that, Mr. Cheney visited the Seattle area and I wondered whether he brought his famous shotgun. He didn't. His public relations team advised against it and told him he was to go bird hunting with a taser. The problem was that his heart couldn't keep up with all that running after quail. So he then considered chasing after a lame duck with his taser. He has another problem though, all that voltage around his internal defibrillator. So he had to wear a neoprene wet suit while chasing President Bush around. There's an image for you.

28. CARL GUSTAV

Sven, my friend in Norway, wrote to tell me that it is not only American leaders who shoot their followers. The late Swedish king, Carl Gustav, loved to go elk hunting. Every new hunting season he got a little more senile, and his court had serious talks between themselves, but he was the king. They had no choice but to place the king on the shooting squad. Of course he would not have accepted a position on the team that drove the elk out of the deep brush into the open and toward the hunters.

On one expedition they were sitting and waiting for the elk to be driven toward them, and a messenger came running up to the king. He waved a letter in his hand with broad movements shouting, "Don't shoot. Don't shoot. I'm not the elk!"

The king emptied his rifle, and the messenger dropped stone dead.

After the poor man had been carried away and the mess was cleaned up, the king's court had another serious talk and decided it was time to discuss this issue with the king. The alderman asked, "Your Majesty, excuse me. Why did Your Majesty shoot the messenger?"

"Why the hell did he say he was the elk?" the king remonstrated.

Thank you for that clarification, Sven. This helps me put the Cheney/Whittington event into better perspective. Dick would not have shot Harry if Harry hadn't waved his arms saying, "Don't shoot. Don't shoot. I'm Dan Quail."

29. SHOOT ME

Hey, no joking here. One of my patients attempted suicide, shot himself in the head, now recovering with significant residual deficits at Harborview Trauma Center. I've known this man nearly twenty years, and this came as a surprise.

He is so very different from me. He is of a very right-wing mind set. His is a narrow, circumscribed heaven. And yet deep inside I know that he is me in the very real sense expressed by John Donne, *No man is an island entire of itself.* So I pray for the end of his psychological anguish.

30. PERSONAL HEAVEN

What if heaven is a very personal thing? What if heaven has only those others in it that any given person wants to have in heaven?

Imagine three men who know each other on earth. Tom likes both Dick and Harry, but Dick and Harry don't like each other. Dick dies, and a short time later Harry dies. After awhile Tom dies.

One day while out for a heavenly walk, Tom meets Dick. They warmly greet each other and reminisce about their good times on earth. Dick remarks that he has not seen Harry, and he actually is quite pleased as he had felt while on earth that Harry should go to hell. Dick also tells Tom that he is surprised how small heaven is. Tom is puzzled by this comment because he has seen many people that he knew on earth, and he has been in heaven for only a short time.

Several days later Tom runs into Harry as he is going out for some ice cream. They are pleased to see each other, talk about the old times while living on earth, and after awhile the conversation comes around to Dick. Harry comments that he hasn't seen Dick and is happy about it. He tells Tom that if anybody deserves to burn in hell it would be Dick. Tom tells Harry that he is sorry to disappoint him, but he had just run into Dick a few days earlier. Harry sours at this news and comments that he hopes their paths never will cross.

Tom remarks that it certainly may be possible as heaven is so very large a place with so many souls, just as he had expected. This startles Harry as he has regarded heaven as being of only moderate proportion.

Dick becomes quite bored. After ten years in heaven he has met only six other people. He isn't a social guy, but nevertheless he thinks heaven is far too small. So one day he goes to complain to God and finds the Great Creator of the universe napping at the park. Dick reports how boring heaven is and asks why God doesn't allow more souls in. God answers that this is Dick's personal heaven, and through his own personal decisions Dick had allowed only six other souls to join him.

Dick becomes anxious and queries how long it will be that only six other people are in his heaven. Eternity! Dick panics and pleads for God to make his heaven larger. God tells him there is only one way for that to happen and that is to return to earth and live another life.

31. WHO? HU?

The April 19, 2006, edition of the Seattle Post Intelligencer pointed out that although the Clinton administration's Northwest Forest Plan was launched to save the threatened spotted owl, a Seattle environmental group said the bird's population in Washington was plummeting. The Seattle and Kittitas Audubon Societies cited five spots where the state allowed extensive logging by Weyerhaeuser near owl nests. The environmentalists contended that this logging violated the Endangered Species Act.

One of my secret operatives donned an owl suit and listened in on a recent owl town hall meeting. "Who, who," began the moderator. "Who?"

Then the owls in attendance nodded, "Who," in agreement. Then all together they said in unison, "Who."

Chinese President Hu Jintao took that as an invitation and decided to visit us. Never underestimate the power of a fowl word. So President Hu said, among other things, that China's rapidly growing economy sure could use more U.S. Northwest lumber.

32. SEX AND VIOLENCE

Never have I advocated putting a condom over the barrel of a gun. That would make no sense at all, except maybe to trigger a victim's laughter before getting shot. No, I'm not advocating that either, getting shot I mean. Laughing is okay. I advocate laughter.

Conservatives and liberals tend to see guns and condoms differently. How's that?

Conservatives in most places will not force you to own a gun, but they want you to have the opportunity to own one if you so choose. They encourage you not to use it illegally.

Liberals in most places won't force you to own a condom, but they want you to have the opportunity to own one if you so choose. They encourage you not to engage in illegal sex, but if you're going to do it, use a condom.

Conservatives don't want you to own a condom if you're under age, as the temptation to use it would be just too great. There's no RIGHT way to handle the consequence of an unfortunate pregnancy.

Liberals don't want you to own a gun, no matter how old you are, as the temptation to use it would be just too great. There's no way, RIGHT or LEFT, to handle the consequence of an unfortunate homicide.

Liberals and Conservatives agree that ample training is important for the safe handling of a firearm. They disagree on the amount of training necessary for the safe use of a condom.

33. SEX AND THE WALRUS

Have you heard enough yet about homosexuality? Are you tired of hearing about it? Maybe not if it's *Will and Grace* or *Brokeback Mountain*. Homosexuality definitely is in the news.

Some people have a hard time with all of this, and their difficulty differs depending on where they stand in regard to personal beliefs about what God wants.

I've discussed this with the Spirit Agnos, and he said he didn't know what God wants, said it's pretty arrogant for someone to say they know what God wants. He said, "Maybe it depends on whether you think God talks louder out of the Bible or out of the mouths of Scientists."

People of Jewish and Christian heritage have to contend with Leviticus 18:22, where it is written that the Lord said to Moses, among other things, *"You shall not lie with a male as with a woman, as it is an abomination."* Leviticus also forbids men from defiling themselves with beasts and women defiling themselves with beasts, but it does not strictly forbid women with women, so maybe lesbians are home free. That is, if we take the Bible literally and God strictly at his word according to the Bible.

What is the law of God? We could argue about that for awhile. I see basically three classifications of religious people in regard to considerations of God and homosexuality. One group adheres to the Old Testament. Another group is progressively New Testament, and a third group resides somewhere in the middle in a sort of meandering vague purgatory of belief they call Grace.

The other day I listened to one of my Lutheran pastors say the law was not a nice thing, and none of us can successfully adhere to the extreme demands of God's law. We're all born sinful and can't escape it. I'm sure you've heard this before, the concept of original sin. Ever since Adam and Eve disobeyed God's instruction, the rest of us have been born dirty, guilt by association. You know guilt by association is one of the things prohibited by the Bill of Rights in our United States Constitution, a piece of inspirational philosophy revered by scholars around the world. But James Madison wrote the Bill of Rights long after the big debate on the concept of original sin back when Augustine engraved it heavily into the consciousness of Christianity. So Augustine just didn't have all the goods at the time to make a truly gracious pronouncement. I still like Augustine though, and I'll admit I'm not perfect, a sin here and there. But it's important for us to be clear on just what we consider a sin, because that consideration is socially powerful and potentially destructive.

Then my pastor talked about homosexuality and said that homosexual Christians are destined always to be unhappy because deep in their hearts they know that what they do is wrong in the eyes of God. This didn't ring true for me. I know Christian homosexuals who are quite happy, and they don't think what they do is wrong, and so my immediate reaction to my pastor's comment was that he manufactured an item in order to make a point. The Spirit Agnos whispered into my ear, "He doesn't really know what he's talking about, does he?"

"Shhhhh," I said. By the way, my horoscope for that day told me to keep my mouth shut, so I did.

Then my pastor asked, "You know, don't you, why gays want to be married?"

An elderly man answered, "To make more of them." I couldn't believe my ears, and I couldn't decide whether to laugh or jeer at this ignorant expression of effrontery. I bowed my forehead into my hands and bit my lip."

Agnos whispered, "Maybe he was just joking."

I shook my head. "I don't think so."

The pastor explained that gays wanted to be married as an expression of acceptance by the church family, but that was a direction he just couldn't go. He was supportive of civil union for gays, as it is right that people be held responsible to one another in long term relationships, and rights should be protected, but he could not see any righteousness in the church blessing gays with the rite of marriage.

Next my pastor said that even though homosexuality is sinful, we all are sinful and so we should not regard gay people as being any worse in the eyes of God than we are ourselves. Sounds nice and forgiving, doesn't it? I mean, it's nice and forgiving in an arrogant self-righteous sort of way, right?

It's like if I told a lion that it is a sinful creature because it eats meat, even though it's an obligate carnivore, but it's okay because I forgive the lion. And God also forgives the lion for being that way because that is the grace of God. God forgives us all for being the way he made us. What a guy, this God fellow! Yeah sure, that's the God I love … not. That is not my God. My God is not as divisive as that. My God has better manners than that.

So let's ask ourselves if Jesus did something more than deliver the message of forgiveness and salvation for us God-forsaken creatures. Did Jesus actually change the law? Pause here and listen to the theme from Final Jeopardy playing in your head. Tom's answer is, "What is YES!" Some examples await you. Read on.

In Mark 7:15, Jesus said, *"There is nothing outside a person that by going in can defile, but the things that come out are what defile."* Then Mark made an editorial comment … . *thus he declared all foods clean.* So you can thank Jesus and Mark the next time you bite into your ham and Swiss sandwich. The law was changed!

Then there is the argument between the Pharisees and Jesus in the nineteenth chapter of Matthew about the status of women. Pharisees came to complain to Jesus about the women who had left their husbands and had come to join his flock. To test him they asked, *"Is it lawful for a man to divorce his wife for any and every reason?"* *"Haven't you read,"* he replied, *"that at the beginning the Creator 'made them male and female,' and said, 'For this reason a man will leave his father and mother and be united to his wife, and the two will become one flesh.' So they are not longer two, but one."* And in so doing Jesus elevated the status of women from being a man's property to that of being fully human with rights equal to a man's. The law was changed!

Recognizing that Jesus did indeed do more than forgive, that he in fact changed the law, what do you think he meant in the tenth chapter of Matthew when he said, *"Have no fear ... for nothing is covered up that will not be uncovered, and nothing secret that will not become known ... and even the hairs of your head are all counted. So do not be afraid."*

In John 16:12-15, Jesus said, *"I have much more to say to you, more than you can now bear. But when he, the Spirit of truth, comes, he will guide you into all truth. He will not speak on his own; he will speak only what he hears, and he will tell you what is yet to come. He will bring glory to me by taking from what is mine and making it known to you. All that belongs to the Father is mine. That is why I said the Spirit will take from what is mine and make it known to you."*

Do you think just possibly Jesus was preparing us for change? Do you think he was telling us that as we understand more and more about the world, we will need to adapt? Do you think, just maybe? Or maybe you don't think? Does God talk through the scientists? Jesus seems to say so.

Here's a sticky part. How do we know when it is God talking? We can't trust all scientists to give it to us straight, can we?

The answer is in Matthew 22, starting with the 35th verse: When Jesus was asked which was the greatest commandment he answered, *"You shall love the Lord your God with all your heart, and with all your soul, and with all your mind. This is the greatest and first commandment. And a second is like it: You shall love your neighbor as yourself. On these two commandments hang all the law and the prophets."* This is your most powerful and reliable decoder ring for all of life, all of the Bible, all of applied science. That's me talking about the decoder ring. Jesus himself didn't talk about decoder rings. That was one of the things the people of his time weren't ready for.

Law that brings people together is God's law. Law that separates people is law created by man.

Science has taught us a lot about how anatomy and physiology differ between the minds of gay and straight people. We see examples of it in animals of the wild, untainted by human law. We understand that it is a natural phenomenon. Do you think God would use such a thing, that he even would create such a thing in order to divide his family?

Here's a final thought for you, and I'm just repeating what already has been said by Jesus and other greats. Don't be afraid of progress. Have faith that as we learn more and as technology advances, we will be guided by adherence to the greatest two commandments. Not to accept change is to be dead. Not to have faith in the future is to cling to a dead faith. In John 10:10, Jesus is recorded to have said, *"I came that they may have life and have it abundantly."*

Don't be dead. Don't let your faith be dead. Grow! Live!

"Wait a minute," Agnos interrupted me. "You're not done here. What about those people who say all sex is sinful, except for sex that is done for the single purpose of making a baby? That would make homosexuality different from heterosexuality, right?"

"What? That's pretty puritanical, isn't it."

"Some people are puritanical," he said.

"What would God have against people giving each other pleasure? If you applied that rule to all things, then we could not dance or give each other massages."

Agnos smiled. "And that's what some people believe."

"But we couldn't hold hands either, or give hugs. This would be one big bastard of a God if we couldn't do that."

Agnos pondered for a moment. "Maybe it's the passion. Maybe we can give each other pleasure as long as we keep passion out of it."

"So then it would be more acceptable to have dispassionate sex with a hooker than for two people to have sex who are madly in love with each other."

"Could be," said Agnos. "Or maybe passion is okay only if two people are married."

"Aha!" I exclaimed. "So that's the real reason why gay people want to get married, so they can have passionate sex with each other instead of dispassionate sex with gentlemen of the night. It also explains why right wing heterosexuals don't want homosexuals to get married. This gives straight people a handle on lording it over the gays. We have something they don't."

Then Agnos said, "Maybe all people can have sex as long as they don't take their shoes off." I was about to glare at him but saw the teasing smirk on his face. "You know," he added, "it's okay to drop your trousers, but it's not really sex unless you actually take them off."

Agnos and I finally worked out what we think makes sense. Sex is wonderful between any two people who love each other and are responsible to each other. It is sinful when one person is coerced or forced to participate. There is sin also when we use differences between people to divide one person or group from others. We are one in God, and when we deny that oneness, we deny God.

The Gospel of John is quite mystical in this regard. In the seventeenth chapter of the Gospel of John, Jesus prays, *"May they all be one. Father, may they be one in us, as you are in me and I am in you ... may they be so completely one that the world will realize ...,"* and the Beatles gave a finish for this quite nicely by saying the world will realize that all of us, taken together as one whole, are the walrus. Fans may point out that John said Paul was the walrus, and of course he was, but so were George and Ringo and the rest of us.

So here I am, one part of the walrus shouting out to you other parts of the walrus. Let us be of a collective mind that keeps our walrus alive and well.

34. A VERY CLEAN YARD

It was the day before we were to go on a two week vacation. I wanted to put fertilizer on the front lawn, and I did the thing my wife has wanted a long time for me to stop. I did it without first consulting the directions.

Once the fertilizer was applied, the thought occurred to me that I really should make sure I did it right, so then I read the directions. The amount I had applied was roughly five times what I should have applied. I did not gasp. I made no sound (I tend to suffer in silence.). My eyes did in fact pop out of their sockets though, sproi-oi-oi-oing. I put them back in because I needed to read the weather report in the newspaper. Maybe if we were going to have a lot of rain my lawn would survive. No such luck. No rain in sight. I was looking at the possibility that after our vacation we would return to a front yard wasteland, a desert.

Quickly thinking, I took the older of our two vacuum cleaners out into the yard and began to suck up fertilizer. At least it was a canister style, not an upright. I got about half the yard done before the vacuum stopped working.

Here's the curious thing. Neighbors walking by on the sidewalk stopped and said hello. Some would strike up a conversation, but they did not ask me what the hell I thought I was doing. Either they were shy about it or else they might have thought this was just Tom being his normal quirky self.

The lawn survived. The vacuum cleaner did not.

35. INTELLIGENT RESIGN

Many of you already know that Federal Judge John Jones III, ruled in Dover Pennsylvania that it is not legal for the concept of Intelligent Design to be made a necessary item for science classes to teach as an alternative to Darwin's Theory of Evolution. Thank God. A deep sigh of relief was heard from the minds of sensible people all over the world.

Jones ruled that Intelligent Design may be taught in philosophy classes or literature or religion classes, but as it is not a scientifically verified concept it doesn't belong in science class.

Intelligent Designers protested, but were they truly intelligent they would intelligently resign themselves to this simple truth, not that there isn't some merit to the argument of Intelligent Design, but science is science and philosophy is philosophy.

Often I wonder at the insistence of right wing Christians to protest new knowledge. I'm pretty sure it happens because they think God stopped talking to humankind after the writing of the Nicene Creed, in which Christians profess that the Holy Spirit has spoken through the prophets.

Do you think if the creed had not been written until today, maybe the authors would have written that the Holy Spirit has spoken through the scientists? That's what I believe. I'm certain that the scientists don't yet have everything exactly right, but I think the evidence sides with them, and I also believe they honestly attempt to make sense of the world. Seek and you will find. Knock and the door will be opened to you. Yes, God speaks through the scientists, whether they realize it or not.

So I think those people who reject scientific accomplishment are in effect snubbing their noses at God's revelations to us. Their faith is dormant. They believe they must protect archaic understandings we used to have of God, and I imagine God shaking his head and saying, "Wake up and look at what I have given you." He'd also say something like, "Look, I really don't need to be protected by you pipsqueaks."

Let me take it a step further. On this issue the far right Christians are committing the same sin that got Lucifer thrown out of Heaven, the sin of arrogance. Lucifer wanted more than what God had given him, wanted his throne in heaven to be higher than God's. He rejected what God gave him, and for that arrogance Lucifer was dispatched from the kingdom. We want what we want, and that's understandable and okay, but when we demand it, when we insist belligerently on having things our own way in opposition to the gifts of God, then we cross the line.

God gave us Darwin's Theory of Evolution, and he stacked all the evidence in Darwin's court. You may even say God is on Darwin's side. That's the way I see it. Far right Christians aren't satisfied with what God has shown us in this theory; they want more. If now I were to write that these far right Christians are anti-God, I'd piss somebody off, so I'll get my point across another way.

Actually there is something that far right Christians and atheists agree on. Both factions believe that God doesn't speak through the scientists. You'd think this would be a rallying point around which atheists and Christians come together, maybe throw a party, but it has turned out not to be a very popular rallying point, so put away the party hats.

Maybe this is circumstantial evidence to make my point. Since God likes togetherness, or at least we strongly suspect that's so, if he doesn't speak through the scientists, then he would have made it so that far right Christians and atheists would bond on this particular point. Since no such bonding has occurred, God must in fact speak through the scientists.

If both atheists and far right Christians start believing that God speaks through the scientists, then we may actually see more togetherness, more parties, and it would make some hard working scientists very happy. Some day when humankind has accomplished what we've requested repetitively from God, "Thy kingdom come," then we all will say to the scientists, "God speaks through you." A puzzled scientist may not know exactly how to answer, so let me suggest an appropriate response: "Thank you, and also through you."

36. HERETIC

"Augustine said only the greatest of souls are born to be heretics," he announced, knowing that I consider myself a heretic. His aim was not to flatter me, and I was not flattered.

How can an eye call itself greater than the other parts of the body? Can an eye go its own way without the rest of the body? If you gouge an eye out of the body, can the eye see? So how can one soul even be itself without the whole?

Of course some of you may argue that this is not a fair analogy, and to that I shout, "Hey! Whose heresy is this anyway?" Heresy can be a lonely thing, except my heresy. It includes all of you in my heaven, even if you don't want to be there. You're stuck with me. Ha!

His aim was to draw me out, and so I answered, "A heretic is willing to march into hell for a heavenly cause," and inside of myself I cringed for having taken the line directly from *Man of La Mancha*.

A heretic has a message of change, critical of current practice and belief. It may seem to observers that he stands shaking his fist at God, but the heretic sees himself as God's fist shaking at the here and now.

The message is not of the heretic's choosing. He simply believes what he believes and is honest with himself. Then either he is quiet about it or a loud mouth.

FOUR

Thanksgiving

37. THANKSGIVING DAY

William Brewster looked out across the damp clearing, watching for the Indian guests who would join his group of about fifty survivors for a three day festival of celebration. Traces of fog still hugged the ground, and as he patiently observed it dissipate, he recalled solemnly the year that had just passed.

He had led 102 passengers of English Separatist Puritans, setting sail in the *Mayflower* from Plymouth England on September 16, 1620, looking for religious freedom and a better life. Here in the new world they had encountered a hard life of bitter weather, the toll of which was softened by the generosity of the native inhabitants. He felt esteem for others in his group, the bravery of John Carver, Edward Winslow and William Bradford, all of whom in years to come would be governors of this new Plymouth Colony. Also there were John Alden, his assistant governor, and Myles Standish, the professional soldier and military advisor who had been instrumental in the safe establishment of this settlement.

The *Mayflower* dropped anchor on November 21, 1620, and an appropriate site was sought for settlement. The 41 men aboard signed the Mayflower Compact, an agreement to enact *just and equal laws for the general good of the colony.* Then it was the day after Christmas when they landed. They found the remains of a village apparently abandoned by its previous citizens, and they did what they could to erect build-ings and other rough shelters for the winter, but harsh weather and illness killed half of them. The half who survived would be prepared better for the coming winter.

It was quite an encounter when the elegantly dressed Indian, Samoset, approached them boldly and stood arrogantly in the middle of their community, with an aura of superiority in his countenance. He surprised them by speaking the King's English which he had learned from traders on the coast of Maine. "You are a curious looking bunch," he said, and from that point on they knew they had something in common. Samoset introduced the colonists to Massasoit, chief of the Wampanoag Indians, and Massasoit received them with gracefulness. Later they met Squanto who also spoke English, learned during several years of captivity after he had been abducted from his home and narrowly escaped being sold into slavery. When he returned to the new world he found that his village had been decimated by disease, and then it was taken and inhabited by these people from Europe. Squanto's role as main interpreter and guide for the Pilgrims, came to him attached with complex emotions. He helped them learn to plant corn, to catch fish and gather fruit.

These three Indians would be arriving soon with close to ninety of their people. It was fitting to share with them the harvest, so much of which was owed to the generosity of these gentle native folk.

Myles Standish stood guard over women preparing food at outdoor fires. He had with him his faithful muzzle-loading musket with a stock stained in a beautiful maroon color. He was fond enough of this instrument that he had named it Mr. Marksman, and he never went anywhere without it. It made him feel manly. It was his manly, maroon, muzzle-loading musket, Mr. Marksman. If given just a lead ball to shoot, Mr. Marksman shot unpredictably crooked. You couldn't hit the hind end of an elk from just fifteen paces, but if you packed it with lots of little stuff, like B-B shot, it could strip the leaves off a gooseberry bush with just one explosion. What would work well, he thought, would be thumb tacks. He wished he had some thumb tacks.

Mrs. Alden supervised the preparation of food for well over one hundred hungry people. It was a daunting task. There wasn't enough cookware, so food would have to be dumped into wooden bowls as they went along, and getting started early was essential. Mrs. Alden was grateful for the sumptuous selection provided by the Good Lord. There were clams and eel, cod, lobster, partridge and duck. The hunters had bagged some swans and eagles. There even would be venison to share. They had flat bread made from flour ground of wheat and dried corn. The gardens had produced pumpkin for stew, but there would be no pumpkin pie, as the recipe did not yet exist. Mrs. Alden had written several letters to Betty Crocker requesting such a recipe, but the letters kept returning as undeliverable. Nobody at the address had ever heard of a Betty Crocker, and there was no forwarding address. Oh well, there were more serious things to worry about. She could be pleased with what they had: peas, beans, onions, lettuce and carrots. They would enjoy wild plums and grapes, walnuts, chestnuts and acorns. They could spice all of this with olive oil, liverwort, leeks, dried currants and Parsnips.

Myles Standish meandered over to where Mrs. Alden was directing the others and wished her a good day. "It smells wonderful, Mrs. Alden."

"Thank you Mr. Standish. With the help of the Lord it will all turn out to the delight of those present."

Standish thought Mrs. Alden talked funny. He always had thought that but never said anything about it. "Is it to your own liking, Mrs. Alden?"

"Oh, Mr. Standish, the food will be tasteful and tender, and we all shall enjoy it, but I wish we could have decorated the houses to show the festival of our celebration. It would have been to the praise of our Lord to have hung streamers and pictures and the like. For that we could have used thumb tacks. By this time in the next year I do hope we shall have procured thumb tacks. Don't you think it would be right to order thumb tacks for our next shipment, Mr. Standish?"

A broad grin appeared on his face as he answered softly, "Why yes, Mrs. Alden, I do indeed think the colony would do well with some thumb tacks."

Nearby, young Miss Sarah Bradford was watching this exchange. She felt warmly about Mr. Standish. A year earlier when she had first met him she thought he was aloof, rather Standish offish, but once you got to know him he was sweet, and his smyles could go for myles (Pilgrim spelling).

Off in the woods not far away, marched the cheerful Indians. Normally they would have walked as quietly as water in a slow pool, and never would they have been heard above the whisper of a gentle breeze through an aspen's leaves, but today was different. Today was a day for merriment and song. Chief Massasoit turned to Samoset and asked if their gifts were packed and brought along. Samoset answered, "Yes Father, you will be pleased by the happiness your people bring to the newcomers."

Then Samoset turned to Squanto, "You remembered the supplies, right?"

Squanto smiled with about three teeth visibly missing and said, "Those supplies aren't the only thing I remembered." He tapped the pouch at his side and winked, "This here's distilled potato spirits. We're going to have a good time."

Samoset looked aghast. "You can't bring that along. They don't drink spirits at all. You'll make a mess of everything."

"There will be a mess alright, but I won't be the one making it. I'll sneak this into their juice, and they won't know what hit them."

Samoset rolled his eyes. "They will smell it, you idiot."

Squanto was unperturbed, "I'll put it in just a tiny bit at a time. I'm sneaky. With them it won't take much. You know, it's not like this is the first time I've played this trick on them." He winked while Samoset buried his face in his hands and shook his head.

When the Indians arrived at the settlement, there was a fanfare of children shouting and laughing. William Brewster extended his hand to Chief Massasoit and welcomed him. "It is with the greatest of pleasure and gratitude that we receive you into our village today, for without you we certainly would have perished. You are earthly angels with no uncertainty brought to our aide by the hand of Our Heavenly Father.

Massasoit answered, "The Great Spirit sees no difference between people, and the land is plentiful for those who nurture it." Then he turned to Samoset and asked, "Did I say it correctly, Son?"

Samoset answered, "That will do Father; that will do." Then Samoset shouted to his group, "Bring forward the gifts of food."

Many men brought all sorts of unusual things the Pilgrims never had seen before. There were turkeys, not like the wild ones in the woods. These were gigantic. There were yams and cans of Ocean Spray cranberry jelly. There was orange jello with marshmallows. There was fruit cocktail stirred up in whipped cream and walnuts. They had pitted black olives and yes, there they were, twenty pumpkin pies. The Pilgrims were astounded and asked where they had gotten all of this.

Samoset proudly revealed the secret of the Wampanoag. "We know the author of this story, and he likes us. He's a real push-over if you can convince him that you really want something. Look here; we even have a can opener."

So they had a big party. Mrs. Alden was a bit put out by how easily the Indians seemed to have come up with all this fancy food. She kept quiet about it until the potato liquor had worked its effect. Her son Johnny was enjoying the fruit cocktail just a little too much, and she petitioned him, "So you like their fruit salad better than mine, don't you?"

Johnny knew he was walking a narrow path, but he rose to the occasion. "I like them both, a lot."

Mrs. Alden muttered, "Yes well, you know which side your bread is buttered on." And she then looked around for the butter which of course wasn't there because they didn't have a cow.

The Indian children showed the Pilgrim children how to put olives on their fingers, and Billy Bradford laughed so vigorously that milk squirted out of his nose.

After dinner they sat around several large bon fires. Squanto laughed and encouraged the children to come over. Then he teased them. "Pull my finger," he said over and over.

On the second day of the festival, Samoset gathered all the men in a huddle and announced, "Every great celebration needs a sporting contest." He produced a very unusual leather ball, shaped like an egg but more pointed on the ends. "Let's divide into teams. One team we will call the Lions, and the other we will call the Bears." The Pilgrims listened a bit impatiently, but Samoset finally won them over. "Come on, just play along with me this one time. I know what I'm talking about. This game is going to be really big some day."

Nobody knows who won that first Thanksgiving Day contest between the Lions and the Bears, but it was a foretaste of things to come.

That was the first Thanksgiving. The friendliness of relations between the Wampanoag and the Pilgrims was not to last. The Wampanoag had in large part been friendly to the colonists as a political ploy to enhance their stature with other Indian nations in the region. Then after Massasoit's death the Wampanoag joined a tribal coalition to eliminate all English settlers, and in the ensuing King Phillip's War the Wampanoag were nearly exterminated, not by military means. No, it was immigrant European disease that proved to be the destroyer of that noble clan.

The Pilgrims never got their thumb tacks. It seems the order got lost until the year 1773, when three large ship loads arrived in Boston harbor. The Bostonians were irritated because this is not what they had ordered. They had requested tea.

There were inefficiencies with the East India Trading Company that exasperated the Bostonians, so they went with a smaller company called, *Represent*. The Represent Trading Company had special package deals, so you could order collections of different kinds of teas. The Bostonians had selected the Asian collection of teas.

When the Bostonians refused to let the thumb tacks be unloaded, the British government threatened to force them to make payment for the tacks anyway. That stirred things up into a dither.

Many of the Bostonians dressed up like Indians, boarded the ships and threw boxes of the thumb tacks over into the water. A cry went out over the land, "No tacks without Represent teas, Asian."

I know; it's a long way to go for a bad joke.

Thanksgiving days were announced from time to time during the colonial period, usually coinciding with a military victory of one sort or another, once commemorating the surrender of British General Burgoyne at Saratoga.

On October 3, 1789, during his first year of presidency, George Washington proclaimed the coming Thursday of November 26, to be set aside as *A Day of Public Thanksgiving and Prayer.* In a very, very, very long winded and incomprehensible run-on sentence, President Washington finally appointed the day *to be observed by acknowledging with grateful hearts the many and signal favors of Almighty God.*

But Thanksgiving did not from that become a regular national holiday. During the 1800s, Sara Hale, a magazine editor, wrote editorials pushing for an annual day of Thanksgiving. She kept at it for forty years. Southerners regarded this as a Yankee tradition and wanted nothing to do with it.

During early July of 1863, the fortunes of the Civil War reversed when the Union turned back the Confederate advance at Gettysburg. Probably related to that, on the same date as Washington had, 74 years earlier, October 3, 1863, Abraham Lincoln wrote an elegant piece, a portion of which I'd like to share. *The year that is drawing towards its close, has been filled with the blessings of fruitful fields and healthful skies. To these bounties, which are so constantly enjoyed that we are prone to forget the source from which they come, others have been added, which are of so extraordinary a nature, that they cannot fail to penetrate and soften even the heart which is habitually insensible to the ever watchful providence of Almighty God. In the midst of a civil war of unequalled magnitude and severity, which has sometimes seemed to foreign States to invite and to provoke their aggression, peace has been preserved with all nations, order has been maintained, the laws have been respected and obeyed, and harmony has prevailed everywhere except in the theatre of military conflict.*

At this point let me interject that President Lincoln was not telling the truth. At the same time as the battle of Gettysburg there was a three day riot in New York City, sparked by resentment of whites against blacks, and in it very many people were killed. It is the way of presidents to put an optimistic, even unrealistic spin on undesirable events. It also is the way of presidents to make appeals to God.

No human counsel hath devised nor hath any mortal hand worked out these great things. They are the gracious gifts of the Most High God, who, while dealing with us in anger for our sins, hath nevertheless remembered mercy. It has seemed to me fit and proper that they should be solemnly, reverently and gratefully acknowledged as with one heart and voice by the whole American people. I do therefore invite my fellow citizens in every part of the United States, and also those who are at sea and those who are sojourning in foreign lands, to set apart and observe the last Thursday of November next, as a day of Thanksgiving and Praise to our beneficent Father who dwelleth in the Heavens.

Lincoln proclaimed just this one day, but it was upon this proclamation that the holiday caught on. The country continued to celebrate every following year.

In 1939, President Franklin D. Roosevelt moved the holiday to the third Thursday of November instead of the last, to extend the Christmas shopping season and boost the economy. People protested, and so in 1941 the holiday was changed again, not necessarily to the last Thursday, but to the fourth.

In 1934, G. A. Richards purchased the football franchise, Lions, and moved it from Portsmouth, Ohio, to Detroit. The Lions did well during their first year in Detroit, but being new in town their fan base was not large. Despite having lost only one game prior to Thanksgiving, the largest crowd had been just 15,000. In the first Detroit Lion Thanksgiving Day football game, their opponent was the undefeated, defending World Champion Chicago Bears coached by George Halas. The game would decide which of the two teams would be champion of the Western Division. NBC radio carried the game coast to coast, and about 26,000 fans pushed their way into the University of Detroit Stadium. The Bears won, 19 to 16. Lions football on Thanksgiving was born as a classic contest.

In the 1920s, many of Macy's department store employees were immigrants who wanted to celebrate this American holiday with the type of festival they had loved in Europe, so they marched in a parade, dressed up in costumes. There were floats, professional bands, and they even borrowed live animals from the Central Park Zoo. Large balloons were introduced in 1927, and the first was Felix the Cat. Tradition during the early years was to release these balloons after the parade, and they would float for days until the lucky people who recovered and returned them could claim prizes. The parade was curtailed during World War II because rubber and helium were needed for more dire demands. The parade resumed in 1945.

I know that there are Indians who resent the Thanksgiving celebration, for obvious reasons. My message to you is that this holiday is not about the pilgrims or the Wampanoag. It is not about the defeat of General Burgoyne or the turning back of the Confederate army at Gettysburg. It pains me to say so, but it's not even about Lions football or the Macy's parade.

Thanksgiving is about giving thanks for our lives, the origin of which is unknown to us at its deepest level, except we know that here we are and for reasons beyond our comprehension. To all of you, this is my gift for Thanksgiving Day. I hope you laughed, and I hope you learned some of the depth of this day's tradition. Bon appetite.

38. JOSHUA'S THANKSGIVING POEM

My son Joshua wrote this when he was ten years old.

Today and forever I am thankful to
Have a family who
Always looks out for me when I
Need comfort and love. I always
Know there will be enough food to
Stop hunger in the family, and
Given that, in a way I am wealthy!
I feel sad for homeless people and
Very thankful that I'm safe, and
I don't have to worry about that.
Nothing though can compare to the thanks for
God Almighty ruling in heaven. He gave me all this.

FIVE

Words

39. PSEUDOFY

On Thanksgiving I overate, sustained a tryptophan induced nap, and while little kids were yelling and jumping all around me, I talked in my sleep. I said, "You're pseudofying." It must have been a euphemism for lying. Cool word. I wish I could remember what I was dreaming.

Someday someone will make scalp electrodes that you can put on somebody while they are sleeping, plug them into a projector and watch their dreams like a movie, record them on a DVD and embarrass them with it. It will be like the atomic bomb, very dangerous in the wrong hands and very popular.

My bit of advice for right now is don't pseudofy while testifying under oath. If you do, you'll be a testiphony.

This is not the same as a pseudophony. A pseudophony is one who pretends to get a telephone call in order to avoid an uncomfortable situation. It works something like this. Pull out a cell phone and mention that it was set on vibration alert. Answer it, and then look horrified. "He did what? He fed Ex-lax to the dog!" Start running away, and yell over your shoulder, "Gotta go; see you later."

You must differentiate between pseudofication (lie telling) and pseudefecation (pretending to go to the bathroom to escape whatever is going on that you don't like).

While it certainly is of questionable manners to make a telephone call from the bathroom, if you were to pseudophone while pseudefecating, then you would be, pseudofiably, a nut case.

40. NUCLEAR

George Bush still says, "Nucular." His advisors encourage this as it makes him more comfortable for common people. This used to drive me nuts. I would jump up and down screaming, "It's pronounced 'nuclear' you idiot" But now I've made peace with it. After all, there are lots of words that are spelled differently than they are pronounced. For example: one, two, geoduck, Bret Favre, not to mention all the *kn* words like knickers. We should become tolerant of such things. Unlike French, a language whose rules are governed strictly, English is a growing and permissive language. The pronunciation, "nucular," may be considered an Americanism. It may not be found in the Oxford Dictionary, but it should be described in our American Heritage Dictionary.

NUCLEAR: The center of something, around which everything else gets busy. Pronounced "noo-kyoo-ler" by down home folks. Pronounced "noo-klee-ar" by frumpy uppity-schmuchs and the English. Pronounced, "unclear" by physics students who have gotten to the point it's not just protons and neutrons anymore. When you have to start learning about up-quarks and down-quarks ... hooo boy! If you don't find yourself in one of those demographic groups, try "noo-kler," a retro style reminiscent of Jimmy Carter and with a connotation that you are over worked and speech tired. On the horizon is the pronunciation "noo-klahr," with accent on the second syllable, for use by those who identify with the arts more than the sciences.

41. TRIBUTE TO GILDA RADNER

I've heard some complaining about week end security at airports. Why wouldn't we want airport security on Saturdays and Sundays? These are very popular travel days, and we need the security. Better safe than sorry. Don't let your guard down for a second. When the cat's away the mice will play. I think some people just need to complain. That's all they do. Complain, complain, complain. If it's not one thing it's another. So now they are telling us they don't want week end security, and I want to tell them to mind their own business. So what if it takes a little more time at the airport. It's good to feel safe. What's that? ... weakened security? ... Oh ... Never mind.

42. IN OTHER WORDS

Other people will judge you by the words you use. It sucks, I know, but that's the way it is.

I am intrigued by the public's recent rampant use of the word, *suck*. Its usage has changed. Once a harmless word, it passed through a period during which it was obscene, maybe guilty by association with other words, and recently it has become widely used and is gaining acceptance, even favor among chronically frustrated people. This thing sucks, and that thing sucks. I'm beginning to think everything sucks but that it's okay.

On the back of the bus we argued about exactly how the word's usage has changed. Some people said the word has changed from a verb to an adjective, a grammatical change, but otherwise it has retained its meaning. Others thought differently, that grammatically it has remained the same, but the meaning has changed. I'm with this second group. To say something sucks is to use the word as a verb. The adjective would be, *sucky*. "Picking up after somebody else's beer party is a sucky job, but somebody has to do it." While doing it you could say, "Why that sucky bastard." To say, "This job sucks," would be using the word as a verb.

So even though my side was correct, this matter divided us, and maybe it's only coincidence but it seemed to divide us roughly down party lines. Feelings about the word *suck* may be an issue deeply dividing this nation during the next major election.

I am convinced *suck* started out as a gentle and good word. Infants suckled at their mothers' breasts. Vacuum cleaners sucked up dirt. We all sucked milk shakes through straws. In one way or another, at some time or another, each and every one of us has sucked. I suck; you suck; we all suck. See, it's a verb.

How did *suck* ever become obscene? Somebody must have sucked something awful, and I can only imagine it must have been old, rancid milk, the most miserable flavor I've ever encountered. Some people on Fear Factor may have tasted something worse, and I bet they said it sucked.

Once there was a bumper sticker that said, *Mean people suck.* I first saw this at a time when I still considered *suck* a base and low word. I almost made my own bumper sticker, *Only mean people say suck.* Since then I've been so bombarded by the word that I've gotten used to it, inured.

Here's some advice. Just like any other word, the power of *suck* is lost when it is overused. Use it only when something really sucks.

For me it's the floors in public locker rooms that suck. I tend to get athletes foot unless I protect myself, so I carry with me a can of antifungal spray. My can of foot spray doesn't suck. It blows.

I've been thinking that maybe the word *suck* itself sucks. There is no question that at least some people regard it as rude. Using words or phrases like these may put two impressions in the minds of polite people. The first is rudeness. The second is that the speaker likely is either too lazy or too uneducated to use more appropriate and fitting diction. So as a matter of public service I've decided to use the following vignettes to share ideas for alternative words.

In recent years our government has favored owners of business rather than the working class. There may be some good reasons for this that are not clear to the average worker. The average worker could say, "This sucks." Or the average worker could say, "Next election I'm going to take a closer look at who is more likely to protect my interests."

Forty million people in the United States are not covered by health insurance simply because they cannot afford it. These people can say, "This sucks." An alternative would be to find some way to sue somebody else. Then they could say, "I'm going to take you to the cleaners." Then maybe they could afford health insurance. A good lawyer can help them.

The Bush administration has made it appear as though it cares about education, making programs with neat titles such as *No Child Left Behind*, but if it then fails to fund these programs sufficiently, parents can say, "This sucks." Or they can decide to home school their children, but that means they would have to stay home from work. Then they won't have money enough for food and shelter. That would give them still another opportunity to say, "This sucks." Maybe they can fake a confusing illness like fibromyalgia, and then if they're lucky they can get on welfare or disability. Then they can say to the doctor, "This sucks," when what they really mean is "Thank God I've got this little bit of something."

The Bush administration finally has admitted there may be something to the greenhouse effect, but it continues to thumb its nose at any ideas that will improve the situation. It has encouraged the Clean Air Act, which takes a position that industry can spew poisons into the air as long as they are either clear or a color of blue close enough to cerulean that they won't disturb the appearance of the sky. A day will come when the clouds are blue. Then we'll have blue skies even on overcast days. Cities will accommodate this by building giant glowing orbs radiating man-made sunshine. We all will be happy until it rains, and the drops stain our clothes blue. Then we can say, "This sucks." Or we can say, "How very interesting."

Current safeguards against spongiform encephalopathy, mad cow disease, are inadequate. They will remain so until the United States decides to get serious enough about this problem that it adopts a system similar to Japan's. In the mean time you can say, "This sucks." Or you can say, "I'm mad as hell." Or you can say, "I'm mad as a cow."

There is another way though. The infectious agent of mad cow is called a *prion*. It is a protein that invades your body very slowly. When it gets into your nerve cells, it changes the shape of all the cell's proteins until the cell no longer can do the things it needs to stay alive. So it dies. Prions cannot be made harmless by cooking, but they can be burned. So the way to protect yourself, aside from abstaining completely from eating any mammalian tissue, is to char your hamburgers completely. I don't mean just the outside. I mean burn them to a cinder. Put a lot of mustard and relish on them, take a bite, and say, "This sucks." Or you can say, "Damn, that Japanese plan sure seems like a good idea."

We are bogged down in a terribly expensive war in Iraq, without end in sight, and that country is stepping on the threshold of civil war. No matter what we do, it seems to backfire on us, sort of like an exploding cigar. We could say, "This sucks." Or we could laugh and say, "Hey look, the joke's on us."

Let's say you're a woman with very righteous intentions about sexual abstinence, but you know you're not perfect so you carry a condom with you anyway. Then one night the unthinkable happens. Your hormones get the better of you, and you do it. But the condom slips off, and you might be in trouble, so the next day you go to the drug store to purchase some Plan B, but the first pharmacy doesn't sell it. The second pharmacy sells it but charges $30, and you have only $25. You could say, "This sucks." Or you could use your credit card that already is maxed out, and so when the bank won't authorize your purchase you could say, "That sucks." Or you could ask your boy friend for five bucks, and he'll probably be happy to lend it to you. Then the both of you could say, "Whew!"

See, there are other ways than using the four letter word. All you need is a little imagination.

SIX

Spirit

43. DUELING OVER THE SOUL

In March of 2005, the entire country became obsessed with the legal battle between the husband and the parents of Terri Schiavo, the young woman dependent on a feeding tube to survive. It was amazing how widespread the argument became.

The country polarized in at least two different ways. One polarization was whether the sanctity of life itself, regardless of quality, outweighed the apparent sensibility of ending the life of a woman who maybe once had said she would not want to continue life in a persistent vegetative state. The other polarization was whether or not it was correct for such an ethical, spiritual and personal matter to receive the urgent intervention of the federal government.

Agnos was quiet about it but studiously watched the hoopla.

I asked him, "What do you think?"

"We don't have enough information to make a decision."

"Why do you say that?" I objected. "Studies showed her brain doesn't have a cortex. She's not able to think. Her doctors say that her utterances are purely basal reflexes and have no cognitive relevance. What more do we need to know?"

"Whether she has a soul."

This brought back memories of a conversation I once shared with a Lutheran minister. I asked him what he had learned about the soul in seminary. His answer was, "Surprisingly little." What he had learned wasn't what I expected. The soul was not considered some phantasm that inhabits a body and gives it spiritual meaning. The soul simply was the person, whole and complete, physical, material. What a disappointment!

Agnos asked me, "Do you believe there is something more to a person than the anatomy and physiology of the body?"

"I do," I answered. "What do you think?"

"Do I have to remind you again? I'm Agnos. Nobody knows the answer to this, but it's important. If the soul is nothing more than the brain's mind, then Terri no longer has a soul. But if the soul is something beyond anatomy and physiology, beyond the mind, then we must ask ourselves whether Terri's soul would still be in that inhospitable and boring domain. If she could escape it, I'm sure she would. Maybe she's trapped. Who knows?"

"Yes, I've wondered about that too. Some people have said that in a situation in which we don't know for sure whether she has some awareness, any error we make should be on the side of preserving life. But another way of thinking would be to make any error to be on the side of kindness."

"Do we know what the kind thing is? Maybe kindness in this case is completely superfluous. Maybe the whole argument of life or death in this case is superfluous."

"What do you mean?" I asked him.

"Sometimes it's nice not to know things. It makes it easier to see inconsistencies in the arguments of people who think they know. For example, if it is the contention of religious people that Terri should be kept alive simply because life is sacred, then where is their faith? If they believe in God, why would they not want Terri's soul to be released into the hands of her heavenly father? It seems that would be the desire of the faithful."

"So you side with her husband that she should be allowed to die?"

"He's inconsistent too. He wants to let her die because he claims that before this happened to her she told him she would not want to continue living in this way. So he keeps fighting for what he says is her will. But if he really believes that she now has no thought processes in her brain, that she has no awareness, then what is he fighting for? He's off the hook. She has no mind to be pleased or displeased, approving or disapproving, whatever happens. He's putting a lot of effort into something that's no more than a memory."

"That's what her parents are doing also," I interjected. "They're putting a lot of effort into something that's no more than a memory."

"Sad but true," said Agnos. "It seems to me that if they really were concerned about Terri's soul, her husband would just sign off because the way it is, her body no longer is Terri. And the parents would want to release their daughter's soul into the eternal love of the being who created her, so that her soul can be rejuvenated."

"They maybe should switch sides in the court battle," I offered.

"Or maybe they just shouldn't care so much," said Agnos. "I never knew Terri, but if I were in her position I would want the people I love to get on with their own lives."

44. TRANSITION

Terri Schiavo died on March 31, 2005. The tremendous outpouring of public opinion on her life had a very important root. In the words of John Donne, taken from his work, *Devotions upon Emergent Occasions*, written in 1624: *No man is an island, entire of itself; every man is a piece of the continent, a part of the main; if a clod be washed away by the sea, Europe is the less, as well as if a promontory were, as well as if a manor of thy friend's or of thine own were; any man's death diminishes me, because I am involved in mankind; and therefore never send to know for whom the bell tolls; it tolls for thee.*

45. EVERY CASE IS DIFFERENT

During the weeks surrounding Terri Schiavo's death, many people from all over wrote and talked about experiences they'd had making the hard decision, life or death for a loved one. While these anecdotes were cathartic and entertaining, from an academic perspective they were not pertinent. Every case is different and warrants careful consideration of its unique circumstances.

As one example of this, many called President George Bush brain dead although, as in the case of Terri Schiavo, there was disagreement about this. Those who claimed he was brain dead cited his decisions on the environment, social security and the Iraq war as evidence. They made a strong but not decisive argument. I asked Agnos, but he didn't know.

I contacted my secret operatives in high Republican places. They told me President Bush was not brain dead, and nobody had considered turning off his life support systems.

Then I contacted my secret operatives in high Democrat places. They told me there had been mutterings about calling an emergency session of Congress to legislate the placement of a feeding tube into President Bush, just so that then it could be pulled out as a gesture of political defiance. The measure didn't make it out of committee. They just didn't have the votes.

Tens of thousands of people rushed out to make a living will. This was a good thing. I encouraged people to be creative, to put into their wills what they really wanted. For example, I would prefer not to be maintained in a persistent vegetative state, but just in case that some day happens anyway, there are certain provisions I'd like to clarify.

At least every two days I want a clean change of clothes, and I want the clothes to be fashionable. Since I won't be able to tell my caretakers whether I have pain, just in case, I want a trans-dermal fentanyl patch, 25 micrograms for the first six months. I want it changed every two days, not every three because we know that the third day is not as reliably effective. Every six months I want my patch to go up by another 25 micrograms, assuming tolerance will occur, and when the overdose of medicine finally stops my breathing, I'll be ready for that.

As a vegetable, I'll want a bed by the window so I can get the sun I need for my fruit to ripen, and if somebody happens to notice that my fruit is ripe, I give my wife authority over whether my fruit gets plucked and by whom.

46. IT ALL IS ABOUT RELATIONSHIPS

Sh-h-h-h. Be very quiet now. I don't want to awaken Agnos. I've waited until just the right moment to let you in on the basic building block of what I believe. He'd make a mess of it. So here goes.

Jesus said, "Where there are two or more gathered together in my name, there I also will be." As a much younger man I bucked against this idea. I asked, "If all the people in the world died except for one, would God then be dead? No! Therefore God is present even when there is just one person."

The group I hung around with (They were called Jesus Freaks.) all said worshipfully, "Praise the Lord." Since then I've often wondered whether their response was one regarding my argument as prophecy, or whether they were praying to guard against the devil that somehow had gotten into me. That's fun to think about. Many people will be divided similarly about the deeper down meanings expressed in this book I'm writing. I don't apologize for the confusing struggle that I will be laying out before you. My assignment is clear. This book is something I must write.

I believe there is an unseen consciousness at work in the universe, and many call it God. I believe this consciousness every now and then assists in the development of new ideas by placing realizations suddenly into the minds of receptive, chosen ones. These realizations sometimes get called *epiphanies*.

I had an epiphany about thirty years ago, and I say it that way because the truth is it was longer than thirty years ago. It was an epiphany about the soul and the meaning of what Jesus told us. It is all about relationships.

The soul is not quite what most people think it is, and yes it does require more than one person. The soul is the inscription of a relationship in the mind of God.

Imagine a doctor talking to a young man about the terrible belly pain the man has with his pancreatitis. Imagine the young man's mother also is there sharing in the support of his treatment. How many souls do you think there are in that situation? Do you think there are three? I say no. Depending on how you wish to count there are either four souls or one.

There is one soul shared by three people. The soul is complete only with the participation of each of the three. Each of the three is influenced by the complete experience of the one soul. Each of the three is aware of only that part of the relationship, the soul, which they can experience from the limitation of their corporeal form, but they each are changed by the interaction and complete experience of the other two people. The part of the complete soul taken by each of them afterward is exactly the same as the part of the complete soul taken by the other two people. Stan the Rev told me that Carl Jung called this shared soul the *collective unconscious* or the *Oversoul*. He cautioned me not to call it the Holy Spirit because that would perturb people. But you know, that kind of is what this book is partly about, perturbing people. So if you want to call it the Holy Spirit then go right ahead. By all means do it.

Imagine the implications of this when one person beats another. Both people are the abusive one. Both are the abused. We live our lives from one shared soul to another.

Imagine the implications of this to the soul of a Hitler who murdered twelve million people. Alas, I lament for the soul you have made for yourself Adolph. You caused God great suffering.

It is the glory of God that such horrors are erased from his own complete soul. He is able to reject the hurtful and save the good. This is his separation of wheat from chaff in the fabric of the universe. Alas, I lament for the soul you have lost from yourself Adolph. You have made yourself small, and you have so much to learn, much to grow.

But here is the beautiful part. Imagine love. Imagine two people intermingling in the act of intercourse, a single soul.

Imagine welcoming into your own being the soul of God, for he said, "Knock and the door will be opened to you." Already you are part of the fabric of the universe, and it has the power to erase the sorrow in your soul. It will happen later unless you welcome it today.

Then Agnos said, "You malign me. I have no problem with the

circumstance that you believe this. These are wonderful thoughts you've shared. But they are not scientifically verified. Don't say that you know they are so."

"But in my heart I do know that they are so."

"In my mind I do not know that they are so. Men are lead by their hearts, but a leader must lead with his mind."

"Then if the mind of the universe is my leader, and if I follow with my heart; is that alright with you, Agnos?"

"It is alright with me only if you accept that since it is not verified, it is belief and not knowledge. Therefore welcome others to believe it if they will, but it would be unfair to them and to yourself if you coerce them. This is a path you have found for yourself. Others may find their own."

SEVEN

Abortion

47. PRO-LIFE DEMOCRAT

We remember him as the ultra-liberal would-be Democrat candidate for president in the 2004 primaries, the one who appeared to throw a sugar-high, overly enthusiastic cheerleading session after his surprise loss in the Iowa caucuses. Then as national leader of the Democrat Party, Howard Dean surprised us again by encouraging greater support for Democrat candidates who are pro-life.

It should not come as a surprise that there are Democrats who are pro-life. It seems a natural consequence of a party that champions the little people, the ones who are defenseless against the perfunctory machinery of society. Who could be littler and more defenseless than a fetus?

The Democrat Party also espouses freedom of choice, freedom of expression, freedom over one's own body. And so, on the topic of pro-life versus pro-choice there arises a discrepancy of philosophies that would stymie a pro-life Democrat. How could a pro-life Democrat make it through the primaries? Or to make the question more interesting, if there were a candidate with charisma and communication skills enough to pull off such a feat, what would that candidate look like?

A pro-life stance would put a candidate at disadvantage in Democrat primaries, and so it would be a topic to avoid until the main election, except it's reasonable to expect the topic could not be avoided. Both the Democrat opponents and the Republican Party would want to draw such a candidate out. Squash the bug before it breeds!

What would a winning candidate look like? A Democrat pro-lifer would not resemble a Republican pro-lifer, and perhaps the essence of that difference would arise from the subtle difference between ethics and morality. In the context with which I'm using these terms, morality refers to the adherence of behavior to a given moral system, whether that morality is that of The Ten Commandments or of a specific religion or a specific society such as the Masons. Ethics on the other hand, in my use of the term here, would consider such moral systems as important in decisions to be made, but would recognize that moral systems differ from one another. Ethics places at its center a goal of the most good for the individuals involved, and considers all pertinent arguments, religious or not. Ethics therefore is more complex, difficult, and it can't be grasped fully. No two people completely agree, although sometimes with a democratic approach whole populations can come to a mutual consensus or agreement on basics. They can agree on a code of conduct, hopefully one dynamic enough to accept its own change as knowledge increases about a topic. Our system of laws is such an example of complex ethics, open to change as better knowledge becomes available.

The ethics of pro-life versus pro-choice is at such a dynamic landmark in history. Knowledge has accumulated enough to show that the conservative approach may be too conservative, and the liberal approach may be too liberal. A winning Democrat pro-lifer will be able to show this is so and will introduce appropriate solutions in a way that is acceptable to a majority of voters. Once again, what will that candidate look like?

I venture to guess that a Democrat pro-lifer would not pull the bait and switch tactics that sometimes have been employed by Republican candidates who have outraged many by claiming to be pro-life in a political ploy to capture right wing votes, only to ignore the agenda of that faction once in power. These politicians have gotten away with such behavior because of the credibility of a shrugged-shoulder position against the apparent dauntlessness of the pro-choice movement. Leaders can look as pure-minded and helpless as their electorate, and they can keep the focus of blame on the pro-choice liberals while at the same time pursuing their other agenda.

What changes could be made to which a majority of voters would agree? Aha! That is what a winning Democrat pro-lifer would know.

Let's peel away the political masks that obscure this topic. It seems the argument usually takes place in the biological arena of deciding when human life begins. This is not necessarily the correct debate arena, but this is the one in which the argument tends to take place, so let's look at it.

At which point does life stop in the process of a human life producing sperm or an egg, to the emergence of a new person? Can it be said that a sperm has no life? If we took a sperm and made damned sure it was dead, maybe dried it out, would it still be able to complete its function? Isn't it life that imbues it with the capacity to become another person? In a successful process, when was it dead?

At which point does an egg, made of a woman's tissue, become something other than human? When was it a chimpanzee?

If we think specifically biological, there is no point at which life stops in the process, and there is no point at which humanity is lost.

But that is not the way the topic is approached by politics. Perhaps the position most compatible with the true biological construct is the one taken by the Catholic Church. The sperm and the egg each are haploid; each has only one of each pair of chromosomes needed to make a complete human. No matter how much a sperm is nurtured and protected, without the egg it will not become a person. That makes sense. A fetus on the other hand, nurtured and protected, will become a person.

However, current law and practice do not agree with that biological argument. By law human life begins at about 23 weeks, and the goofy reason given is that it is about that time when, with advanced medical assistance, a prematurely born baby has an inkling of a chance to survive. Let us please be a bit more honest and say forthright that the 23 week mark is practically useful because it allows discovery of congenital deformities that society would best like not to have to deal with, and gives medical providers time to terminate those pregnancies at the request of the parents.

Earlier I mentioned the biological debate may not be the most appropriate for deciding this issue. Two other items may take precedence. They are the onset of consciousness and the ultimate ethical standard of kindness.

Consciousness often is defined as awareness of one's own existence. As yet we do not understand how this occurs. We do not know how a human brain accomplishes this feat. So we get no help from this very important concept, except to say that the onset of consciousness occurs at some time well after the mingling of an egg and a sperm. I bet it takes more than sixty-four undifferentiated cells to reach consciousness. It takes more than 1024 cells, or does it? Does it take only one cell? We don't know.

In an attempt to achieve meaningful kindness for both the mother trapped in an undesirable situation and a fetus trapped in an undesirable mother, there is another piece of information we can use. Pain. When can a fetus feel pain? Although anatomical and physiological studies implicate that the cellular and neurochemical workings of pain can be identified by ten weeks, other studies indicate that the ability of the fetal brain to appreciate pain is not established until well into the third trimester. So decision making is confounded here as well. What if we were to be careful? On the question of pain, which way should we err?

One of my patients, a Democrat pro-lifer, gave me a pin of tiny hands made from a mold of a ten week fetus. I wear it on my coat lapel. Those hands are meaningful to me.

If ethics tells us to be kind to both the potential mother and the potential baby, what is the solution? The following are my recommendations. They fall short of the absolutism of right wing pro-lifers who would be satisfied with nothing less than strict adherence to their moral system, but these are recommendations that would improve our society and would allow us to look in the mirror again without shame. They seek to provide pro-life incentives rather than force a moral code.

I propose that except in cases of significant fetal abnormality, any legal abortion must take place before the fetus has reached eight weeks. Such abortions would be taxed heavily but also according to the mother's income level or the income of her parents or legal guardian. Abortions wouldn't come cheap. Proceeds would be used to fund agencies for family planning, well-run orphanages, adoption agencies, foster home programs, day care facilities, education. Mothers who choose to carry their babies to term would be given generous tax incentives, the first time. In the case of the congenitally deformed fetus, current laws would remain.

The aim is kindness. The aim is to have a plan that actually would work. The aim is to be consistent with the world as we now know it.

I'm looking for the Democrat candidate who will take a stand like this.

48. KINDNESS?

Agnos said, "You almost got it right, man."

"What are you talking about?" I answered.

"That kindness bit. You had me humming along with you until the end there when you said the aim was kindness."

"The aim is kindness."

"You really believe that. I mean you really do, don't you?"

"Of course I do. What are you coming at me like this for?"

"Kindness for whom? What kind of kindness does this plan show for a 22 week fetus with Down's syndrome? Doesn't that conscious, possibly pain-feeling fetus have any say in all of this? The aim isn't kindness. Think about it. The aim is something else."

Damn it! Agnos was right. One thing you can say about Agnos. Maybe it's because he doesn't know much of anything that he can see right through an inconsistent argument. You can't very easily pull the wool over his eyes.

"The way I see it," he continued, "is that if kindness is the aim, then congenital anomalies can't influence the decision."

I was three counts from being pinned in this wrestling match. I needed a miracle. When arguing with Agnos you're not going to go very far by getting mystical, but I was desperate. "What if by aborting a deformed fetus you give that particular soul a chance of being born in another whole and healthy body?"

He looked at me with contempt. "You're really stretching now. You already know my answer, don't you." It wasn't even a question. "We don't know that there is anything such as a soul. You can believe it, but you just don't know. Do you think you'd be doing a fetus a favor by killing it based on that argument? And what if there is a soul? Who says it has an opportunity to live more than once or to choose different bodies?"

I was silent.

"You lose, Buddy," he said. Then after a pause he asked again. "So what is the aim if it's not kindness? What is the aim of terminating a deformed fetus?"

One … two … three. He pinned me. "It's the only way to sell this plan to the left wing of the voting populace," I answered.

"Bingo."

"So it's politics rather than kindness," I added.

He nodded. "Also convenience."

"Well, at least it would be a step in the right direction, wouldn't it?"

He nodded again. "Not for the 22 week old deformed fetus."

"I've got an idea," I beamed. "We can tax those abortions too."

49. AFTER THE FACT

It has happened to all of us. Only a matter of hours after an argument an idea pops into your head about something you wish you would have said. There is more to the termination of a 22 week old deformed fetus than just politics and convenience. Have you ever toured a nursing facility for the severely, congenitally disabled?

It is not ethically appropriate for us to make a judgment of the quality of another person's life. There is no way we can put ourselves into another person's mind to determine whether that life is or is not worth living, and I want you to know I realize that.

As a society we have limited resources. Resources are required to take care of the severely disabled, and we must ask ourselves whether those resources may be invested better in other social programs. What is kinder, to spare the life of a severely deformed 22 week fetus, or to have money and manpower to care for an indigent person suddenly afflicted with multiple sclerosis or diabetes, or spinal cord injury? Of course we would prefer not to have to choose between such things, but our society has not shown the kind of generosity necessary to help all people afflicted with terrible hardship. We have no choice other than to choose. This transforms the question of kindness into a question of logistics and priorities. Maybe the way to decide is to ask what distribution of resources will most benefit society. How do you answer a question like that? What would we most value? Financial benefit? Spiritual benefit? Productivity? There are not clear answers.

Spirits do not cast shadows that you can see with your eyes, but during the writing of these few paragraphs I sensed a presence behind me, and I looked. It was Agnos, and he was smiling.

"All I said," he explained, "is that the aim is not kindness."

"Agnos, it's like we have to play God. Circumstances force it on us."

"That is why there are moral codes, systems of morality. It is not that they are right or wrong, but they are clear cut. That makes them easy, especially if the making of a moral code is ascribed to God. Then followers of that morality can divorce themselves from responsibility. They are spared the challenge of thinking and the remorse of having made a decision."

50. WOW

Dan Kurti called me: "Your topic reminds me of Dr. Rick Strassman's book, *DMT, The Spirit Molecule.* In it he describes his research on intravenous DMT in volunteers. Besides describing sessions and their implications, he made other comments, particularly on how individuals and groups may either like or dislike his conclusions based on their own agendas.

"Specifically concerning the abortion debate, Dr. Strassman suggests that both sides of the abortion rights debate may have problems with his proposal that DMT released from the pineal gland, at 49 days after conception, identifies the entrance of a spirit into the fetus."

"Wow," I responded. "What is DMT?"

"DMT is di-methyl-tryptamine. Tryptamine, as you know, is a derivative of tryptophan, an amino acid. When you add two methyl groups to tryptamine you get DMT. Serotonin is 5-hydroxy-tryptamine. Melatonin is N-acetyl-5-methoxy-tryptamine. All these are very natural neurotransmitters in the brain."

"Wow," I responded.

"DMT is a psychedelic, and so you've got to wonder a bit why it is naturally produced within the brain. It exists in very tiny quantities at any one time. In his experiments, Dr. Strassman administered a thirty-second intravenous infusion of 0.4 mg/Kg. His subjects had profound psychedelic trips, as intense as LSD, mescaline (from peyote cactus), or psilocybin (the active ingredient of magic mushrooms). The body converts psilocybin into psilocin, and psilocin differs from DMT by only one oxygen. Dr. Strassman refers to the psilocybin/psilocin tag-team as the *orally active DMT.*"

"Wow," I responded.

"Another important tryptamine is 5-methoxy-DMT, and it differs from DMT by the addition of one methyl group and one oxygen. Plants and fungi containing DMT quite often also possess 5-methoxy-DMT. These psychedelic plants usually are smoked to get a high. Experiments suggest that LSD, mescaline and DMT, among others, exert their primary effects on the serotonin system of the brain. Research in the 1960s and 1970s heralded DMT as the first discovered psychedelic chemical produced by the human brain. Dr. Strassman pondered the same thing I'm pondering. What is DMT doing in our bodies? He proposes that DMT is the *spirit molecule.* In one of his chapters he suggests that the mysterious pineal gland is the *spirit gland,* the production factory of DMT."

"Wow," I responded.

"Furthermore, the number 49 is interesting and not just because it's seven squared. The *Tibetan Buddhist Book of the Dead* suggests that 49 days is required for the soul of the recently dead to reincarnate. Seven weeks are necessary after the time of death for the life-force to rebirth into the next body. Dr. Strassman points out that 49 days landmarks two important events in formation of the human embryo. At 49 days after conception, the human pineal gland first appears. It's also 49 days when the fetus differentiates into male or female. Dr. Strassman offers a theory that the pineal acts as an antenna for the soul. He believes in a soul, but until the 49th day celebration of events, the fetus doesn't have one. Therefore, maybe the fetal age of 49 days should be considered when an individual sentient becomes a spiritual entity."

"Wow," I responded. "I thought the ultimate answer to the questions of life, the universe and everything, was 42. Well, anyway, it was close."

51. SOUND BITES

My good friend, Tom Sproger, wrote to me: Such reasoned thinking. You make a lot of sense. Where does human life truly begin? If you look at a fetus it starts out as what, a couple of cells, then becomes a fish, a lizard and a person, roughly in that order. Okay, so that's a terrible oversimplification. So let's agree it's okay to terminate the life of a fish or a lizard, as we do already kill fish, cows, sheep and pigs that we eat, and deer and elk and all that stuff on Fear Factor. But it's not okay and never will be okay to end the life of a human being just because its existence is inconvenient or imperfect. I can buy that, and I bet a lot of Demos would buy that.

But it never will fly. How would a politician convey the complicated arguments to justify your proposal in twenty second sound bites? That's why extremism on both sides prevails. The media will not grant sufficient time to this or any subject, for reasoned argument, for someone to build a case step-by-logical-step.

But you knew that. Didn't you?

52. SOUND BITES RESPONSE

You're right about the principle that ontogeny recapitulates phylogeny. This basically means that during embryonic development the human shows its evolutionary phases, starting with something like a fish, then a tadpole, a salamander, a warthog and finally the finished product along with diaper rash. This has given me pause to wonder about exactly when our mammalian characteristics began. Were we hairy fish? Were we tadpoles with breasts?

Twenty second sound bites would be a problem. The argument may end up sounding as though George Bush were the one saying it.

1. Howard Dean threw a sugar-high, overly enthusiastic cheerleading session.
2. Democrats who are pro-life also believe in a woman's right to freedom of choice over her own body. They are flip-floppers.
3. Democrats talk about ethics, but they pooh-pooh morality.
4. No two people fully agree, especially if they are Democrats.
5. Democrats talk about a code of conduct, but then they want it to be changeable when the mood suits them. What did I tell you about flip-flopping?

6. Democrats say there are other things that take precedence over human life.
7. It is an unfortunate baby who gets trapped in an undesirable mother. Protect the baby.
8. Right wing pro-lifers will not be satisfied with anything less than strict adherence to moral values.
9. All Democrats ever want to do is tax, tax, tax. The only things you can rely on from them are Death and Taxes, and there's nothing better to illustrate that than this whole crazy proposal.

I must admit I'm puzzled, frustrated and pessimistic; but maybe I can overcome my despondence. The Spirit Agnos tells me I pretend to know too much, and that's my problem. Maybe ignorance is bliss. If I could admit I just don't know the answers, then I'd be happier. What do you think?

EIGHT

What Next?

53. LIFE AFTER LIFE

Pastor Stephen Guttormson gave me the idea for this piece in a sermon he preached decades ago. It has stayed with me.

Two fetuses, twins in the same womb, talked with one another. One queried, "Do you believe in life after birth?"

The other answered, "There must be life after birth. We can hear all those sounds coming from the darkness that lies beyond."

"But we don't know for sure, do we? We can believe there is life after birth, but there's no proof of that, is there? It really is a matter of faith, right?"

Then the other fetus turned to face its twin directly. "What is your name?"

"I don't know."

54. BELIEVE WHAT I SAY

My spirituality does not require you to believe one way or another. My spirituality wants you to be honest with yourself. People are what they are. Each of us was born with a set of genetics given by parents. Neither they nor we had any say in what genetics we ended up with. Thank you, God. During our formative years as children we had little control over the environment in which we developed. These two great things, genetics and environment, are the most crucially important factors determining what we are and will be, what we believe. We really have nothing to do with it. We emerge from our genetics and society bearing them as gifts with which we interact with the rest of the world.

Therefore how can I agree with that favorite of Bible verses? John 3:16: *For God so loved the world that he gave his only begotten son to die for*

84

us, that whosoever believes in him shall not perish but have everlasting life.
What a beautiful verse! What a coercive motive! What an ignorant revelation! I love it. It has deep roots for me.

A God who loves would not allow you to be punished for being what you are. He would not on that basis withhold his love and salvation. He made you what you are. He would not punish you, or withhold life from you, based on what you believe. He made you believe what you believe. Friends, be gentle with yourselves. And if you are both honest with yourself and inquisitive, you must realize that God has to have a different intent for his creation and our salvation than a demand that we believe.

"If you do not believe who I am, then at least believe what I say because then you will glimpse the kingdom of heaven." You are saved regardless of who or what you are. If you believe that, then heaven will come to you now, no waiting.

Jesus told the parable of separating wheat from chaff. Self righteous people make that mean good people are saved and bad people are not. I'm telling you God can have it both ways. From each and every one of you he will save what is good, what he wants, and he will cast away what is bad. Be good, and more of your life's experience will last to the end of days and beyond.

All of you are in my heaven: Atheists, Catholics, Muslims, Jews, Protestants, Hindus, Buddhists, Don Juan, Elton John, Mother Teresa, Michael Jackson, Gandhi, Hitler, Charles Manson. By the way, in my heaven Gandhi and Mother Teresa are of gigantic proportion, and both Hitler and Manson are smaller than Topo Giggio, but they are still there. My mom and dad are there, and I talk to them. In my heaven God would not be God if he rejected you, and if you believe this, then heaven will come to you now. No waiting.

So there you have it. No proselytizing, not really. It's no skin off my nose what you believe. Just take care of each other. The world is structured in such a way that it will work smoothly only if each and every one of us loves and nurtures the others, only if we share with others all that we have and all that we are. Tall order. It will take some time to get there.

Also take care of the planet because it will be our home for many lives to come.

55. REINCARNATION

Have you ever stopped to think what a difficult problem arises when a self-righteous and intolerant religious person contemplates the possibility of reincarnation? What if such a person were to reincarnate as an atheist or a homosexual? Would God actually do that? If God's anything like me he would, and Genesis clearly points out that I was made in God's image. So God and I have our similarities, and maybe this is one of them.

It's sort of like the Native American admonishment not to judge another person until you have walked a mile in his moccasins. I knew a guy who did that once, walked a mile in someone else's moccasins. Afterward he said his feet hurt, and then he turned to the owner of the moccasins and said, "No wonder you're such an asshole."

How about living a lifetime with someone else's genetic and environmental make-up? That's Karmic justice for you. I like that. Imagine a rerun of our world with Rush Limbaugh playing the role of Elton John.

Reincarnation does play a role in the history and mystic elements of the Jewish and Christian religions, but not so prominently as with Hinduism and Buddhism. Hindus believe a person can be reincarnated as a cow. Do any of them worry that they will reincarnate as a homosexual cow? What about simply a cross-dressing cow or one with gender confusion? Are Hindus okay with that?

It is interesting that the goal of each of the major religions, the four just mentioned as well as Islam, is to escape the woes of this world and to reach heaven. These religions arose out of impoverished societies in which misery was commonplace. This of course makes sense. Anyone trapped in a horrific world would want to escape. Reincarnation for a Hindu or a Buddhist is not a desirable thing. It is forced upon people until a certain degree of spiritual maturity has been achieved that will allow them to stay in Nirvana for awhile, removed from the turmoil of this world.

A branch of Buddhism teaches that it is selfish to escape from this world when others of less spiritual development remain. The truly holy of this sect, the Bodhisattvas, choose to continue reincarnating even after they reach Nirvana. These truly holy people return over and over again to this world in order to teach others and to bring others along to Nirvana.

Bodhisattvas parallel the saints of Catholicism in that each one may be thought of as a specialist in a certain virtue. Avalokiteshvara is famous for compassion. Manjusri is the bodhisattva of wisdom and memory. Manjusri literally means "sweet splendor." Maitreya is the bodhisattva whose name means "the friendly one." Maitreya lives in his heaven (tushita) now but will be the next Buddha to appear on earth, sort of like the second coming of Jesus, I guess. Maitreya will establish a new era on earth and will lead us all into salvation. Yep, he's the Buddhist Jesus alright.

It is paradoxical that in his last incarnation the great Buddha himself declared that he would not be returning to this earth again, not for a very long time. He said his work here was done. That wasn't very Bodhisattva of him if you ask me. I think there's still a lot of work to be done. Just look at this mess. I suppose Buddha's decision to depart us could be explained by acknowledging he had been bodhisattva long enough. He was tired and it was time for retirement. Nobody's perfect; not even Buddha. Okay. I still like him.

Contrast these eastern concepts of reincarnation with those of religions emerging from Native American societies in which people lived their lives in spiritual harmony with the world around them. For them reincarnation is a natural event and wonderful. Heaven is not a future unseen kingdom. Heaven is this world here, now and forever. One should not feel a need to escape from this world. One should not feel a need to escape from heaven.

Thy kingdom come. Thy will be done on earth as it is in heaven.

What if we all believed in this way? What if we all believed that we now are making the world in which we ourselves will be living forever? Would we take better care of our environment? I bet we would. This just goes to show you that we do not yet love our neighbors as ourselves. At least we don't love our descendents as ourselves. Once again, the attractiveness of reincarnation is its cosmic justice.

If the American Indians were happy with their world, and the Christian European settlers wanted to escape from it into some unseen promised heaven, what is the meaning of this difference between societies? One of the societies seems to have treated its people better than the other, and when considering this sometimes I think dejectedly that the wrong society prevailed in the new world. But then I get a happier thought. The spirituality of the world is changing. We are ever more environmentally aware, and we are beginning to care. It is as though the American Indian spirituality, against all odds, is in the process of assimilating us.

Beauty and truth cannot be suppressed.

56. KARMA

Isn't it interesting that people who believe in reincarnation and believe they can remember previous lives, always seem to remember themselves as somebody special? For the rest of us who believe in reincarnation and can't remember previous lives, maybe the reason we can't remember is that we are certain our previous lives were drab, uninteresting and not worth the effort of extensive meditation to uncover. I suppose in a previous life I might have been a bus driver with a back problem, and before that I was a coal miner with a lung problem. Maybe I was a kid hiding behind a post on a pier in Boston, watching a band of men, dressed as Indians, board three English merchant ships and throw boxes of tea into the harbor. Maybe that was the most exciting thing that ever happened to me.

Once I wanted earnestly to find out about my previous lives. Meditation did not yield the answers. So I went to a psychiatrist friend of mine, DK from the heartland, and I asked him if he would hypnotize me and regress my memory back to before I was born. He said no. He refrained from saying anything like, "Tom, it would just be too damned boring." Instead he advised that the experience might be too traumatic. "Do you know what they used to do to boobs in the olden days?" I might learn something about myself or I might experience again something that could cause psychological difficulties in my present life.

Since then, in my conversations with Father, I learned simply that I am who I am.

One of my friends who remembers several or maybe many previous lives, recently was telling me a little bit about what he knows of himself from his previous life experiences. I told him the same thoughts I've written for you above, and then I asked him, "Wouldn't it be horrible to find out that in a previous life you were Hitler?" How could you live with yourself then? How would you recover?

I also told him that what I know of spirits is that they are like pendulums, some of them with great energy and capable of swinging from one extreme to another, while others cut arcs of smaller dimensions. Did his concept of reincarnation allow for a possibility that he who was Jesus also was he who was Hitler?

His response was that Hitler had dug for himself a karmic debt so deep that it would take eons for his spirit to recover. Hitler's spirit now likely was reincarnated as something like a rock on Mars. Although that was in a small way comforting to me, it was not something I could believe.

If Hitler's spirit has such karmic debt, it would be more like a loving God to put that spirit into a position in which it could redeem itself. The energy of such a spirit given the physical genetics and environment to nurture it toward goodness, could work wondrous acts for betterment of our world.

Or does it indeed work the other way? Did Hitler's heinous acts in the physical realm cause his spirit to lose nearly all of its karmic energy? Is it indeed a tiny insignificant pebble in the hot sands of the Sahara Desert? Bum trip, man.

Or maybe I am the reborn Hitler. And maybe so are you. Maybe we all are, just as we all are the reborn twelve million people that he murdered. If we are the holographic reproduction of the universe, then the entire universe is inside us and the same as each and every one of us. Oh wait, I haven't written to you about that. Really that's okay because I don't understand it very well myself.

We indeed have done despicable things to our self. Now it is time, as it always has been time, to do right by our self. Let us redeem our self by loving our neighbor as though our neighbor is our self.

Agnos tapped me on the shoulder. "You think you talk with God?"

"Sure. It's not so very different than talking with you."

"I'm not God. I'm very different than God. Remember, I don't know anything of any importance. My guess is that there are very few people out there who think that is the correct way of describing God."

"But when talking with you, I am using all my focus to be honest with myself. In that way talking with you is very much the same as talking with God."

"I'm special."

"You are honest. Like a child you admit that you don't know these things. True spirituality begins with the admission that we don't know. Jesus said, 'Let the children come to me, and turn them not away, for of such is the kingdom of heaven.'"

57. HAPPY COWS

Having sprouted from roots in the Wisconsin dairy land, it's not unusual for me to enhance my plate of spaghetti with about a pound of parmesan, but this time I paused between my second and third shovels of cheese. I pondered. Is it true what the obnoxious commercials tell us about how the balmy California climate makes cows happier than cows in northern climates? And if they are happier, does that necessarily mean that they make happier cheese?

I asked my cheese, "Are you happy?" My cheese was silent. Talking with cheese can be a lot like talking with God. You must be quite sensitive to telepathic transmissions, and then you must be careful with interpretations because, let's face it, whether from God or cheese, telepathic messages can be hard to fathom, and frequently mistakes arise.

This time, in the back of my mind, I could hear the Beach Boys singing, "I wish they all could be California cows." Then I couldn't get the song out of my head, and the question pursued me. In the grand scheme of things, should we even care about whether cows are happy?

Again in the back of my mind it was either God or my childhood friend, Mickey, who said, "It would be nice to care about cows. They're pleasant animals, and look what they've done for you." Instantly I thought of ice cream, pizza, and then French onion soup layered with cheese, then chocolate milk and peach flavored yogurt.

Yes of course, I care about whether cows are happy.

I remember watching my Uncle Ray milk cows, and the farmyard cats would come around, and sometimes Uncle Ray would teasingly shoo them away by squirting at them directly from the cow's teats.

This may seem like quite a jump, but this memory reminds me that not all Hindus are as gentle and peaceful as Gandhi. Hindus believe their ancestors may reincarnate as cows, and one day a crazy Hindu guy rushed into my Uncle Ray's barn, waving and shouting, accusing Uncle Ray of fondling his grandmother. These impressions stay with me.

It is right to care about the happiness of cows.

California cows enjoy a gentle climate, but they also are steeped in the party life and California dreamin' fantasy world of the LA movie crowd. Cows are susceptible to such things. Do California cows ever ponder the deeper meanings of life?

If you want cows with core values, heartland and home grown common sense, then pay attention to the stoic and disciplined nature of cows honed by harsh winters. These cows are grateful when you give them homemade knitted caps and sweaters, although it's hard to get their legs through the sleeves. These cows appreciate it when a farmer warms his hands before touching them. Cows notice these things. Actually now days it's all done by machine, but I bet the Wisconsinite operators of udder-sucking machines pay attention to the temperature factor.

The phrase, "How now brown cow," which by its color discrimination is inherently racist, now has been supplanted by another rhyme. "There now, there now, gentle cow. Winter storm, hands are warm. There now, there now, holy cow." This can be sung in time with the sounds coming from the sucking machine, and cows like it when you sing. Here's another, this time taken from Franky Valli and the Four Seasons. "Big Cows Don't Cry."

By way of saying so long, imagine Roy Rogers and Dale Evans singing, "Happy cows to you, until we meet again. Happy cows to you;

keep smiling on 'til then. Happy cows to you, 'til we meet again."

58. RAM

Fearless Leader had to put his Scottish Terrier to sleep because of unrelenting cancer. "He left his paw print on my heart." The dog's name is Ram.

As a child I heard a story that once Martin Luther was asked whether dogs go to heaven. His answer was that if dogs don't go to heaven then there will be a lot of unhappy dog lovers in heaven.

I've been thinking. Isn't it supreme vanity for us to think God's favorite animal in this world is the human? That's pretty smug and arrogant, isn't it? What if when we get to heaven we find that the place is owned and operated by dogs?

At the pearly gates we'll be greeted by a handsome German Shepherd. We will be surprised that we actually understand his barks and whines. We also will be surprised that he can read the list in front of him.

Fearless Leader will wait patiently until the Guardian Angel of Heaven's Gate looks up and says, "We have here a very nice recommendation from our friend Ram. He speaks quite highly of you. He looks forward to seeing you again, and he'll be in Golden Canine Park. He'll be waiting for you near fire hydrant number 1,764, which just happens to be the square of 42. I'm certain this will be an auspicious reunion."

NINE

Christmas

59. THE LORD'S SUPPER

It was the first Sunday of Advent, the season of anticipation and preparation for the birth of Jesus, the entry of light into the world; and at our church we ate and drank of the Lord's Supper. This is a small wafer of unleavened bread and a thimble-sized cup of wine. Different beliefs abound about what this wine and bread are. In the Lutheran Church one cannot escape the vitalistic perception that there is essence in the bread and wine beyond what can be measured objectively by current scientific method.

Vitalism derives from the Platonist view that concepts and spirit are the reality of our universe, and that the physical, sensual, measurable things that surround and occupy us are merely manifestations or projections of the spiritual reality. As I said before, this is where you've got to go if you are Lutheran or Catholic or Episcopalian, or any one of a number of churches. These churches believe that Jesus the Christ is present in the bread and wine and enters us as we eat and drink it. This is why the Romans suspected early Christians of cannibalism.

The alternative to this vitalistic philosophy is the mechanistic philosophy, the origin of which is attributed to Aristotle who said no, that the material world around us, the sensible and measurable world, is in fact the real deal. It is upon this mechanistic view that science has been founded and which, in turn, has nurtured its Aristotelian beginnings.

Current technology owes more to the mechanistic view than to the vitalistic view, although the mechanistic view has not always been correct. Robert O. Becker, M.D., assisted by the gifted eloquence of Gary Seldenquite, nicely wrote about this in the superb book, *The Body Electric*, in which he pointed out that it was the mechanists who thought there must be an entire little human being in a single sperm, who merely had to grow larger. The vitalistic idea that a human could be made from nothing but a conglomeration of chemicals was regarded absurd. Read that book. It's fascinating.

So back to the Lord's Supper; the problem with it is that red wine often gives me a headache, and on this particular Sunday even the tiny thimble-full seems to have worked its magic. Mind you, it was just a thimble-sized headache, but nevertheless I had the distinct impression that this headache was a gift of the Lord.

My wife had partaken of the flesh and blood of our savior on an empty stomach, much because of the rush to get to church on time, and after the service she told me that Jesus had given her stomach cramps.

Vitalistically my wife and I were just fine, filled with the spirit of God the Son. Mechanistically we were a bit uncomfortable.

I explained to my wife that when I was a kid, it was the rule of our household not to eat breakfast before the Lord's Supper, so we always ate and drank it on an empty stomach. The idea for this fasting before the Lord's Supper was to keep us from burping on the body and blood of Christ, unseemly to be certain.

Then my wife asked if mine had been a family that commonly burped after breakfast, a family that commonly talked about burping after breakfast, especially as pertained to church activities; and my truthful answer was yes. That was a characteristic of the family which raised me. I remember one very important discussion we had about passing gas in church, probably a topic prompted by either Stan or I farting during the sermon. My dad, smart as he was about other things, gave us the wrong answer. He told us to hold it in until the church wasn't so quiet. Maybe we could fart while everybody was singing. My sister insisted no, that if you try to hold the gas in it only makes the fart louder. The desirable technique was quietly to let the gas out a little at a time. That was the gas debate. Now with my credibility earned as a doctor of medicine, I can declare my sister as the winner. It's a paradigm for life. Stay quiet and sneaky, and you won't embarrass yourself.

What are we to learn from all this? First we have learned that through the ages there has been a boxing match between nearly opposite philosophies called vitalism and mechanism, and this boxing match continues. Sometimes it has seemed as though the vitalists have been on the ropes because of the tremendous practicality of the scientific method and its nurturing influence most of the time for the mechanistic view. However, we've also learned that the scientific method has from time to time pulled a great reversal on the mechanists, and so the boxing match continues. The next reversal may be shaping up at this very moment.

Watch the field of quantum mechanics. It's going to show us some very surprising and maybe upsetting things. So the message to be learned, whether you define yourself as a mechanist or a vitalist or someone somewhere in between, is don't be too smug. In the boxing match of life, smugness goeth before a mandatory eight-count.

Back to the Lord's Supper, and very specifically to the one on this particular first Sunday of Advent, 2005; Stella, my then five year old who could not yet eat and drink at the Lord's Supper, asked her older brother Joshua if he put the bread in his pocket. We laughed, of course, but it brought up another great question to explore. If one were to save the body of Christ for later, would it be the same?

60. MARY HAD A LITTLE MAN

At the age of six and just before Christmas, Stella sang, "Mary had a little man, little man, little man. Mary had a little man. His name was Jesus."

Maybe Jesus wasn't so little. Have you noticed in manger scenes how large the infant is compared to his mother and father? What if this is a realistic depiction, and Jesus was bigger than life?

During labor Mary screamed out, "Jesus Christ Almighty," and ever since then people have been saying that.

When Joseph first saw Jesus' head appearing he was startled and exclaimed, "Holy Mary, mother of God," and ever since then people have been saying that too.

61. CHRISTMAS IN SEATTLE

In many ways Christmas resembles spicy food. People tell me they love Christmas, but Christmas doesn't love them. They take Tums for Christmas.

Waiting in the rain at the bus stop, someone said, "At least it isn't snowing." When it snows in Seattle everything shuts down. Even with an all-wheel drive vehicle you can't get anywhere because the traffic will stop you. Seattle is not a snow oriented community. There aren't many one horse open sleighs. There aren't many people in the meadow building a snowman and pretending that he is Parson Brown. Maybe there are people conspiring as they dream by the fire, but you wouldn't know it.

In New York people know that Donald Trump is conspiring his firing; they know that. Jack Frost nips at their nose, and people dress up like Eskimos. In Seattle people are dressed like the Lewis and Clark expedition. When Jack Frost visits he turns into a drip. Instead of people donning their gay apparel, they don their rain gear. Instead of trolling the ancient yuletide carol, they troll for salmon. That's Seattle for you.

In this city, Jingle Bell Rock turns into Jingle Bell Grunge. That's the way it is.

In other parts of the country, every mother's child is going to spy to see if reindeer really know how to fly. Boeing employees' children think *big deal. We don't need no stinkin' reindeer.* There are a lot of Norwegian immigrants here and they eat reindeer meatballs. They call the dish *Yoika.* You want Rudolph? He's in there. Okay, so I just overdid it. I apologize to all you Rudolph fans.

With all this going on in Seattle, why do we stay? It is because we love it here, and we are as quirky as the weather.

62. SANTA CLAUS

Even though there are parallels between the stories of Santa Claus and Jesus, people find it much easier with Saint Nicholas to sort out what is historical from what are mythological legends. With Jesus' stories it is different and more difficult. Admittedly people easily reject as fantasy the legend that Jesus caused Pontius Pilate to grow bat wings and a Pinocchio nose, but other than that people tend to choose to believe the fantastic legends of Jesus and to reject those of Santa Claus.

The name, Santa, means saint just the same as in Santa Cruz or Santa Anna. Claus is a nick-name for Nicholas, and so there you have it.

Saint Nicholas was a Christian bishop of Myra, in Lycia, a province of Byzantine Anatolia in what is now Turkey. He lived during the fourth century and was renowned for his generous gifts to the poor. He was particularly revered for having bestowed dowries upon three daughters of an impoverished man so that the women would not have to survive by working as prostitutes. One other possibly truthful legend about him is that at a time of epidemic disease, while people were quarantined in locked houses, he still delivered packages of food and clothing to the poor by lowering them with ropes down chimneys. So it's true!

I find myself wondering if Santa is nicer than Jesus. He is at least less demanding. For example he will continue to bring presents even if a person doesn't believe in him. Even if a child is naughty, generally Santa will bring toys anyway. Santa is very forgiving.

In some Germanic folklore Santa is depicted as being so loving and nice that he could never bring even naughty children such things as a lump of coal, and so there was talk about a Moorish slave who followed Santa around. In Dutch this evil being was called *Zwarte Piet*, meaning

Black Peter. Zwarte Piet might take away the toys Santa had left, or he might beat bad children with a rod or even steal them away from their homes.

This is sort of like how many people imagine God as not possibly being a creator or cause of all the horrible things in our world. God cannot at all be responsible for that evil. It must be the Devil.

There is this little matter of believing in Santa Claus, and when a child is roughly ten years old his parents begin to wonder, *should we tell him?* And the child is concerned that if his parents find out he already knows, maybe he will get fewer presents. So parents and children go through this amusing little charade, dancing around each other on the issue of whether Santa Claus is real.

At Christmas Eve dinner, Granny told my children, "Yes, certainly leave cookies out for Santa, but don't forget his reindeer. Maybe you should put some carrots in the yard for them, and some water too."

Later as I was carrying a bucket of water and a plate of carrots out into the yard, my son Josh said to me, "Dad, actually we need to put plates out here for eight reindeer, nine if you count Rudolph."

I answered, "One plate of carrots is enough. They can share."

"I don't think so," he said. "They'll be in a hurry with all the deliveries they need to make. They won't have time to share."

Nine plates of carrots later, and only three buckets of water because after exhaustive search that was all the buckets I could find, my son relented. "That will do. We can use cereal bowls for the rest."

Do you know what happens when you leave carrots out in the yard overnight in rainy Seattle? They get covered with slugs. Slugs love carrots.

So it was some time shortly after midnight when Santa's reindeer, clad in garden clogs, sneaked out into the yard and tossed the slug-laden carrots over the fence into the woods. *Clever reindeer*, I thought to myself. Then I dumped out three quarters of the water and retreated into the house to enjoy cookies and a glass of milk.

The day after Christmas is notorious for sales and mark-downs on the price of Christmas supplies, and so our family went shopping. Joshua noticed that the very same paper that Santa had used to wrap presents was right there in the store, 40% off. "Santa must like shopping at Hallmark," he observed.

Eventually Joshua will come to understand that Santa continues to bring goodies whether or not a person believes in him. We as families play the role of Santa. We even play the role of Santa for those we don't know. We give presents to the homeless and otherwise disenfranchised members of society. They are relatives of our larger family.

Is this another parallel to God? Does God forgive us and love us and save us even if we don't believe? Only if he is as nice as Santa Claus, and only if we are as nice as we want God to be.

Some of you may think I'm being blasphemous. If you think that, I want you to reflect on what you are saying when you pray, "Forgive us as we forgive others." We do not play passive roles in God's acts of forgiveness and beneficence. A friend of mine, Suzy, told me that every day and in every choice we make, we are living either heaven or hell.

Hell, I like Santa a lot. How about you?

63. ELLIOT EVERGREEN

Everything green has been touched by elves,
and perhaps you have seen that they're green themselves.
As if by magic, green to green,
it is they and their fingers who green the string bean,
and trees in the summer, the grass in the spring,
the eyes of some drummers and most living things.

Of course there are red elves, blue elves and pink.
Some elves are dull elves, and some like to think;
but of all of these elves let us think of just some,
and of all of these some elves in particular one.

His name is Elliot Evergreen.

He is quick, and he's clever; he's cunning and keen,
and you know if you've seen him he's also quite green.
He lives in a forest near Knotted Wood Square
and sun up 'til sun down makes green the trees there.
He nurtures the fir trees. He shines up the pines.
He spruces the spruce trees and keeps them in prime.
When other elves leave in the crisp autumn air,
let their trees change, drop leaves, become bare;
Elliot stays and works through the fall
to keep his trees' branches the greenest of all.

This is a story of once long ago
how hard working Elliot wanted to know
where in the world the other elves dallied
when other trees changed in the Knotted Wood Valley.
Every September the maples turned gold.

The oaks became red with the onset of cold.
The elms all turned yellow and later to brown,
and then in October the leaves fluttered down.
The elves who all summer were keeping them green
of a sudden in autumn could nowhere be seen.
Where did they run to? Where did they fly?
How did they get there, and most of all why?

Elliot wondered. He wanted to know,
and once in an autumn decided to go.
He followed two others named Sumac and Oak.
The one was an acorn, the other a bloke.
He followed them out past the knotted wood homes,
north through the tundra where nobody roams.
He followed them far to a land full of snow
where the sky was quite dark, and the winds were ablow.
This land full of darkness, this land full of ice,
for all of its shiver was still very nice.
For elves the cold winds were not at all bitter.
This land full of ice was a wonder of glitter.

Away in the night they could see a small light,
and chase it they did 'til a house came in sight.
It lay in a snow bank, its walls white and red.
On the door there was holly, in the garden a sled.
"There it is," announced Sumac. "I see it," said Oak.
"So do I," ventured Elliot, "and who are the folk?"
"You'll find out; you will meet them. You'll like them.
    They're fine.
They work hard and sing songs and love all mankind."
The three in the snow bank rap-tapped on the door.
Then inside they went to meet elves and galore.

The front hall was snow-wet and cluttered with clothes.
Ice-beaded mittens and coats there unfroze.
From within there arose a clamor, a din
of wood cutters cutting and hammers on tin,
with bing bangs and cling clangs, with whistles and hums,
sing songs and ping pongs, with trumpets and drums.
Squeaking of rocking horse on sawdust floors,
a thousand or more elves were all at their chores.

"Hurry," said Sumac, "It's time to begin.
First shout a hello, and then let's check in."
The clerk at the desk addressed them in formal
and snootily called their arrival abnormal.
"Long summer," said Sumac. "Late frost," added Oak.
"Never mind that; don't worry," the formal clerk spoke.
"But here's a discrepancy, answer me this;
there's no elf named Evergreen here on my list."
"I'm a very good worker. I'm fast and I'm strong.
If you choose then to keep me you cannot go wrong.
Do you want me or don't you?" Our green friend replied.
Stay there he would; he would not be denied.

It was time then to muster all nissen and elves,
cluster all new toys in groups on the shelves.
"Listen all workers; you've three friends to greet.
Then off to the kitchen, it's time now to eat."
They marched to the kitchen in lively parade.
Some of them danced, and more of them played.
Some gents and lady elves turned in a waltz
while others more limber performed somersaults.
A vaulting small youngster was first to pop in.
The last elf, a grandpa, had hair on his chin.
This grandfather elf was as tall as a man,
but gentle as cotton and head of this clan.
Amusement and kindness were part of his air,
and he wished a glad night to all who were there.

The cook elves who came with their clattering platters,
light, cheerful laughter and talkative chatters;
proudly presented great cauldrons of juice,
fruit from the gardens and vegetable mousse,
barrels of berries and barley supreme,
mugs of hot chocolate and coffee with cream.
Before this proud passage of procession grand
a great elfin grandma exerted command,
directing them rightward and leading them left,
presenting the delicacies she had cheffed.
The great elfin grandpa's great elfin dame
gave out the cuisine that had earned her great fame;

and there she sat herself down by her man,
the great elfin grandpa of this joyful clan.

Elliot questioned the persons he knew,
who were these elf hosts, these grandparent two?
"What on earth!" answered Sumac. "You're kidding!" said Oak.
"Where have you been that you don't know these folk?"
And then they all sang, that kindred throng.
The kitchen hall rang out in lively sing song:
"Santa Claus master is ruler of elves.
He knows what their thoughts are, inside their minds delves.
He knows correct answers to questions of heart.
He brings souls together when they've been apart.
Santa Claus master is planner of plans.
He lists sincere wishes; the whole world he scans.
He loves little children and flies his reindeer
to bring toys and goodies and plenty of cheer."

"Mrs. Claus mistress is magical too.
When urgency calls she is able to do
all the wonderful wonders that Santa performs,
even flying the reindeer through Christmas snowstorms."

After the sing song they danced a fun jig.
Some of them played on a fiddle-dee-fig.
The jig saws were jumping. The thing-thaws were thumping.
The toys on the shelves were rubbing and bumping.
Whiskers were flying. Shoes went ka-thunk.
The toys that were sleeping jumped out of their trunk.
They danced. They pranced. They made lots of noise,
those rambunctious elves and their living live toys.

Then it was done, the dinner and dancing;
finished the singing, the swinging and prancing.
Then it was time for all elves to sleep,
to lie like the snow, drifting far, drifting deep;
as deep as the night, as dark as the sky,
as quiet as breathing a slumbering sigh.

When they awoke it was still arctic night.
The sun in its heaven was way out of sight.

Cuckoo clocks cuckooed, and some beds were shaken.
That's how the elves knew it was time to awaken.
They stretched. They yawned and wiped sleep from their eyes.
After that a small breakfast helped them to arise.
So up they got and then off to work
building toys for good children; 'twas no time to shirk.

This was the order for all who stayed there,
to work hard and play hard and most of all care.
They all worked together with good cheer and fun.
If one was unfinished then no one was done.
This was the secret they liked to point out,
to live life with pleasure, to work without doubt
that the end of the day would have its reward.
Work without wanting, and speak with accord.

Elliot stayed, and he lived by these rules.
He worked with his fingers, his magical tools.
He worked without wanting and spoke with accord,
and the colors he made there the others adored:
the greenest of greens, the bluish greens too,
the yellowish ones as well as green true.
Santa was pleased as well as the others,
the elfin clan sisters and elfin clan brothers.
These were the prettiest greens they had seen.
They marveled and praised Elliot Evergreen.

So when Santa heard about the great scare,
the great forest problem near Knotted Wood Square,
he knew where to look; he knew just the one.
He knew what Elliot Evergreen had done.
"Elliot," he said, "It's time for a walk,
and while we are walking it's time for a talk.
Have you heard that the trees in Knotted Wood Forest,
all the evergreen trees are looking their poorest?
They've lost all their needles and turned sickly brown.
The needles are dropping; they're all falling down.
The children in Knotted Wood Square have a fear
that there will be no Christmas tree trimming this year.
Why do you think good Elliot, friend,
that these fine Christmas trees have come to their end?"

Now Elliot saw the cost of his fun.
He'd left his evergreen duties undone.
When he ran away in the crisp autumn air
he'd abandoned his Christmas tree friends that lived there.
But now, though he'd learned of his wretched mistake,
he hadn't a clue of what steps he could take
to make it right, a remedial plan.
"I want to. I do. I will do what I can."
That's what Elliot Evergreen said,
and he blushed 'til his evergreen turned slightly red.

Santa looked upward at the North Star.
"We'll import Christmas trees on my sled from afar,
and you, Elliot, will join this endeavor.
You will make these trees' colors the greenest green ever."
They raced away speedily, fast as two jets,
to gather up trees to pay Elliot's debts.
Eight magic reindeer and Santa's great sleigh
flew along with them southward without a delay.
Toward forested woodlands the Christmas crew chased
over mountains and meadows with dazzling haste.
They found trees and felled them, greened them and Santa'd them,
and in their place tiny seedlings were planted then.

Now certainly curious readers will raise
a question about that curious phrase.
What does it mean to Santa a tree?
It means make it smaller times ten thousand three.
This is one method that Santa employs
to deliver at once all his candies and toys.
All of these things he miniaturizes,
and takes them at once to the kids he surprises.
He also can do this, make smaller himself,
this wonderful, marvelous, magical elf.
That's how he fits down the chimneys he pleases
and does it without any dark sooty squeezes.
That's what he did with the trees they got there
and carried them all to the Knotted Wood Square
where children all laughed with sparkling eyes
replacing the salty tears left from their cries.

Resolved was the crisis at Knotted Wood Square,
the scare of the problem of knotted woods bare,
but what about next year, the next and those after?
How would they keep up the smiles and laughter
if every year with the autumn's arrival
Elliot elf didn't tend the survival
of green in the needles of each of his trees
but rather departed with autumn's cold breeze?
Elliot looked downward, troubled and doubtful.
To tell you the truth he even looked poutful.

Santa then winked and he said, "There are ways
to keep you still coming while green in trees stays.
but it requires some changes, if changes you can,
if northward to help me remains your plan.
You'll no longer tend to the Knotted Wood Forest
nor any one woodland we see before us.
Other elves can do those deeds,
fulfilling each separate forest's needs.
For you, your trees will grow far and wide,
but just one kind will be your pride.
You will be master of tamarack trees
which stay green in summer but brown at the freeze
of autumn's crisp air when you'll fly north to me
to touch some of my toys with your green wizardry.
As certain as there will be toys in my sack,
When anyone looks at these trees tamarack
they will know the reason the needles have dropped
is that Elliot Evergreen's magic has stopped,
and he's flown north to Santa to be one of mine
whenever it's soon to become Christmas time."

And with that and a glitter, a sparkle or two,
Santa and Elliot Evergreen flew
back to the Arctic's cold wintry night
to fabricate toys and to color them right.
So now there is happiness both here and there.
There is happiness even in Knotted Wood Square.

TEN

Mythology

64. A TERRIBLE DAY AT THE COFFEE HOUSE

DK from the heartland wrote, I'm trying to make sense out of Isaiah 14:12-17.

How you have fallen from heaven, O morning star, son of the dawn? You have been cast down to the earth, you who once laid low the nations! You said in your heart, "I will ascend to heaven; I will raise my throne above the stars of God; I will sit enthroned on the mount of assembly, on the utmost heights of the sacred mountain. I will ascend above the tops of the clouds; I will make myself like the Most High." But you are brought down to the grave, to the depths of the pit.

This was written by the prophet upon the collapse of mighty Babylon whose king, Nebuchadnezzar II, had destroyed Jerusalem and enslaved Jews for fifty years between 588 and 538 B.C. The Persian king, Cyrus, released captive Jews and allowed them to return to their homeland in Judea. In these verses Isaiah blew a raspberry at the descendants of Nebuchadnezzar.

Some have interpreted these verses also as connecting to a story of God throwing Satan out of heaven because he was getting too big for his britches. Maybe there's more to tell of the story.

Many Gnostic Christians believed the universe was so much of a mess that it had to have been created by someone other than God. God would not have made it so. The world was fashioned by a lesser god who was powerful, but also arrogant and blind. He could not see the true God above him.

Gnostics believed that God would not have done and said many of the things attributed to him in the Old Testament, so they had to have been performed by this lesser god who was called by various names such as Samael, Sakla, Yaldabaoth, and even Yahweh. Gnostics in the early centuries of the church said some not-so-complimentary things about the God of the Old Testament. No wonder their books were burned by the Orthodox Christians.

Orthodox view was and is that evil relates to the fall of man. God created man perfect, but then man blundered. So much for perfection! The Gnostics believed that God would not create such an imperfect creature, and so such an imperfect creation, evil in the first place, had to have been created by Samael, not God.

With this in mind, please read DK's story.

Lucifer breathed a sigh of relief as he stepped out of the courthouse, ecstasy keeping his fatigue at bay. Tonight he would sleep soundly. As Father's top prosecuting attorney he had been in a number of high profile cases, but this was the pinnacle.

He made his way toward the coffeehouse on Fifth and Heaven Way, a quaint and favorite meeting place for his family on special days and celebrations. Father, Josh and Agnos already would be there waiting for him.

Lu thought about the case as he strolled along. Samael had been charged with extreme disregard for the creatures of his universe, for the slaughter of uncountable numbers who fell victim to wars waged in his name. He had been charged with blasphemies against the divine and resistance to attempts of rehabilitation. Samael was known by various names throughout the eons, names such as Sakla, Yaldabaoth, and he was even depicted as The Snake. But the blasphemy that irritated Father most was Samael's having taken the sacred name of Yahweh.

The bottom line was that Samael had become known as *The Blind Fool, The Blind leading the blind.* He had made ridiculous pronouncements such as when he said of his messengers, "Thou shalt not bow down thyself unto them, nor serve them, for I the Lord thy God am a jealous God, visiting the iniquity of the fathers upon the children unto the third and fourth generation of them that hate me." Such pronouncements, echoing eternally in the Akashic Field, had caused terrible confusion in the universe. Creatures on new worlds, just starting their enlightenment and naively opening themselves to messages from above, had thought they were hearing these directives from God. But these were perversions of the Akashic Field and not from Father.

Not just on Earth had wars started when tribes and nations felt they were the select race with authority and responsibility to convert or abolish "inferior races."

It there was one significant defect in the universe, it was that once a statement was made it would be part of the Akashic Field forever, for better or worse. In the case of Samael, it had been for worse, and his influence now would be echoed until this universe ends and the Akashic Field could be cleansed for the next Age.

Lucifer shook his head. The Family had tried diligently to rehabilitate this gigantic realm. Missions usually had been specific, to individual worlds that had become mired in utter confusion. Each son and daughter of God had made missions with various degrees of success. Lucifer the first born, Maria, Agnos, Jo, Joshua and Sophie, all had had their assignments. But for as long as Samael had been free to rape the universe with his excesses, missions were fraught with hardship, and some had failed. Now because of his most recent and ultimate success, Lu hoped things would turn around.

He was jubilant, but also an uneasiness lurked inside him about Father's having questioned his ardent efforts for bringing maximum punishment against Samael. Still, Lucifer could not help smiling. Samael would be imprisoned for the rest of eternity, that is, for the remainder of this Universal Age. Father had opined that a sentence for a millennium should be sufficient. Well, what if Sam was not rehabilitated after completion of so limited a sentence? Sam may thwart all of their planned efforts for rejuvenating the realm. While Samael did not have the power of Josh or himself, and certainly not the omnipotence of Mother or Father, still he would certainly appear to be the Almighty to confused citizens of the realm.

Alas the rule of Free Will. It prevented direct eradication of the spoils that could be caused by Samael. The Family only could enter minds to provide an alternative thought. Individuals still could choose for themselves what to believe.

Lu stepped up into the shop and there they were, Father and his brothers, savoring their favorites. Father had a cappuccino; Josh sipped a mocha, and Agnos enjoyed an espresso. Lu ordered his own favorite, a medium latte with a touch of honey, and then he slumped in his chair awaiting the inevitable onslaught of questions with a broad grin on his face. Everyone at the table could have read his mind, perhaps, but they were too polite for that. They obviously could read from his expression that the verdict had gone well for him, but they didn't know how well.

Agnos was first to pipe up. "Well?"

"Well, I won. And I won big. Uncle Samael is detained for the duration. You may say that he's interned for eternity. Throw away the key." Lu was high on himself and wanted to inject more levity. "He's allowed to write from prison, but he must use only lower case letters," he laughed.

As he continued to share the details of the verdict and to collect congratulations from his brothers, he felt a powerful tension building in his father. Finally he asked, "Father, what do you think?"

Father took some time to answer, choosing his words carefully to avoid misinterpretation. "Lu, you are happy with your victory, and I am happy for you. However, don't you think you asked for too harsh of a sentence? We are no longer about an eye for an eye and a tooth for a tooth. That was Sam's way, not ours."

Lucifer also was careful with his reply. Quietly and in an uncharacteristically monotone voice he answered, "You know how much I wanted the maximum sentence. With Samael out of the way, our rehabilitation of the universe will progress much more smoothly. His minions will not dare to interfere too openly or vigorously, knowing a similar fate may await them. Countless wayward planets depend on us to set things right. The confusion in the Akashic Field is tremendous, and these poor helpless beings need for operations to go correctly now, and not for just a little while. For always."

"Yes, yes I know." Father countered, "but the noninterference principle is not just a right for mortal beings on planets but also for creators and messengers above. Samael has a right to get on with his journey, after of course a definite period of thoughtful reflection. Lu, you went too far. Don't you have compassion for him too? Is your compassion limited only to the creatures on planets? Being locked up for the rest of the Universal Age is too much for anyone to bear, even a divine being. Look into yourself. Don't you think you were acting on a personal vendetta because of the misery he caused when your own personal missions have failed?"

Lucifer's anger swelled. "Are you choosing sides now? Must I contend with you now like I had to contend with him? He HAD rights, Father. Past tense. He sacrificed his rights by his own felonious behavior. You know as well as I do that a huge correction was required, and that was my role. I should be commended."

Josh and Agnos looked anxiously at one another, and then Josh butted in, "Father and Lu, settle down. Cool heads need to prevail so nothing gets said that later would be regretted."

Lu ignored the advice. "Father," he shouted. "How dare you judge me. Don't you understand how deep my compassion is for mortals? Am I not a 'chip off the old block?' Isn't everything I say and do a manifestation of you? So if anyone lacks compassion it is you! Samael is a big boy; he can take care of himself. He's responsible for so much chaos that we can't begin to understand its depth. Show your compassion for the mortals. Who will take care of them? From what I've just heard it won't be you. Have you lost your senses? Maybe it's time for me to take over. I'll visit you at the retirement home!"

The explosion of tempers was overwhelming. Josh and Agnos retreated to watch as the walls of the coffee house blew apart with shouts of rage from one to the other of the combatant deities and from both of them at the same time. Then suddenly Father afflicted the space with a silence so deafening that only his own voice could be heard. "You are a disgrace. I never want to see you again. You are banished from my home."

Next there was a flash so terrible it blinded them, and when at last Josh could see and hear again he saw nothing of the neighborhood but devastation. Agnos looked shocked and Father was weeping. Lucifer was nowhere to be seen.

Josh tried to console his father who lamented, "What I have done is not pardonable. I am a pathetic being. Lucifer was right; I have no compassion, particularly for my own son."

Quickly an idea and plan came to Josh, a mission beyond anything ever attempted before, a mission of love without limit. As he shared it he saw hope reappear in Father's eyes.

Lucifer awakened in unfamiliar surroundings with both his mind and his body feeling numb, both his soul and body in painful anguish. Alone. He was no longer in his father's domain, and for the first time in his life he experienced nearly limitless fear. The space around him was hard and dense, much more so than even Samael's creation. Then as his mind began to work again, to remember the events at the coffee house, his fear changed to bitterness. He was banished.

Alone with no one to hear him, he shouted, "I'll show you. I will be as sly as a serpent. I will teach the creatures to be strong and self reliant. They will be as gods themselves, and they will fashion their fears creatively." Then he pondered himself. *I am compassionate. I will teach them with tough love, and these creatures will have no need for Father. They will not be his sheep. Instead they will be cunning as my wolves. They will know the depths of good and evil, and they will use both with craftiness. I will reject none of them. All of them will be acceptable to me and I will empower them to see both the light and the darkness in themselves and in others. I am the son of the morning. It is I who made the earth tremble and who shook the heavens. I will do so again.*

65. A STONE TO YOU, LUNCH TO ME

Agnos was pleased to have been included in the coffee house gang. "DK made me one of the deities," he smiled.

"Yes, he asked me if he could borrow you; nice of him to do that. I think he wanted to point out that even from the beginning there have been people honest enough with themselves to admit they don't know answers to the great questions. That questioning honesty may in itself be worthy of worship."

"Worthy of worship?" Agnos was taken aback.

"Yes well, if we're going to worship things."

"I'm just pleased to have been noticed. Really that's good enough for me."

"You're so humble. Look, Dan wrote to me some more of his series that he calls *Brothers*. He doesn't look at the struggle between Jesus and Lucifer as being the same as the struggle between good and evil. It will be fun to read it together, you and me. Instead of you arguing with me about what I write, for a change you and I together can criticize Dan."

"Are you telling me I argue with you about everything?"

"Yes, something like that. It's sort of your make up, who you are."

"Sort of like you're a boob, right? Something like that?"

"Let's read his letter."

Hi Tom. Here is my next story, an obvious account of Matthew 4:1-11. You know, Satan always has been a mystery to me. Why would anyone actually want to sabotage everything God wants for us? Peace. Harmony. Forgiveness. Eternal Life. It doesn't make sense. What kind of twisted mind operates like this? There has to be a revenge factor and bitterness behind it, and suppose Satan thinks he is doing good for the humans that he's tempting.

I guess there are two ways to look at Satan. One would be a fallen angel, a being who has a specific plan known only to him. The other is to realize that Satan is a process of the mind, and not just an individual mind but the collective mind, the Mind of God. So he cannot be completely banished, but he can be driven deeply into the unconscious. Then he is those evil thoughts with which we don't want to deal, hidden away out of our awareness but awaiting an opportunity to bite us in the butt with slips of the tongue, conflicts, physical symptoms.

Perhaps this is why I get stuck developing a story line for mythological characters, Satan, Christ, etc. I think in more abstract terms.

I'm not implying Jesus is not historical. Well maybe, to some degree. I do think there was a man from Galilee, a wonderful man from whom fabulous legends have been made.

"May I say something?"

"Yes, Agnos."

"The whole idea of being able to blame Satan for the crap that goes on in our heads and our behavior, it's a very handy thing. We're lucky to have him."

A STONE TO YOU, LUNCH TO ME

"We meet again. What brings you to this rock?"

Lucifer replied, "To visit you Josh. I've come to make you an offer. After all you are my brother. When I heard about your incarnation, I just had to see you. Well, you are a fine looking young man; never mind the shabbiness you've inflicted upon yourself. The clarity and intensity of your eyes! Just looking at you, I can see how persuasive you would be with these mere mortals."

Josh asserted, "You know Father misses you. He would like ... ."

"Stop it!" snapped Lu. "How dare you bring this up, after what he did to me. Did you suppose I would want to have anything to do with him? He is the last being I want to see. You have no idea what I've contended with these first few eons, but I have made the best of the situation. I've taught a tough love and a fierce independence to the creatures I've encountered, and here on earth I've had great success. Admittedly I haven't reached everyone, yet, but you won't find these humans easy to convert to your starry-eyed kind of love. Beyond the fear that the name Satan arouses, there is a curiosity and an admiration for me. Being called the Prince of Darkness suits me fine."

"But don't you see what you're doing? You're leading these poor creatures down the worst one way trip possible. How can Father reach them with the venomous lies you spread?"

"Lies?" Lucifer smiled. "Truth? Ah yes, names. What is truth? Whose truth, yours or mine? Must I be untrue to myself to please you? Your simplicity disappoints me, Josh. But really Brother, all this discussion is beside the point. I have a proposition for you. How about a partnership, you and me? You're forgiving. I'm cunning. Have you any idea what miraculous changes we could make together in this world?"

Joshua appeared weary. Lu said, "With your extended fast, you must be famished. How long has it been, forty days? That is not healthy behavior for this body of yours. Let's have lunch. Change these stones to loaves of bread, and when we have eaten we will reminisce about the good times."

"Don't you understand? Even as a human I don't live on just food. What is life about? Life is the words of Father."

"Clever answer, little brother. You have matured, starting to rival my own wit. But you know how I feel about Father. He is an ungrateful has-been, and the future could be ours, yours and mine." Then Lu quickly changed the subject. "Come with me to the holy city. You will love it there, and I want to show you something beautiful."

"Before they run off to the city," interrupted Agnos, "I'd like to comment on this business of stones to bread magic. In the Bible it was written that Jesus said, 'Man does not live by bread alone, but by every word that proceeds from the mouth of God.' Isn't that just what a person would say if he had tried to convert stones to bread and failed? It would be like sour grapes. It's like Jesus saying, 'It would have been bad bread any way, pieces of sand in it. I don't need no stinkin' bread. I've got God.' Okay, now you can go on with the story."

"Agnos," I said. "Don't you think it could be Jesus recognizing that he fundamentally was a spiritual, not a physical being? I mean, he was physical, but that isn't where his life was. His life was his spirit, nurtured by words of God."

"Forced into it I'd say. Remember what you used to say back when you were poor, right after your divorce?"

"Oh yes. I used to say I was spiritual because I couldn't afford to be anything else."

"That's my point, my second one. Of course that's probably why Jesus went into the desert in the first place. He knew it was where John the Baptist learned to free himself from depending on the pleasures of life. Jesus was searching for himself. Let's go on."

Lucifer took Joshua to the city, and Josh wondered what his older brother was up to as they walked up the stairs of the temple to its highest point. Lu said, "So you are God's favorite son, or so it has been said. But you have told me that he misses me. I am his prodigal son for whom he would celebrate if I returned. There is power in my position, little Josh. Are you Father's favorite son? You don't know that for sure, do you? You have some doubt; don't deny it."

"What does that matter? Father loves all his children equally. You know that. You spent so much time with him; how could you possibly question his love. How could Father have a favorite if his love is infinite for every one of us?"

"Let's see his love in action. Jump. You have come into this world on some magnificent mission that depends on your human body. If you have no doubts then you know he will command his angels to catch you. Do it. Not even your foot will be bruised. Here in this body of yours, you have doubts. I know. I've been watching. Let's see this God in action." Lu began to chuckle.

Joshua answered. "My doubts were left behind. You know as well as I know that if we have faith in the Lord there is no need to put him to the test. To test him would demonstrate a lack of faith. I have no doubts. You also know the Holy Word inside and out, Lu. Put your complete faith in the benevolent nature of God. Father will accept you again any time."

"Circular reasoning," Lu said flatly, and he decided to change tack again. "We will go to the mountain where the view will inspire us."

"Before they go to the mountain," interrupted Agnos, "don't you think Lucifer had a good point? What harm would it have been for Jesus to have jumped, or maybe to have slipped and fallen accidentally. If he didn't have any doubts, why was this passage written in the first place? This passage of writing is precisely about Jesus' doubts. There's no other reason for it. It's a story about how Jesus decided to do the right thing. He didn't commit suicide."

"I don't know what to say. Agnos, sometimes you're impossible. You can suck the fun out of anything."

"Nothing personal; it's my job. Go on with the story."

Lu brought Josh to the summit. "Look out on the world. All these kingdoms; yours and mine. All this splendor; we can share it, and not just here on Earth. Gaze upon the stars. They twinkle like rejoicing eyes wanting to be yours. Humans will bow down to you just as they have bowed down to me. Forget your allegiance to Father. His way demands too much of you and you will have little compared to what you could have with me. Come Josh, a simple bow to me, and it's all yours!"

Joshua felt exasperated. How could Lucifer stoop so low? My brother, the Morning Star, the Son of the Dawn. The materialism! The admiration of the crowds! How did he get so wrapped up in these unimportant matters? These things Lu talked about, they were only toys. Who was the child here? Josh told his brother, "Serve the One. Our wills are unimportant. See the greater good. You have blinded yourself with greed. Look into yourself, at what you have become. You have taught, 'See the darkness within,' but when you see the darkness within, don't succumb to it. Overcome the darkness. I'll show you the light, the way to return. If you cannot do this, Lu, then get away from me. Satan! I have my work to do."

Lu was startled by how strong Joshua had become, and he saw the loving light shining in his eyes. It had been a long time since he had experienced such pure compassion, and it frightened him. Almost stumbling in his speech he said, "I'll go away now, but I'll be watching you.

The toughest test is yet to come. How will you react when all your friends abandon you? I'll be there, Josh. I'll be waiting for you, and then you will see. You don't need any of them, not even Father.

Lu left Josh on the mountain.

He's such a stubborn brother, Josh thought. He wished Lu would lose his bitterness, and Josh himself would help with that. He also realized that his friends indeed were fragile, and although he had displayed a strong faith in God when tested by his brother, he also knew that he too was human and had frailties. Would he succeed in his mission? Even if he did succeed, how would his friends react? How would the people of the world react? Would the mustard seed grow and blossom?

66. JOSH TEACHES COMPASSION

The small crowd and the disciples sat still in the vanishing darkness of the new day. Josh finally stood up and watched the rising sun just starting to peek over the horizon. He turned to the crowd and exclaimed, "Look at the sun!"

He watched the sun as it climbed higher. "Feel its warmth. We are so blessed. The sun gives us life. It shines upon all. It matters not if one is young or old, rich or poor, man or woman, arrogant or humble, a warrior or a peace maker. We all receive its warmth and life.

"So it is with Father's love. It is bestowed upon all. There is no judgment that one will receive it and another will not. It is given equally to each and everyone. We are truly blessed. We do not have to do anything to receive His love. Nothing to sacrifice, nothing to achieve, it is given freely and can be received just as freely. We all are his children. Soak in His love as you soak in the warmth of the sun. Soak in as much as you can, and when you think you can hold no more, allow his love to spill over to all around you. Give it to everyone.

"Make no judgment on whom will receive your love, just as the sun makes no judgment on whom will receive its warmth, and Father makes no judgment on whom receives His love. Be as compassionate as Father is compassionate. This is how heaven is achieved. No more wars. No more strife. No more killing. No more revenge. No more bitterness. May your compassion be a beacon of light for all to see, for all to receive.

"When the light is turned on inside of you, darkness dissolves. Just as the world changes from night to day as the sun rises and shines, you are the light of the world."

It appeared to the crowd that Josh himself shined as brightly as the sun. They gasped in amazement. As Josh continued, hardly anyone actually heard his words, transfixed as they were on the blazing light emitted from him.

"Live the life of compassion.

"Be born of the womb of compassion.

"Drink the milk of compassion.

"Receive the mother's embrace of compassion.

"Take the first step of compassion.

"Run with the speed of compassion.

"Play with the joy of compassion.

"Learn from the books of compassion.

"Fall in love with the romance of compassion.

"Mature in the ways of compassion.

"Give the embrace of compassion.

"Teach the rules of compassion.

"Age gently in the years of compassion.

"Die in the transition of compassion.

"Meet Father in the heaven of compassion."

Hardly anyone realized when Josh stopped speaking and sat down. The sun was at its zenith and had become hot.

Everyone returned home, and as they experienced events of the upcoming weeks they realized they were no longer the same. Their lips smiled more than ever before. The town was more peaceful, more serene and more compassionate. Interestingly very few remembered the day that Josh taught about compassion. Only his mother, aunt, girl friend and brother recalled that day, but of course they knew him from before the foundations of the world were laid. They knew about his mission when he came home from the coffee shop.

They, his family had been such a comfort to him as everyone else viewed him as special, so strange. He thought, if only he could touch the soul of his lost brother, Lu. Then his family would be complete again.

Lucifer did watch the events of that special day, hidden from the crowd, and in the bottom of his heart something started to stir again. Well, he thought, this makes me ponder. My brother is tender hearted, and each day he gets stronger. But what about my compassion? I know these people. They are better served by the mission I have undertaken. Inside he started to have doubts.

67. JOSH TEACHES ASTRAL PROJECTION

DK wrote: I believe the Man from Galilee taught some form of astral projection to his disciples. Reading in the Bible the events after the crucifixion would lead a discerning mind to the conclusion that something unusual took place. One conclusion is to take literally the events in agreement with traditional Christianity, that he was resurrected physically and came back to meet the disciples wearing his physical body.

There are several alternative explanations. The first is that the disciples might have lied. It was to their political advantage to make up a story and steal the body from the tomb. But would the early Christians put their lives on the line over a lie?

The second is that they might have hallucinated. However a group hallucination seems far fetched. Certainly they were grief stricken, but was it of an intensity to induce group psychosis?

A third explanation is that they might have witnessed some other phenomena that later authors twisted either mistakenly or on purpose.

I propose that the disciples had become proficient in a technique in which they communicated with their teacher across the border that separates the physically living from the physically dead.

During the last couple of centuries various psychic phenomena have been written about in parapsychology literature, including the somewhat antiquated term of being a medium, then replaced by the term of channeling. Then there is the phenomena referred to as out of body experience, near death experience and astral projection. In years to come we may discover a biochemical explanation, maybe related to the DMT molecule. Maybe these experiences are related to tapping into the unconscious mind that sits deeply within our psyches, and maybe it only mistakenly is recognized as communicating with another being, dead or alive; or exploring a landscape beyond our familiar surroundings. Can we differentiate between the individual unconscious mind and the collective unconscious? Is it possible that we can connect with a greater mind beyond our individual minds, or tap into some type of mental/psychic network in which we share our thoughts with others, living or dead?

The Galilean healer's disciples were able to explore some type of altered state of consciousness. Here is the account from Matthew 17:1-9: *Jesus took with him Peter, James and John the brother of James, and led them up a high mountain by themselves. There he was transfigured before them. His face shone like the sun, and his clothes became as white as the light. Just then there appeared before them Moses and Elijah, talking with Jesus. Peter said to Jesus, "Lord, it is good for us to be here. If you wish, I will put up three shelters—one for you, one for Moses and one for Elijah." While he was still speaking, a bright cloud enveloped them, and a voice from the cloud said, "This is my Son, whom I love; with him I am well pleased. Listen to him!" When the disciples heard this they fell facedown to the ground, terrified. But Jesus came and touched them. "Get up," he said. "Don't be afraid." When they looked up they saw no one except Jesus. As they were coming down the mountain, Jesus instructed them, "Don't tell anyone what you have seen, until the Son of Man has been raised from the dead."*

Next is the account from John 20:10-18: *Then the disciples went back to their homes, but Mary stood outside the tomb crying. As she wept, she bent over to look into the tomb and saw two angels in white, seated where Jesus' body had been, one at the head and the other at the foot. They asked her, "Woman, why are you crying?" "They have taken my Lord away," she said, "and I don't know where they have put him." At this, she turned around and saw Jesus standing there, but she did not realize that it was Jesus. "Woman," he said, "why are you crying? Who is it you are looking for?" Thinking he was the gardener, she said, "Sir, if you have carried him away, tell me where you have put him, and I will get him." Jesus said to her, "Mary." She turned toward him and cried out in Aramaic, "Rabboni!" (which means Teacher). Jesus said, "Do not hold on to me, for I have not yet returned to the Father. Go instead to my brothers and tell them, 'I am returning to my Father and your Father, to my God and your God.'" Mary Magdalene went to the disciples with the news: "I have seen the Lord!" And she told them that he had said these things to her.*

I urge people to look at these accounts and others with an open mind. Many passages of the Bible are up for various interpretations, and a fundamental Christian approach is not the only way of looking at things.

If the Man from Galilee taught his disciples meditation and astral projection, it would have been fun to eavesdrop on the very first session. His bewildered students might have acted like first graders. I have been lucky enough to apprehend a written report of that very first class. It was already translated into English when I got it, which is a very good thing because I don't know any Aramaic. Let's peek in just after Josh had provided instruction in a meditation trance, and his disciples were practicing his technique.

JOSHUA TEACHES ASTRAL PROJECTION

Pete squinted, pretending to continue his practice session, and he noticed Matt was peering around. He blurted out, "No fair, Matt! Hey everybody, Matt has had his eyes open. You know what Joshua told us. The technique needs a lot of concentration with shutting down visual stimuli."

Matt countered, "How did you know Pete? You had to be looking too. Aren't you being quick to judge? It takes one to know one."

John interrupted, "Guys, stop it. How are the rest of us going to get anything done with all this childish behavior?"

Tom snored.

Then John turned to Joshua, "Master, why are we learning this technique? Could you enlighten us again? I think it would motivate us further if we could understand the whole purpose behind this."

Josh said, "Okay. Brothers and sisters, your attention please. Meditation allows a clearer perception of any given situation. It slows down and clears the mind, relaxes the body and invigorates the spirit. You can see your own faults better and recognize ways to change yourself. It is harder to condemn others when you see the same faults in yourself. How can you see the light if the darkness confuses and overwhelms you? Meditation will help you to be truly compassionate to your friends, your acquaintances and your enemies. This is how Father's kingdom truly is achieved.

"Further, when I have died and gone to Father, my comforting spirit will be ever present to guide you. With a clear mind and a pure, compassionate heart, you will recognize me in the time to come, for I will be with you forever."

Pete jumped to his feet and interrupted, "Master, how can you talk like this? This shall never happen to you. I will make sure of it. I will protect you."

Joshua turned and said, "Pete, it's clear you have not read the end of the book. This is exactly the reason you need to practice this meditation technique. How will you grow spiritually without developing a compassion that knows no bounds. When you behave this way you are a stumbling block to me, and you will not understand me until later. So until then you will deny me. Then after that you will understand. Please understand. My mission is hard enough as it is."

Joshua answered many more questions and finally felt satisfied that his friends had a better grasp of what he wanted them to accomplish.

68. JOSH DESCENDS INTO HELL

DK and I worked together on a piece entitled, "Josh Descends into Hell." I showed it to Agnos.

"Nobody knows what hell is all about," said Agnos, "unless you include hell on earth; then there are plenty of people who know about it. That's something to think about, but if you're talking about hell in the afterlife, it's anybody's guess."

In the Apostle's Creed, Christians profess to believe that Jesus descended into hell, but there really isn't much at all about this in the canonical Gospels which more or less just say that on the third day Jesus arose from death. However, in the Gnostic text, *Dialog of the Savior,* Judas talks to Matthew about how difficult it would be to climb down to the bottom of the abyss, *for there is a tremendous fire there, and something very fearful!* Yadda yadda yadda, and then the Son of Man told them that somebody powerful was *deficient*, yadda yadda, and went down to the *abyss of the earth.* Then God *sent the Word to it,* and the Word *brought it up into his presence,* so that it *might not fail.* And because of this the disciples *concluded that it is useless to regard wickedness.* I think that means God won't let wickedness and hell keep the wicked. He rescues the wicked. Purchase the book if you want to read this passage without all the yaddas.

JOSH DESCENDS INTO HELL

The pain of the torture and the cross was now subsiding. The ache persisted in his wrists and feet, but the severe, stabbing jolts no longer tormented him. His headache had dulled. Meditation helped.

It was the emotional anguish which refused to diminish. He felt pity for the mocking crowd and the Roman soldiers who did not understand even their own motives. It is so easy for one person to assail another when the deep thorn of self-hatred isn't recognized.

Where was his brother? During recent months, the more Josh had been convinced about the coming of the Kingdom, the less he felt any emotional connection with Lucifer. Now he cried out, "My brother, my brother, you also have forsaken me." Those around him were puzzled and wondered, what did he say?

Lucifer watched from a distance, distraught, hardly able to think. He felt sorry for Josh, but he could not make himself move to rescue him. His whole body felt paralyzed, and he was ashamed. Was this the selfishness of love he felt? There was nowhere to turn. He had alienated his family, and it seemed Josh had given up all hope in him. He asked himself, is this my end as well as Joshua's? My influence on these humans has come to this, and by destroying Josh have they destroyed me as well? I must escape to where no one will find me, to the very depths of hell.

Josh knew he would join his family soon. The ties to his body were loosening, and his time on earth was slipping away. The Kingdom would come as he had pledged, and the Son of Man soon would arrive with power and glory. Certainly this generation would not pass away before it happened, and justice soon would prevail for the poor, the mourning, the meek, the hungry and thirsty, the persecuted. All would be comforted, filled and rewarded. His mission was finished, and he felt himself drifting from his body toward the light.

He awoke! This was not heaven. The landscape was bleak, and in the distance a few, lonely and dejected souls meandered without direction. There in the distance also was Lucifer.

Josh's mind began to clear. *Why am I here? What has Lu to do with this?* He moved toward his brother, but it was not the instant think-and-arrive travel he remembered of heaven. This was agonizingly slow. He began to wonder if he might never arrive.

Lu called out to him, "They need the Kingdom, Josh. The poor, the sick, the hopeless; they need the Kingdom, but this is not how the universe works. Free will, such a wonderful gift, but is the will free when they cannot comprehend the consequences of the choices they make? No wonder the Kingdom has not come, nor will it come soon, Josh."

Josh thought of his disciples who would be awaiting his soon return in glory, but here he was passing through the loneliness of hell. *Yea though I walk through the valley of the shadow of death, I will fear no evil, for thou art with me.* He tried to move faster but could not. Each step was effortful.

Then he recalled his own words. *If thy whole body therefore be full of light, having no part dark, the whole shall be full of light, as when the bright shining of a candle doth give thee light.* Then so filled was he with light that it shone from him, and the path before him was clear.

Lucifer said, "Go away. I have not earned the right of your presence. I don't deserve you. Please leave."

Josh replied, "Lu, why would you say that? I love you and will do what it takes to bring you home. Look at me."

Lucifer lifted up his head, and Josh saw that the face was nearly unrecognizable. Lu's eyes had grown blank, without emotion, and his brother did not look at him. This was not the Lucifer who had been passionate in his job as Father's chief prosecutor. This was not the arrogant Lucifer who had appeared to him in the wilderness with schemes of temptation. Lucifer said, "For what I've done to our family, to Father's creation, the anguish I've caused; I deserve to die. But, as you know, I'm an eternal being and cannot die. So then I deserve this hell forever."

A brilliant light appeared, brighter than a thousand suns, and both Josh and Lu knew that Father was with them, had himself descended into the depth of hell. Father spoke. "Lucifer, my son, it is only through forgiveness that we may be reconciled. Do you forgive me?"

Lu was amazed by this. The Creator of the universe was asking him for forgiveness. "I don't understand," he mumbled.

"It is only through forgiveness that we may be reconciled. Do you forgive me?"

"Do you forgive me?" Lucifer returned.

"You have been forgiven from the start."

"But you cast me out of heaven."

"Even as I cast you out of heaven, I forgave you. Even as I cast humans out of Eden, I forgave them."

Lucifer's heart thawed then, like the first spring day after a severe winter. "I forgive you." The words felt strange. "I am so very sorry. I love you so much. Yes, take me home with you."

They embraced and the light was made mellow, still bright and still beautiful.

The three of them ascended out of hell, together, Father in the middle with Josh and Lu on either side. "Dad's two boys!" exclaimed Father.

And the foundation of hell itself collapsed, for the foundation was loneliness. God in this moment destroyed the separation of one soul from another. We were bound together by forgiveness given from one to another.

Josh found himself alive in his body again, for where there is eternity there is no limitation by time, no separation of past from present or future. There was a multitude of people before him, and he said to them, "You are so blessed, beyond anything you can imagine. Blessed among you are all those who are poor of spirit, persecuted by their self-accusations, mourning for so long. Please join us in our banquet. Please eat, drink and be merry. We love you all."

And Josh saw that each person in heaven and in earth and those who were brought up from hell, were different than they had been before. They had within them the Holy Spirit. He saw both himself and Lucifer in each and every one, and he marveled at the magnificence of Father's solution.

Instantly there were tables and an abundance of food for all, and this no longer was earth. Everyone was with him in heaven, and they all ate until they were satisfied and more. "Come stay with us," Josh told the crowd. "We want you with us. Each and every one of you makes our lives meaningful."

The barrier between heaven and earth was broken. The barrier between hell and heaven was broken. The barrier between Father and Son was broken. The barrier between God and human was broken.

"Ah," said Father, "At long last this creation makes me happy."

69. GOD'S MEETING

A few people might have noticed the grizzly old gentleman sitting alone at a table in the back room of Sal's Deli in Burien, Washington. His clothes were only mildly soiled, and a small amount of cologne masked the otherwise faint smell of urine. His eyes smiled as he patiently savored his sandwich and cup of coffee. A few people might have noticed, but they had no idea of what was happening within him.

Lucifer and Joshua watched Father devour his Sicilian sandwich. "This is not to be believed," Father raved. "Simply out of this world. It's the marinated onions; they're heavenly."

"Thank you," said Josh.

"Oh, you're such a glory hog," chided Lu.

"Am not."

"Are too."

"Boys!" Father interrupted. "This is not something to get testy about." He took another bite of his sandwich. "Mmmmmmmm, this is to die for."

"As a matter of fact, I did." Josh smiled.

"Would you knock it off!" Lu shouted. "Sometimes you're insufferable. You just lord it over us all the time."

"I forgive you." Josh laughed.

"Boys! Can't a guy once in awhile just eat a meal in peace?"

"Do you mean the peace that passes all understanding?" Josh smirked.

Lu silently glared at his brother.

Father said, "I'd like you to meet one of my operatives. Come over here son." A hovering spirit approached, and Father introduced him. "Boys, meet your brother Agnos. He's been doing a little extra duty for me. Hi Agnos. How are things?"

"Oh, I don't know."

Father broke out laughing. "I just love that about you, Agnos. Some times you slay me. How is that book coming along that I commissioned to be written?"

"Again I must say, and please take me seriously, I really don't know about this book. These guys, T the splogger and his friends, they're pretty imaginative."

"Chips off the old block," Father countered.

"Yes, I guess you can say that. Well, I can't tell whether these guys know what they're talking about or not. I just don't know."

"Does it matter, Agnos?"

"Beats me."

"I can help you with that." Lu chuckled while the other three turned and looked at him in somewhat concerned bewilderment. Lu argued, "Look, it's not easy always being the black sheep of the family. You ought to appreciate that I do some things for you in this world that your dainty little hands won't do. You know, like the times I tamper with evidence so criminals won't get away. I'm very useful from time to time."

"Sometimes you really puzzle me," said Father.

"Yeah well, you made me this way so the truth is you puzzle me too. I wouldn't be so surprising to you if you'd take a good hard look at yourself."

Josh closed his eyes and gently shook his head. "How do we ever get anything done around here? All we ever do is bicker."

Agnos piped in. "You know you were very successful at accomplishing that, making humans in your image. They're always bickering too."

"Yes," said Father, "and it's quite entertaining. Agnos, I agree with you. That part of creation pleases me. I enjoy the bickering, the give and take of ideas, even the seemingly meaningless ones. It's like reality television only it's real. Humans like it too. They're like me." He sat back in his chair looking pleased with himself.

"So that's that?" Lu asked, "You're satisfied with the world the way it is? It's enough for you that it's ... entertaining?"

"Oh, I'll admit it's a little rough around the edges, but you know, it's not bad."

"It sure as hell is!" Lu objected.

"For once I have to agree with him," said Josh.

"What do you think, Agnos?"

"Oh well ... um, I don't know. I guess it depends on what you're looking for, what you want to get out of all this ... at the end I mean."

Father considered the bit that was left of his Sicilian sandwich. "Damned good sandwich, that one. Next time I'll have it with a beer. I'll let you in on a little something that is so simple it's almost embarrassing. In the beginning of all this, all I wanted was to taste a sandwich like this one. I wanted to cuddle a baby, and I wanted to feel wind on my face. I wanted to be two people making love to one another. I wanted to be two people in discourse trying to figure out the meaning of all this. That's all I wanted. It became so much more than that."

"As well it should have."

"Lucifer my son, you are right. We have become so much more than we were. We are a complex lot. You may talk about truthfulness and deceit. You may argue about whether, in any given situation, it is gentleness or forcefulness that is the most effective means of behaving. You may be horrified at many of the things that have happened in this world, and of course I am as horrified as any. Hopefully we are learning from all of this."

"Is it possible that the world can become pleasant?" Agnos asked. "I mean can it happen that some day there will be no sorrow and no fear?"

Josh said, "That is part of the wonderfulness of this creation. Yes. Even though there always will be heaven and a bit of hell in each of us, we are able to live in whichever of them we desire. We need only to go there. John Milton said it well. *A mind not to be changed by place or time. The mind is its own place, and in itself can make a heav'n of hell, a hell of heav'n.* As for your life to come? That choice is made for you with the greatest of Father's love. Agnos, if you believe this I will grow inside you like a meadow of wild flowers."

"He means weeds," needled Lu. "He prefers mustard plants, but really any hardy weed will do."

"This is difficult for me even to understand, much less to believe," said Agnos.

Father put a tiny dot of mustard on the last bite of his sandwich and put it into his mouth. "Here," he said. "Take this back to the people you know, and see if it makes them cheerful."

After the grizzly old gentleman had stood up from his chair and shuffled out of the deli, the waitress clearing the table noticed he had written a message on his napkin. *This is to be sung to the tune of "For He's a Jolly Good Fellow." There's a hole in the fence at the nut house, a hole in the fence at the nut house, a hole in the fence at the nut house; and that's why we're all here. Please turn over the napkin.*

The waitress turned the napkin over and there was another message, a poem.

What is God?
God is Love.
Love who?
Love God.
Who is God?
God is Love.
Love who?
Love you.

70. LITTLE VINCENT

This is a song, and maybe some day I'll be able to sing it for you.

Can you imagine yourself with wings, little Vincent?
Imagine yourself with wings.
For God and his glory you'll fly in the winds
with a harp and a halo,
where everyone sings for God and his glory,
you'll fly in the winds, little Vincent.

Why did you want to go home, little Vincent?
Why did you want to go home?
Your brothers and sisters you left all alone
with a tear and a smile,
and everyone prayed for the brothers and sisters
you left all alone, little Vincent.

Straight way to the chapel did your mother run.
Straight way to the chapel she ran.
A candle for Vincent, a candle for prayer,
with a flame ever burning,
and everyone prayed with the candle for Vincent,
a candle for prayer, little Vincent.

Why did the candle go out, little Vincent?
Why did the candle go out?
Relighted, it darkened. Relighted again.
With a flame ever ending?
And everyone wondered, a flame never burning?
Relight it again.

Were you on the altar with tricks, little Vincent?
Were you on the altar with tricks?
The candle went out, and your vision appeared
with flashing eyes and a smile.
Sat Vincent on the altar, snuffing it out.
Sat Vincent, snuffing it out.

Can you imagine yourself with wings, little Vincent?
Imagine yourself with wings.
For God and his glory you'll fly in the winds
with a harp and a halo,
where everyone sings for God and his glory,
you'll fly in the winds, little Vincent.

ELEVEN

Demons

71. SVEN'S LETTER

Sometimes I receive letters that are so extraordinary I want to share them. Sven Conradi is one of my pals in Norway, a physician, rehabilitation specialist at Norway's National Rehabilitation Hospital, Sunnaas. This is the hospital where I worked for one year, 1990/91, and where I met this charming, inquisitive and incisive man. In this letter you will see language that gives Sven away as a Buddhist. Isn't it fun to see from another's perspective!

Hi Tom,

I've just arrived home after two weeks in Jordan. The first seven days were spent in a seminar, Sunnaas Hospital's continuing cooperation with Palestinian health authorities, meeting with health workers from Jerusalem, Bethlehem and Ramalla. Our Gaza friends were not given permission to pass-through. They all are in a permanent, 1.4 million population sized jail, not allowed to move from their 40 x 15 kilometer strip.

The seminar was on brain injury and rehabilitation, probably useful to them as they have many of this group. Many of the Palestinians were depressed though, and several suffered from PTSD (post-traumatic stress disorder) and had problems with concentration. All have histories to tell of personal tragedies.

The second week I spent as a holiday round about Jordan. I visited Petra and the old Roman town, Jerash, close to the Syrian border. I spent two days in the desert, sleeping out in the open under the stars with the Bedouins. I rode a camel on the sand.

In the north of the country I was close to the village where the story goes that Jesus cast demons out of two men. Often I have wondered about this story. According to the script, Jesus went about it carelessly enough that the demons immediately went into a herd of pigs that rushed over the edge and into the Tiberias Sea where they all drowned. This can make one believe that Jesus didn't like pigs. That is not strange since he was a Jew, but since he is at the same time supposed to be God, this places God in a rather awkward light. Does God dislike pigs? So much that he wants to harm or punish innocent ones? Are pigs inherently sinful so that they deserve to be haunted by demons and brought to a violent death?

Another thing that puzzles me about this story is Jesus' acceptance of and belief in the existence of demons. Most present time people I know don't believe in demons (or trolls or gorgons or elves) any more. They think such beliefs belong to old societies with other more primitive conceptions of the world.

How is it that Jesus, who presumably had an eternal and all-encompassing knowledge of the cosmic connections, went around harboring a primitive world view? There are of course several possibilities.

1. Demons really existed in those old days. If so, his belief in them was of course adequate, and it must be considered highly beneficial that he drowned the last pair of them, together with the pigs.

2. Demons still exist. Maybe they survived the near-drowning and still ramble around doing mischief. Now maybe they are demons with anoxic, demonic brain injury.

3. Demons never existed, even in year 30 CE, but Jesus met two men with anoxic brain injury, maybe from near-drowning in the Tiberian Sea. In that case Jesus' belief in demons reflects the human temporal part of his dual human-divine nature, and tells us that the human part of him, at least on that day, had a holiday away from its usual symbiosis with the divinely illuminated part.

4. Maybe Jesus was only a Jewish man from Galilee who believed both in demons and possession by them as an explanation for anoxic brain injury behavior and the impurity of pigs.

Sven

Hi Sven,

At the time this story took place, people thought pigs were unclean and therefore expendable. Jesus gave us permission to eat pigs, and we've liked them ever since.

t

72. PSYCHOLOGICAL DEMONS

DK so very much enjoyed Sven's letter about the pigs and demons that he wrote and sent to me five different manuscripts, four of them serious and one of them silly. He went hog wild. I liked the silly one most, and I'll press him to give me permission to share it. This following piece is academic. We see what we see because of where we stand. One of Dan's professions is psychiatry.

Hi Tom,

Having wondered about the pigs as well, I'm glad Sven emailed his concern. Healing of the possessed man always has haunted me as it seems to shine a bad light on Jesus, at least in the minds of modern humans of the animal rights persuasion. Can you imagine the protests against a modern healer doing a similar act?

Biblical stories are complex. Many scholars would tell us that there are many different levels of understanding one story. One way to look at a specific story is to see each element as a symbol, similar to dream analysis, in which every element of the dream has personal meaning for the dreamer. The dream then would be analyzed with each symbol representing an aspect of the dreamer's personality. For instance if someone dreams about a dilapidated house it may mean the dreamer feels that way about himself.

Mark 5:1-20, New International Version: *They went across the lake to the region of the Gerasenes. When Jesus got out of the boat a man with an evil spirit came from the tombs to meet him. This man lived in the tombs, and no one could bind him any more, not even with a chain. For he had often been chained hand and foot, but he tore the chains apart and broke the irons on his feet. No one was strong enough to subdue him. Night and day among the tombs and in the hills he would cry out and cut himself with stones.*

When he saw Jesus from a distance he ran and fell on his knees in front of him. He shouted at the top of his voice, "What do you want with me, Jesus, Son of the Most High God? Swear to God that you won't torture me!" For Jesus had said to him, "Come out of this man, you evil spirit!"

Then Jesus asked him, "What is your name?"

"My name is Legion," he replied, "for we are many." And he begged Jesus again and again not to send them out of the area.

A large herd of pigs was feeding on the nearby hillside. The demons begged Jesus, "Send us among the pigs; allow us to go into them." He gave them permission, and the evil spirits came out and went into the pigs. The herd, about two thousand in number, rushed down the steep bank into the lake and was drowned.

*Those tending the pigs ran off and reported this in the town and coun-
tryside, and the people went out to see what had happened. When they came
to Jesus they saw the man who had been possessed by the legion of demons,
sitting there, dressed and in his right mind; and they were afraid. Those who
had seen it told the people what had happened to the demon-possessed man—
and told about the pigs as well. Then the people began to plead with Jesus to
leave their region.*

*As Jesus was getting into the boat, the man who had been demon-pos-
sessed begged to go with him. Jesus did not let him but said, "Go home to your
family and tell them how much the Lord has done for you, and how he has
had mercy on you." So the man went away and began to tell in the Decapolis
how much Jesus had done for him. And all the people were amazed.*

What might be the symbols?

Pigs = innocence (inspired by Sven's comment)
Demons = wild, uncontrollable, unacceptable thoughts
    plaguing someone
Lake = the unconscious (from psychoanalytic theory/symbols)
Jesus = plea for help/salvation (Yeshua/Joshua means "God is
    our salvation")
Pigs drowning = loss of innocence/wild, unacceptable
    thoughts driven from the conscious mind.

Without going through all the steps in the process, the story can
be interpreted as ridding one's self of wild, uncontrollable, unacceptable thoughts through a plea to God, reducing the pervasiveness of
thoughts emerging into conscious awareness, allowing one to regain
psychological equilibrium and function in society. The unacceptable
thoughts might be incongruent with the image one has of one's self
and how one wants to portray one's self.

Why do I say there is a loss of innocence? As the mind accepts these
unacceptable thoughts, there is a change in self image. The individual
no longer sees himself as innocent, as someone incapable of thinking
such violent or perverse thoughts, but has gained significantly in being
able to manage them, as these thoughts now are known by him to be a
part of his mind. This is a great advantage, as no longer would there be
a tendency to use the primitive mechanism of projection, making someone else the villain who harbors such bad thoughts. It would allow this
person to have more harmonious relations with those around him. Others
would not have to be seen as evil and therefore needing to be converted
or destroyed. Just think, the world would be a much more harmonious
place as more and more peaceful, mature individuals inhabit it.

It certainly may be argued that this is not how Mark perceived this. This is not how people of his society 2000 years ago would think. In a society of angels, demons and evil spirits possessing an individual causing illness and dysfunction, the story would be explained in those terms. They would not explain these events in terms of the unconscious, psychological equilibrium, function in society, psychosis or interactions in the mind. But I suggest that it doesn't prevent us from seeing this story in the light of modern explanations of how the mind operates. The story thereby can relate to us here and now.

Another way to view this story is in a less abstract way, as Jesus healing another human. Then it would be fair to say that Jesus was thought to be a healer of souls. He could be considered, among other roles, a psychiatrist. The roots of the word psychiatrist are *psyche*-(etymology: Greek, from breath, principle of life, life; soul) and *iatry*-(etymology: Greek -iatreia, art of healing). So psychiatrist means breath-healer or soul-healer. Isn't that what many would consider Jesus, a healer of souls?

Isn't it interesting that psyche, soul, breath and life all mean about the same? It may be fun to go to a psychiatrist and say, "Please heal my soul."

In ancient times the man in this story would have been described as demon-possessed. Today his behavior would be described as some sort of psychosis, functional or organic. Since he responded well to intervention, probably it was a functional psychosis (i.e. psychological rather than brain injury). Of course the dividing line between these two classifications is not so simple as we used to think it was.

After having been healed, the wild man no longer displayed psychotic behavior, no longer experienced his wild, uncontrollable thoughts. What happened to these thoughts? From a psychoanalytic perspective it appears that they were driven deeply into the unconscious of the disturbed man. No longer consciously experienced, at least in an uncontrollable manner, the thoughts no longer haunted him. In symbolic terms the unconscious mind was likened to a sea. So Jesus, through suggestive psychotherapy, effected a cure or at least a remission in that man's psychosis, allowing the demons to be driven into the lake. The previously conscious, wild thoughts now were deep inside, less likely to be experienced consciously, now controllable, and the man could function again.

A generation or two ago psychoanalytic psychotherapy was one of the mainstays of psychotherapeutic techniques. In psychoanalytic approach the goal is to uncover, rather than cover, the disturbing thoughts. Once uncovered the disturbing thoughts can be worked through and resolved. Several problems occur, however. It is quite time consuming, expensive, and it doesn't work well on more disturbed patients. While psychoanalytic therapy still is available, many psychiatrists focus on drugs and supportive psychotherapy. The goal is not to gain the patient's complete understanding of the mechanism of his problem but rather, simply, to do whatever is needed to restore function in society and hopefully to recapture happiness.

Jesus accomplished this in one session! A modern psychiatrist would be elated if such a disturbed patient became sane and functional with just one session. And Jesus did it without drugs! At least none were mentioned in the story.

DK

73. RYAN'S LETTER

Ryan is my nephew, son of Stan the Rev.

Uncle Tom,

I have to wonder if this story actually is supposed to be literally true or if it is, in fact, meant to be allegory to teach the listener/reader a specific point. Clearly you (DK) have broken it down in an allegorical fashion, but you state that Mark probably didn't perceive it as such. I suspect he might have. Otherwise I worry that it's too coincidental that a true, real life story could be so perfectly broken down into symbolism. At the least it is likely that parts of it are not exactly as they are told now.

I'm inclined to draw a parallel between this story, or even biblical stories in general, and the oral tradition of Africa, mostly because I took an African storyteller class recently. In Africa there is a cultural phenomenon of traveling storytellers. They pass their lives in this way because they are so adept at the art. When they tell stories and change them, embellish them, they are doing so with the intention of making a specific point. Often that point is buried deeply such that the listener understands it on different levels over the course of their own life, as they hear it many times over, perhaps from different storytellers and with different details.

Mark, in writing his book down in the Bible, is fulfilling the role of storyteller and quite likely had the intention of providing one or several moral lessons to his readers, and in so doing likely did not stick exactly to the facts as they happened.

All that having been said, I want to comment further on how you (DK) broke down the story. I suspect strongly that the pigs do not initially represent innocence. My feeling on this is actually influenced by one of your previous splogs, when you noted that the people at the time viewed pigs as unclean. Mark would have had this perception of pigs and therefore would not have used them to represent innocence, and the killing of them the loss of innocence. If that had been his goal, perhaps he would have used a lamb, which can be seen as innocent and then would have represented Christ symbolically, and their death would have echoed Christ's death to carry away our sins.

But this story isn't really about Jesus. It's about the man and his path to God, or perhaps it's about the townspeople. African stories often portray the family society of the main character as being corrupt or out of balance in some fashion. Then the story is about how the main character grows and eventually either leaves this society or redeems it by taking it over, or by destroying and rebuilding it.

As such we could draw a parallel between the pigs and the society. Pigs were unclean. The fact that this society raised them and presumably ate them portrayed that the society was out of touch with God. The townspeople were more comfortable with the man when he had his demons, and again this showed that they were out of tune with God. When Jesus cleansed the man and cast his demons into the pigs, and when the pigs ran into the lake and died, we could see this as the society taking a step toward God. The man himself moved completely into the faith, and in the non-existent part two of the story maybe we would see the man lead the society more fully onto the path of the righteous.

It seems clear to me that this is what Jesus intended. In any case, these are just my thoughts.

Ryan

74. REV'S RESPONSE

Stan the Rev wrote: Well, isn't this nice.

Ryan, have you taken any classes in exegetical analysis of scriptures? What you say in your reply is first class exegetical analysis.

Too many Christians today interpret scripture from the mindset of today rather than from the mindsets of both those who wrote scripture and those to whom they were written. The opposite of exegetical is isogetical analysis, putting a spin on the scriptures from our modern day perspective and coming up with conclusions that would be off the mark for, in this case, first-century Christians. That's why isogetical work is frowned upon by any serious theologian. It is the same as taking scriptures out of their original context and putting a false twist on it; in other words doing the same thing that political spin-doctoring is done today by politicians.

Pigs were considered by Jews to be totally unclean and offensive creatures. Their religious laws prevented them to even come near pigs. Jesus and his disciples coming as close as they did to them possibly would have broken a religious law. Also the ancients believed that the seat of the soul was in the heart which also ruled the emotions.

The Jews also were frightened of large bodies of water, believing that they were the abode of demons. So when Mark is sharing and possibly embellishing on the story of the healing of the demoniac, he is making a point to his contemporary readers that with Jesus casting the demons out of the heart of the man and into the hearts of the pigs, and sending them back to where they belong, that they must remain true to the ways of God. In the mind of Jews, including Mark, pigs were of kindred spirit to the demons.

This means that Mark was telling his readers not to do the same things as the gentiles who were involved in the evil ways of the world but rather stay true to Jesus and his teachings because Jesus has the power to overcome the world and heal those who are repentant and wish to return to the ways of God.

Ryan, I enjoyed your analysis.

S. (Dad)

75. A LEGION OF DEMON PIGS

Clearly there are many takes on the story of Jesus removing a legion of demons from a demoniac and allowing them to take refuge in pigs which then couldn't handle the craziness and ran into the sea and drowned.

The subsequent fearfulness of the local people, and their having asked Jesus to leave the area, gives the story an air of credibility. Something likely happened as a seed to this story, but my belief is that it was then embellished. The embellished story took its current form some time before Jesus' death, even though it remained in the oral tradition for decades until it finally was written in the gospels.

Remember the time. The main focus of the Jews was to throw off the yoke of Roman occupation. To capture a little bit of the feeling of it, imagine the American occupation of Iraq right now.

The Jews believed in and yearned after a messiah who would free their homeland and reestablish a kingdom of God-like justice, resembling their memory of the reign of King David. This was their hope with every messiah-wannabe who came along, and it is what they wanted from Jesus.

In this story, the demoniac man is a symbol for Israel possessed by Romans (demons). Jesus drives them out of the man (Israel) and allows them to show themselves for what they really are, pigs. Then with Jesus' blessing the Demon Roman Pigs did exactly what they should do. They threw themselves into the sea and drowned.

Couched in these symbols, people could call the Romans pigs without risking themselves being slaughtered for the insolence. And it was a way also to spread word that here they had the messiah for whom they had been waiting.

The people of the town, fearing a Roman backlash, of course wanted Jesus to get away from them.

"Who started this damnable, terrorist story."

"Well now, I couldn't really tell you. That healer fellow, the one who started this mess, he's long gone now. Don't rightly know where he went."

76. WRIGHT COUNTY GAZETTE September 30, 2006

TRAVELING MINISTER DROWNS PIGS, FARMERS RIOT

Yesterday brought a high level of excitement for the residents and surrounding farmers of Maple Lake. A traveling preacher, Josh Anderson, was preaching next to the cemetery near the beach. As he was putting on a show for the crowd, he edged closer and closer to the graveyard. He caught the attention of local wild man, Jimmy Olsen, who was just discharged from the Anoka County Mental Hospital three weeks ago. Olsen reportedly stopped the medicine prescribed by his psychiatrist last week, according to trusted sources. A heated exchange of words occurred between Anderson and Olsen. Eyewitness Harvey Johansson told this reporter that the next thing he saw was the herd of pigs in the nearby field getting very excited, and then they rushed into the lake.

Traveling minister continues: A7

LOCAL PSYCHIC WARNING

A local psychic warned the residents not to swim at the local beach at Maple Lake. Mary Swanson felt bad vibrations this morning by the beach after the incident when the traveling minister drove evil spirits into the pigs yesterday. The pigs rushed into Maple Lake and drowned. Swanson now feels the lake is haunted and needs to be exorcised. She said when interviewed this morning that it will take a lot of work and many days to drive the evil spirits away. She is buying some additional crystals to help with the healing work. She told this reporter that if swimmers disregard the sign and swim anyway, they are doing it at their own risk.

"I don't want to have to exorcise those spirits from half the kids in town," said our local spiritualist. "Please don't make a bad situation worse." Swanson will need to close her new age shop temporarily while she is healing the lake, and is requesting compensation from the local government.

Psychic continues: A5

LUTHERAN MINISTER UPSET ABOUT PREACHER'S SHOW

"Hogwash," is the way our local minister, Matt Jorgenson, described the show put on by Josh Anderson yesterday. Jorgenson went on to say ...

Minister continues: A8

SHERIFF'S OFFICE BARRAGED BY TELEPHONE CALLS

The deputy sheriff told this reporter that the telephone was ringing off the hook yesterday afternoon. As soon as he finished with one call, the phone rang again. The pig farmers in particular were more than just a little upset ... Deputy continues: A3

77. BED DEMONS AND ANTISTUFF

During my writing hiatus in the summer of 2006, my mind wasn't dormant but continued searching for outrageous truths.

My family spent some time along the Oregon coast. My youngest two children had traveled little as yet, so I wanted to make this vacation special, as though we were on an adventure to an exotic land. Just before we crossed over the Columbia River I told them, "You may notice that people in Oregon speak a little differently from us in Washington. They're farther south, so they may say things like, 'Hi y'all. Y'all are from Washington aren't you? Have s'more grits.'"

We rented a suite in Seaside and separated ourselves into a girl's room and a boy's room, so of course there was time for boy humor in the dark just before we fell asleep. We were saying our goodnights, and the old saying about bed bugs came to mind, but this was an unfamiliar hotel, and I didn't want my sons to think there may actually be bed bugs, yikes! I told them, "Don't let the bed demons kick you in the nuts."

I continued, "You laugh because you don't believe in bed demons. You've never seen one; you've never even heard of them before. We don't have them in Washington, but Oregon is a different place. So put your hands down over your privates. This is the way you have to sleep in Oregon.

Later my eldest, Christoffer, suggested I should write a book about bed demons. That's a good idea. I can write it from a bed demon's perspective, like Anne Rice's *Interview with a Vampire*. I can explore the whole history of bed demons, how they came to be and why they are the way they are.

Once I had a scary, realistic dream about a demon I taunted out of a possessed patient of mine. The demon assaulted me, and I awoke with my heart pounding. Even while awake I felt the demon's presence, and I told it that it had no power over me as I was protected by Christ. The demon became quieter but did not leave until finally I came to a realization that evil has no business in God's kingdom. I said to it, "You don't even exist in my world," and it disappeared. My nuts were spared.

Both my friend Dan Kurtti and my brother Stan suggested that instead of taunting the demon I could have had a better experience by inviting it into conversation, much the way Jesus would talk to demons. That sounded good; maybe next time. I'll wear a cup.

One night in late July I was awakened by fireworks exploding somewhere in the neighborhood. I looked at the clock and there it was, 3:16. This is remarkable because there was a time when I would awaken once or twice a week, look at the clock, and it was 3:16. So this was one more time. I took this to mean John 3:16, and there was something I was supposed to learn about this verse.

Then during the first week of August, my son Joshua attended basketball camp and collected a lot of great autographs on his t-shirt. Next to coach Lorenzo Romar's signature was written, *John 3:16*.

John 3:16 is all over the place. *For God so loved the world that he gave his only son to die for us, that whoever believes in him will not perish but have everlasting life.*

Again I nestled into my cozy conversation with God, and this time he told me something different.

I said, "Please God, don't make me say that."

He answered, "Now that you know, I would think you'd want to share it with others."

That's when I called God a turd, and you may think I was being blasphemous, but God laughed, acknowledging the uncomfortable predicament into which he had put me. He also knew my true disposition. *The searcher of hearts ever knoweth the mind dwelling in the spirit.*

Just as one easily can find both Christ and antichrist in the Christian Church, so can one find both Lincoln and antilincoln in the Republican Party. Also, just as both Christ and antichrist use the Bible to promote agenda, so may both Lincoln and antilincoln.

On June 16, 1858, in Springfield, Illinois, the Republican State Convention selected Abraham Lincoln as their candidate for the U.S. Senate, running against Democrat Stephen A. Douglas. That evening in his address to Republican colleagues, Lincoln said, "A house divided against itself cannot stand ... I believe this government cannot endure, permanently half slave and half free. I do not expect the Union to be dissolved; I do not expect the house to fall; but I do expect it will cease to be divided. It will become all one thing or all the other."

Many of his colleagues thought the comment was premature and too strongly stated. It did not instigate, nor promote, but it did predict war. It was widely understood that the enduring stand-off between the North and the South would not be resolved peacefully. It would be resolved by dissolution of the United States or war between the factions. So this was a bold statement by Lincoln. Still, it did not advocate war.

Historians point out that Lincoln's election to the presidency, known as he was to be sympathetic toward the abolitionist cause, drove slave states beyond their tolerance and made inevitable the progression toward war. But it was not Lincoln who struck the first blow. He carefully made it necessary for the Confederacy to make that historic transgression into hell.

"A house divided against itself cannot stand."

Compare this to Matthew 12:25, in which Jesus said, *"Every kingdom divided against itself is laid waste, and no city or house divided against itself will stand."*

Or Jesus in Mark 3:24-25, *"If a kingdom is divided against itself, that kingdom cannot stand. And if a house is divided against itself, that house will not be able to stand."*

Or Jesus in Luke 11:17, *"Every kingdom divided against itself becomes a desert, and house falls on house."*

The antilincoln said, "Either you are with us or you are against us." Political analysts have described this as a technique called *the false choice*. After all, there can be a middle ground, neither for nor against, but the antilincoln refuses to acknowledge this. It is a statement that divides, misleads and provokes.

Compare this to Revelation 3:15-16 (there it is again, 3:16). *I know your works; you are neither cold nor hot. I wish that you were either cold or hot. So, because you are lukewarm, and neither cold nor hot, I am about to spit you out of my mouth.*

I'd like to say that Jesus isn't the one who said this, but then some-one would say, "Yes he did."

And I'd say, "No he didn't."

And then they'd say, "What about Matthew 12:30 and Luke 11:23."

And I'd have to say, "Says Matthew and Luke."

And they'd say "Are you saying Matthew and Luke made this up?"

And I'd say, "It's either that or Jesus was a novice at logic. Make your choice. Frankly I'm fine with either one."

By the way, Jesus was a Jew, so he liked to argue because that's what Jewish spiritual men do. No scripture is regarded holy unless it can be interpreted in at least three different ways. In this way Jews are more like Jesus than most Christians. Jews feel obligated to argue their spiri-tuality in a search for truth. Christians feel obligated to follow their master like sheep after their shepherd. That's just an observation.

Just as you can find Christ both inside and outside the Christian Church, you also can find Lincoln both within and without the Re-publican Party. Here is one example. In his fireside chat on Christmas Eve, 1943, Franklin D. Roosevelt said, "The doctrine that the strong shall dominate the weak is the doctrine of our enemies, and we reject it."

The antichrist is sneaky. Christians are fond of saying, "We are one in Christ." If by this they mean everybody in the world is one in Christ, even the nonbelievers, the atheists, the Jews and Muslims, Hindus and Buddhists and others; then this is a concept of unification consistent with what Jesus taught us.

On the other hand, if by saying, "One in Christ," Christians mean only believers, if they mean believers versus nonbelievers, us versus them; then this breaks apart Father's body, and it is antichrist. It is respon-sible for wars and hate crimes.

From the Gospel of Thomas, saying 72: *A person said to him, "Tell my brothers to divide my father's possessions with me." He said to the person, "Mister, who made me a divider?" He turned to his disciples and said to them, "I'm not a divider am I?"*

From the Gospel of John 17:22-23, Jesus prayed, *"The glory that you have given me I have given them, so that they may be one as we are one. I in them and you in me, that they may become completely one, so that the world may know that you have sent me and have loved them even as you have loved me."*

If Father created all of the universe and all of the beings in it, then any one of his creatures is as dear to him as any of the others.

Did the event of Jesus change the very fabric of this universe? Did it make us eternal beings? If so, then it was a change that was made not for just some, but for all of us. Many in the Christian Church diminish this. Citing John 3:16, they make salvation a psychological function of belief and acceptance. Instead of an act of God they make it an act of man, an act of man's psychology.

Scientific study has shown clearly that personality is determined by genetics and environment, and some people are simply unable to believe. This is the way God structured his creation. When believers separate themselves as being more special in Father's eyes, they deny his creation.

I thought God would be pissed off by this, but when I asked him he said, "What do you expect? These are humans."

"Why don't you fix it?"

"I did fix it. I gave you an eternal spirit. Now you've got time to work all this out."

I didn't say anything then, but I must have looked puzzled because God laughed. "Yes, but ... ," he teased me.

78. DEAD ENOUGH

There have been times when I was despondent enough that I found myself requesting God to just let me die. Father answered, "Give up your selfishness, the cravings you have that you describe as needs. Let those desires die, and you will be dead enough. Give yourself in service to others, and you will be alive."

79. 666

There was a lot of excitement about June 6, 2006. 06/06/06, the number of the beast, or I should say the second beast, the one who would kill those people who do not worship the first beast. Here it is out of Revelation 13:15-18. *He was given power to give breath to the image of the first beast, so that it could speak and cause all who refused to worship the image to be killed. He also forced everyone, small and great, rich and poor, free and slave, to receive a mark on his right hand or on his forehead, so that no one could buy or sell unless he had the mark, which is the name of the beast or the number of his name. This calls for wisdom. If anyone has insight, let him calculate the number of the beast, for it is man's number. His number is 666.*

This is great material for movies like *The Omen* and *Rosemarie's Baby*. Apocalyptic terror.

I went through a phase once during which I thought this phrase out of the Bible was blatantly anti-Semitic. 666 referred to the Star of David, with its six points, six little triangles and a hexagon in the middle.

This would be very interesting indeed because it would mean that the phrase itself, being anti-Semitic, was the spoken prophecy of the antichrist beast itself. That just screws us all up. Got to think backwards and inside out.

Then Stan the Rev corrected me. He does that a lot. He said that 666 referred to the study of numerology, and with numerical regression the beast's name is supposed to yield 666. If you want to know, Jesus' number is 888. So that's cool. Later in the book I'll talk about the struggle between sixes and eights.

If you look into this numerology business you find out that it can be done in different ways, and various arithmeticians have shown evidence that implicates such people as Hitler and FDR. It can be made to fit almost anyone. I'm sure I'm on the list too. But wait a minute. FDR fought Hitler. And I'm fighting something too. I wonder what it could be. Since you can attach 666 to just about anybody, I've decided numerology is a dead end lead, and I've gone back to thinking this is one more piece of anti-Semitism.

Well, let me side track a little. There have been a lot of bears coming into human neighborhoods here in the Seattle region. They tend to be allured by garbage, and then when people see them and scream, the bears run away and climb trees. Then somebody comes and shoots them. All in all it's hard on the bears.

And coyotes too. Coyotes have been biting little kids. Recently I read an article about how very adaptable coyotes have shown themselves to be. They've been found in every bit of real estate in the contiguous 48 states, with the exception of Long Island, and there have been reports of coyotes trying to swim the channel to that local as well. My secret operatives have told me coyotes are building a boat in the basement of an urban dog house, but so far they can't get it out through the door.

So this begs the question. Where are the bears and coyotes all coming from? If you see a bear wearing a dark blue jersey with orange trim, that's easy. That would be a Chicago Bear. But these bears around here have been naked. And I have no clue at all about the coyotes.

The other day I looked up in the sky, and I saw six bears parachuting down out of the heavens, and I looked again and there were six parachuting coyotes. Then I looked down and saw that more than half of my six pack of beer had been drunk. Six, six and six; could it be a sign of the end?

This brings me to a confusion I've had concerning the definition of two very important words. *Eschatology* is the branch of theology having to do with the last things, such as death, resurrection, judgment, immortality. *Scatology* is the division of zoology having to do with the study of feces. It is important to keep these terms clear in our minds because they help us with such questions as whether a bear is Catholic, or what does the Pope do in the woods, questions like that.

Also we need always to ask ourselves whether people are delivering us a load of eschat or a load of scat, mainly because it makes a difference.

In the Seattle Times there was a story about 3 year old Muhammed Hussein, here for doctors to do what they can to repair the terrible damage to his face caused by an AK-47 fired at close range. There was a great picture on page A16. Maybe you want to look at it or others like it because this is a part of our American legacy in Iraq. There's a 666 story for you.

If the Holy Spirit is the resurrected God within each and every one of us, and I'll talk more about that later, then it follows that in war, God suffers. So then let us ask and answer the question, when is war justified? It is justified when the war between the Holy Spirit and the antichrist finds a battle of such importance that it is worthy of shooting baby Jesus in the face, not just once but many times. This is the standard by which we should make decisions about this and any war.

My ten year old Joshua came down from his bedroom at 10:30 in the evening. "I can't sleep. I can't stop thinking about all the violence in the world."

His mother set him to reading a light hearted book to distract him.

I thought a long time before approaching him, and then I said, "There once was a man named Gandhi, and those who admired him gave him the name *Mahatma*, meaning *great soul*. Gandhi taught us, *we must be the change we want to see in the world.* Joshua, you will have so much to give this world, and you will be a force to change it for the better. But now it is your job to be patient, and to learn, to develop skills. And as for now, here in this house, in this family, you are safe. God already has won the battle here."

So on that day of reckoning, June six, two thousand six, I suggested to all who would listen that they should consider 666 as a little bit of scat. But you know, just leave it to both Christian and Muslim fanatics to make the scat hit the fan.

80. EGO

Certain behaviors and words spoken and facial expressions were unusual enough that they caught my attention, and I wondered about them until the puzzle seemed to fall into meaningful place.

Unverified suspicion ruled a region of my mind where ego was not defended, and to cry out for help would have handed my soul over to the demon. There was no solace to be had from without myself, so where should I look for solace from within?

I was responsible for the welfare of this creature over which I had been given dominion. Its happiness depended in part on realization that its own ego was no more important than any other. Ultimately I could not justify my own existence without the existence of others.

With God's eternity a gift already mine, I needed not to ask for anything more.

81. STAN'S DICTUM

The only power evil has over us is what we ourselves are willing to give it.

TWELVE

War

82. JUST WAR THEORY

The parameters by which war may be justified, most often are ascribed their beginnings in the writings of Augustine, but the topic was talked about in the times of the Old Testament. Perhaps the first mention of it by anyone of the early Christian Church was by Paul in his letter to the Romans, chapter 13, where he wrote, *Everyone must submit himself to the governing authorities, for there is no authority except that which God has established. The authorities that exist have been established by God. Consequently, he who rebels against the authority is rebelling against what God has instituted, and those who do so will bring judgment on themselves. For rulers hold no terror for those who do right ....* Yes Paul, tell that to the Jews of the holocaust. Whether Saint Paul intended the implication may be debated, but it has been inferred from these verses that if the government sends you to war it is your duty to comply. I suspect that at the time he wrote this, Paul's left nut was in the jaws of a vice grip held by an officer of Rome.

If Paul's exhortation resembles anything that Jesus said, my best guess would be Jesus' answer in Matthew 22, when he was asked whether Jews should pay taxes to Rome. He said, *"Give therefore to the emperor the things that are the emperors and to God the things that are God's."* So money belongs to the emperor. To whom belongs a person's soul?

The fact that Augustine found no recorded excerpts of Jesus' teachings that dealt directly with the problem of one nation warring against another, might have indicated to him that a relatively permissive attitude toward the inevitability of war was reasonable, given humankind's imperfect condition. The saying has been ascribed to Jesus that, *"There will be wars and there will be rumors of wars,"* a statement that also acknowledges the inevitability of these horrors.

Inevitability does not validate nor justify war.

Why would Augustine write about situations in which war would be justifiable? Maybe he was influenced by Jesus' exclamation in Matthew 11:12, *"The Kingdom of Heaven has been subjected to violence and the violent are taking it by storm."* Augustine had a concept of the Roman Empire as the *City of Earth*, and the Kingdom of Heaven as the *City of God*. He saw parallels. His hope for the destiny of humanity, particularly the Roman Empire, was for the City of Earth to become or to mirror the City of God. But there were insurgent barbarians at the borders of the Holy Roman Empire, and they were particularly threatening because of the professed pacifism of the empire's Christian citizens. This was Constantine's blind spot at the time he proclaimed himself emperor of the Christians, of whose religion he was at the time ignorant. Ironically this master warrior, Constantine, left to his successors an empire of conscientious objectors.

Seen in this light the pragmatism of Augustine's rules for justifying a war is at least understandable. In his *Contra Faustus,* 22:75, Augustine wrote about the necessity of war sometimes for maintenance of a peaceful state. *When war is undertaken in obedience to God ... it must be allowed to be a righteous war.* Critically analyzing Paul's statement in Romans 13, he acknowledged that there is no power except what is given by God, but he also considered what should be done by a person serving an ungodly king. *It may be an unrighteous command on the part of the king, while the soldier is innocent, because his position makes obedience a duty—how much more must the man be blameless who goes to war on God's authority.*

Augustine counseled that a just war was limited by its purpose (to maintain or restore peace), its authority (only the rulers of nations because of their obligation to maintain peace), and its conduct (basically following rules of necessity and avoiding acts of revenge or barbarism).

Probably never having been able to reach a comfortable acceptance of war as sometimes being justifiable, but still observing that situations arose for which there was no alternative if peace were to be preserved, Augustine's writings tended toward dualism. He wrote about how it was possible to love an enemy even while killing him. He wrote, *we go to war that we may have peace. Be peaceful, therefore, in warring, so that you may vanquish those whom you war against, and bring them to the prosperity of peace.*

For Augustine war was an occasionally necessary business, but we should never let our emotions get the better of us. *The passion for in-*

flicting harm, the cruel thirst for vengeance, an unpacific and relentless spirit, the fever of revolt, the lust of power, and such things, all these are rightly condemned in war.

In other words Augustine was of an opinion that warriors needed to be something other than human because the human psychology does not stay in control when the exigencies of violence require step over step escalation for those who want to win. In situations of life and death, humans do not constrain themselves.

Thomas More also pointed this out, that war in the abstract is different than the reality of war. In his Utopia, or ideal society, More allowed for war in defense against an aggressor, but stated that in reality no war that he knew of was just.

Thomas Aquinas followed similar lines of thinking as Augustine, and both regarded it necessary sometimes to punish people *with a benevolent severity in order to purify them of their sins.* Aquinas added detail to Augustine's arguments, but remained of the same school of thought.

Later specialists in the art of finding ways of making war palatable included Vitoria and Suarez. They along with many similar thinkers regarded a defensive war as entirely understandable and not needing any special moral justification. A war of aggression required the three points of Augustine and Aquinas, plus two more. An aggressive war must be fought only as a last resort and in a proper manner, without killing innocent people.

Since then experts have worked on specific rules of war such as don't bomb a church unless it is being used for military purposes, lots of specific rules.

In my review of Just War Theory, it seemed to me that scholars have tended to be of widely differing opinions, and as of yet there are no clearly correct answers, so I decided that instead of further consultation with those who are in the know, it would make sense to ask the one person I know who isn't in the know.

"Yeah," Agnos yawned. "What can I do for you?"

"Agnos, what kind of war is justifiable?"

"I was having a pretty nice dream there, and you wake me up for this?"

"You're a spirit Agnos. You don't really need to sleep, do you?"

"Not exactly. I just like to take an occasional holiday, to take flights of fancy. Let's see, Just War. I have no idea how you can justify a war. I don't know. How's that?"

"Don't you at least have some insight?"

"Well, Jesus is a problem. Not so much for non-Christians because they don't believe he's God, so they can take or leave what he says, but Christians have a hard time with Jesus. Before Jesus war wasn't such a bad thing in the eyes of God. God just wanted his army to win. So to justify war then, all you had to do was to be on God's side, and of course since both sides believed they were on God's side, God could be happy with whatever happened. War worked pretty well before Jesus came along."

"How did Jesus change all that?"

"Mainly, I think it was that people misunderstood him."

"Was that his fault, poor communication?"

"When you're God you get blamed for everything. It goes with the territory."

"So how was he misunderstood?

"Every little thing he said was generalized to have some all-encompassing morality to it. For example, Jesus told Peter to put away his sword and not to defend him against arrest, knowing Peter would be killed if he resisted. Jesus said 'He who takes the sword will perish by it.' Christians read that and interpreted it as meaning all wars should be unlawful, but Jesus just didn't want Peter to get killed. When you're famous and important you have to be very careful what you say because you never know what people are going to do with your words. Augustine felt he had to make a special interpretation of this little bit of scripture to protect the interests of the government. He wrote that it is okay to use the sword only if given permission to use the sword by an authority figure. Jesus didn't give Peter permission, so he couldn't do it. However, if the Holy Roman Emperor gave Christians permission, they had better do it."

"So you think Jesus was okay with war?"

"Oh hell no. Remember we're supposed to love both our friends and our enemies. I guess if you think like Augustine you can love your enemy as you push a sword through his throat, but that sheds a whole new light on the golden rule."

"Can a war be just?"

"Well I'm glad it was Churchill and Roosevelt leading us against the Nazis rather than Gandhi. If there were any justifiable war in memory, that would be it. It wasn't a pleasant matter though."

"But it was justifiable."

"Why do people want to justify war in the first place? War is war. It is a breakdown of the peaceful order of things. At the point war starts, the system already has been broken. Instead of feeling guilty about the waging of war, we should be concerned about the situation leading up to and causing the perceived need for war. Humans should feel guilty about the conditions that bring us to the point of violence, so let's ask ourselves why we don't spend more time on that."

I thought about it and answered, "Greed, inequality, revenge, religion."

"Yes, and some others too."

"Rules help to keep war more sane though, don't they?"

"Who follows the rules? The more powerful combatant follows the rules. Weaker combatants would be nuts to follow the rules. Then the violence escalates because nobody wants to lose. I kind of think of it as two brain injured people in an argument. Have you ever seen that? They can't control their emotions, so they keep getting louder and louder, and more and more aggressive until someone gets hurt. We all are like that. We all are brain injured in this way, or maybe it would be better to say we all are brain weak in this way. Like you said at the very beginning of this book, we need to evolve."

"So what is all this discussion about Just War Theory?"

"Politics. It's the art of persuading peaceful, ethical people that God is willing to have them play a role in the violence of one nation pitted against another. It works."

"It does work, doesn't it."

"For awhile, until we remember the horror of war. Then we stop the war if we are able, and we enjoy peace for awhile until we forget. Then we fight again until we remember. This is the natural order of things."

83. BATTLESHIP

Awhile ago when asked if he had requested his father's advice before attacking Iraq, George W. answered that he had consulted a higher father. I wish I could have been a fly on the wall during that conversation.

God and George were enjoying a game of Battleship, and George said to God, "Aha! I know exactly where you are. H-4."

"Miss. George; you have no idea in the world where I am. Let me see here. How about C-9."

"Damn it, Lord! That's a direct hit. God, I wish I had your intuition for this game."

"Yes George. Well, it is handy to be able to see correctly what lies right in front of your eyes. It's your turn."

"Lies you say? Yes, I can see the usefulness of that. How about C-4?"

"Another miss."

"No, I mean like the explosive, heh heh. You know, C-4 the military explosive. Kaboom!"

"C-4 is still a miss. Let's call it an explosive miss."

George smirked. "Right, an explosive miss kind of like a fart without a projectile in it. Thunder and awe!"

"Sort of like that. It's my turn. B-9"

George's eyes shifted back and forth. "Nope, there's nothing benign about it. No siree."

God raised an eyebrow. "I know you have a ship on B-9, Mr. President. Who do you think you're playing with here?"

"I distinctly remember you telling me about lying. You said lying right there in front of my eyes. That's what you said, and that's all I'm doin.' I'm lying about what's right there in front of my eyes. My turn. Um … M-16."

"There's no such thing as M-16 in this game. What's going on in your head, George?"

"No M-16? I'm sure I heard somebody talking about an M-16. Well then, I'm guessing B-1. You know, like the bomber. Boom! Ha! Gotcha."

"No , you didn't get me. That's another miss. Next I'll select D-9, because there's no denying that on my next turn your battleship will be sunk."

"Oh no. Dear Lord, don't sink my battleship. I've got a better idea than this game. Let's attack Iraq. Hey, I like that. Attack Iraq. It's got a nice rhyme to it."

"Why would we want to do that?"

"Because of that Sadam fella. He's a bad guy."

"A bad guy?"

"Yes he does evil things, like the time he invaded another sovereign nation, Kuwait, just for the hell of it."

"Just for the hell of it?"

"Well actually, he said that Kuwait historically belonged to Iraq anyway, so he invaded and occupied it. What he really wanted was to control the Middle East. It's a pretty important place, you know, with all that oil. My Daddy took care of that mess, spoiled the oil so to speak, heh heh. Just making a little joke there. Dad should'a finished the job though."

God interrupted, "Did you know it's your turn?"

"Yeah, that's what I was thinkin.' Gotta go back in and finish the job."

"No, I'm talking about this game of Battleship."

"Oh, pardon me. Let's see. B-4. I can see it in your eyes. I've got to declare it before you have a chance to hide the evidence. Be-Fore! Get it? You've got your weapons of mass destruction on B-4, and I'm declaring it Be-Fore I declare war on Iraq. I'm just full of 'em to-night, aren't I."

"It's a sorry problem when you have to explain your own bad jokes, George. I got it the first time. Just because I wasn't laughing didn't mean I didn't understand it, but it's another miss. And now, are you ready for my own bad joke? A-9, as in an ace and a nine, as in ace 'n nine. Asinine! Do you get that one George? Your battleship is sunk, Mr. President. It's time to stand on your head and wiggle your toes. That's what we agreed on. Wait a second; let's make sure the photographers are ready. Georgie Porgie, pudding and pie, drove a ship and watched it die." God did a little dance. "Hoo-hoo. Sorry if I'm carrying on a bit, but this is fun."

GeorgeW. reluctantly put his head and hands against the floor and lifted his legs into the air, but then he got a kick out of it. "You look funny this way, sort of like you have a mouth in the middle of your forehead. I wonder if this is the way people look in Australia, upside down."

"Wiggle your toes, George." God sounded stern. "Okay, that will do." When George got back to his feet, God continued. "Now tell me George, why is it you want to attack Iraq?"

"Would you believe it's to find weapons of mass destruction?"

"That's just an excuse, Buster, a miss. Try again."

"Would you believe it's to spread democracy into that part of the world?"

"George?"

"Well, I want to spoil the oil too."

"What do you mean by that, little fellow?"

"Sadam's not playing by our rule book."

"Our rule book?"

"Yes well, you see, we put that smart ass, upstart puppet into office in the first place. He should show some respect for his betters."

"Respect for his betters?"

"Yes! My God, don't you see. His playing around with the control of oil threatens our American economy. And then he also threatened my Dad."

"Somebody's put you up to this, haven't they George?"

"Sworn to secrecy, God. Can't say a thing about it."

"You still don't understand who you're talking with, George, do you? I know what's going on. I'm asking you these questions to find out how much you're willing to open up about it to me. Do you understand that?"

"You're asking me what I know about all this, yes, I know that. How about, 'nothing ventured; nothing gained.' How about that, Lord?"

"You can pull the wool over your own eyes, Mr. Bush, but the truth will always be known somewhere. Maybe you doubt that?"

"God, you know there are people being tortured and treated monstrously in Iraq. You know that. Americans can make a difference there. We can stop all that horror."

"Can you? Can you really?"

"Well, I guess we're going to find out; aren't we?"

"George! There are horrors in many other places of the world as well. The difference between those other places and Iraq is your own desire for controlling the region. Admit it, at least to yourself, George."

"Iraq is the birthplace of civilization, God. It's the original Garden of Eden. I want to take it away from that hellion and give it back to heaven again. You can understand that, can't you?"

"The gates to Eden were closed by me because of the insistence of humans that they know better than I do. Don't make the mistake of thinking you can open the gates by war. I'm the one who closed the gates. I'm the one guarding them, and so you'll have to come to Eden another way. I'm not about war."

George looked frustrated and perplexed. "Are you sure?"

"George, in Sunday school they taught you about the trinity. Do you remember what they told you?"

"Heh heh, sure do. Father, Son and Holy Ghost; who grabs the fastest gets the most."

"George, you've heard that God is love. Do you understand this? It's as simple as that."

"Shock and awe, God. Simple as that."

"Shock and awe?"

"You bet. Put the fear of the Lord in 'em. They'll love us when we win. They'll love us because they'll see how good we are. We're the good guys."

God sighed, "How can I get through to you? I'm not going to give up."

"Right!" George bubbled, "That's because you're on our side. God loves America. God bless America."

"Sometimes I get weary of hearing that. It's all take and no give. Can you give a little bit of your love to me?"

"E-3."

"What's that?" God asked.

"The game; I'm guessing E-3."

"Oh. That's a miss."

"Say Lord, would you mind talking with your son, Jesus, about something?"

"What about, George?"

"Well you know, with all the prisoners of war that we'll be getting, maybe Jesus could help us with the interrogation. Do you think he'd participate in a little good cop bad cop?"

"That's not the sort of thing Jesus has any interest in doing, and certainly he has no experience. C-1."

"You mean see one, and then do one. He needs a little on the job training. Yes, that can be arranged."

"No George. I meant the game. I'm calling you on C-1."

"Oh, let me see here now. Oh damn. It's another hit."

84. WMD

For a *while* of *major duration*
President Bush *was much distracted*
by the *wicked, malicious dictator,* Saddam Hussein.
He *watched* the *madman daily.*
On a particularly *wonderful, magnificent day,*
spy plane photographs saw *woozers, maybe doozers,* in Iraq.
From the CIA, agent Fwudd reported,
"WASCALS MAKING DESTWUCTOWS."
So President Bush *went, much determined,* to the American people
saying, *"WASCALS MAKING DESTWUCTOWS."*
And the American people repeated, *"WASCALS MAKING DESTWUCTOWS."*
He went to Congress
saying, *"WASCALS MAKING DESTWUCTOWS."*
And the Congress repeated, *"WASCALS MAKING DESTWUCTOWS."*
He sent Colin Powell to the United Nations, where the *world makes decisions.*
General Powell said that in Iraq there were
"WASCALS MAKING DESTWUCTOWS,"
and he showed them the photos that saw *woozers, maybe doozers.*
But the United Nations was not impressed.
It did not repeat, *"WASCALS MAKING DESTWUCTOWS."*
Instead it sent to Iraq some *waboomba mazoomba detectives.*
These detectives reported that there were no *wascals making destwuctows* in Iraq.

In fact, they said there were more *women making dungarees,*
more *wild monkeys doodling* and more *wombats marching dutifully,*
more *whirling marimba dancers* than any destwuctows in Iraq.
President Bush *was much displeased.*
He went to the American people
saying, *"We must decide. We must do."*
He went to the Congress
saying, *"We must decide. We must do.*
We must determine what *war may deliver."*
And Congress repeated, *"War may deliver."*
When men deployed to Iraq, they looked at each other
saying, *"We may die."*
But Iraq put forth the *worst, miserable defense,*
and *we made* our *destination,* Baghdad.
There were *whiskered men dancing* in the streets.
A statue of the *wicked, malicious dictator* was toppled.
The *wretched misanthrope* himself *disappeared.*
Warriors, many, dispersed.
There *were many distractions.*
There *were many disruptions.*
There *were many detractors wishing more destruction* in Iraq.
When months and *days* later the *wicked, malicious dictator* was found,
he was found transformed into a *whining, miserable, disheveled* ghost,
worried and *marred* and *demented.*
The *war machine declined* to stop.
Wicked, merciless, dirty terrorists *waxed more dangerous.*
Wounded men died.
Weeping mothers drowned in blood shed by their sons and daughters.
Wailing, mourning daughters were left fatherless and motherless.
We all *mourned* in *distress.*
The *world mouthed discent.*
Was the *world more dangerous?*
Did the *world much desire* a *war made democracy* in Iraq?
Would manufactured democracy wield a *manufactured design*
of peace for the world?
Would insurgent *wishers* of *more destruction*
make a permanent battle ground of Iraq?
We may have *dreamed* that *we* could *make* a *difference,*
but we *were much disenchanted* with *war made desperation,*
and we wondered.
Would it *matter down* the road?

152

Laugh on the Way to Heaven

Would it *matter definitively?*
Would it *matter decisively?*
Would it *matter* what we *decided?*
In the end *We made doo-doo.*
We martyred the *dictator,*
that *wicked, misanthrope demento,*
and *we meandered directionlessly,*
and *we massively destroyed* Iraq.
Our children, *we mourn* their *deaths.*
We miserably disabled their generation.
But one thing *we may dispense* with now is this question
of whether *WMD* are in Iraq.
The question of *whether? meanders depending* on its definition.
What you *may define* it as, *will most determine whether* you *may detect*
WMD in Iraq.

85. MARKING TERRITORY

I heard a story about homeland security, a true story. A man I know breeds dachshunds, and a week earlier than this story one of his females, in heat, rode in the back of his pickup truck. Then a week later he took this same truck onto the Washington State Ferry System. Twice the bomb sniffing golden retriever came over to the truck excitedly, and then the officer managing the dog asked if my friend had hauled any guns or fireworks or anything of that sort in the truck.

When the officer learned the reason he said, "Oh well, that explains why he's peed on the wheels. He's never done that before. He's marking his territory."

Imagine if people were like that. A man passing by a truck that one week earlier had carried a squad of cheerleaders all wearing Channel No. 5, might say, "Wow, I like the smell of this truck. I think I'll pee on the tires."

People aren't like that though. We mark our territory with smart bombs and patrols that lose control of their behavior. It's not quite the same as peeing on something to mark our territory, but then again it is.

86. GEORGE'S PSYCHOTHERAPY

On August 21, 2006, in an address to the nation, President Bush appeared finally to admit that Iraq was a mess. But we must stay there. To leave "would be a huge mistake," meaning of course that he believes our presence there now is more helpful than harmful in the goal of calming that land of division and violence. Not everyone agrees with him. That's the argument now.

We're damned if we do and damned if we don't. President Bush's legacy will be that of the damnable dilemma. What to do now? No desirable choices.

I wonder if he's known this for awhile, underneath his shell of denial, and now the shell no longer is impenetrable to the searing realization of thousands of American's killed, tens of thousands of Americans wounded and disabled, and way over one hundred thousand Iraqi's killed. For a loving soul this realization would be horrible.

I brought this to T2B2, Think Tank on the Back of the Bus, and I suggested that we need a fund raising drive to collect money for George's psychotherapy. He's going to have to work through a lot of internal conflict. T2B2 wasn't all that sympathetic. Some suggested a car wash. We could charge extra for a wax job, sort of like we paid extra for the wax job we got in Iraq.

Others of T2B2 didn't want to help George at all, so I negotiated on his behalf. Finally they yielded to the notion of paying for group therapy and suggested he could do something like Jimmy Carter, lead the way for a charity like Habitat for Humanity, only George's efforts would be in Iraq. He could build houses for Iraqis. That seems fair, reparations for harm done, expiation and hopefully atonement.

So next I asked T2B2 if they'd be willing to let George drive around Iraq in a Humvee with armor. They said, "No, give him a camel or a bicycle." Through my extraordinary diplomatic skills I was able to negotiate their generosity up to a 1963 Corvair, exploding gas tank be damned. I could say that George owes me one, but really my fellow Americans, we need to learn how to find within ourselves more generosity than this.

87. ANGELS

When angels and demons battle,
why must angels die?
As goodness sheds its earthly shell
we wonder.
Some of us, bereaved,
pray we've not been deceived.
Bitterness lives in demon breath.
Bravery breathes an angel's death.
Committed, calm, in noble role,
selfless, grander as the whole,
an angel gives itself, its soul,
not for gain itself to hold.
An angel acts for goodness and good alone.

If there is a heaven, ours to hone,
then it is the honing and the heaven and the battle fought
that are immortal.

88. SHE SITS AT THE WINDOW

She sits at the window watching the rain
thinking the weatherman must be insane.
She traces out time in a line with her finger
and wonders what later the morning will bring her.
She sips from her china a puddle of tea
and nibbles her slices of apple and Brie.
For a change, she waits with patience and poise,
smiles, amused at the rhetoric noise.
She plays her Sinatra, Chicago then too.
Some things are timeless and carry her through.
A candle for fragrance, to chase away fear,
she prays that the innocent are safer next year.

THIRTEEN

The Christian Church

89. GOOD SMOKE BAD SMOKE

On the morning the new pope was elected, my radio announced there had been at least four billowings of black smoke over the Vatican, and then later I learned Cardinal Joseph Ratzinger was elected on the third ballot. My initial reaction was, good for them. This process should take some time, like the World Series. We would be disappointed if these things were decided by just one game or one vote. Things with this kind of gravity rightfully require time for us to appreciate the weight of it all.

There were one or two reasons, or a dozen, why I was not a member of the College of Cardinals voting that day, but I imagine the cardinals also felt an appreciation for the importance of not getting this over too quickly. They were secluded *con clave*, under lock and key. Nobody knew what they did in there. I wouldn't be surprised if the first vote was whether to just burn some black smoke for the joy of it. "Let the world be entertained," they said to one another. And that spoke well for their good understanding of the situation.

It was all secret, but the Vatican missed a great opportunity for increasing its wealth and popularity. They could have opened the process for the world to watch by making it the most magnificent of reality TV programs. They could have started with twelve popular cardinals, twelve because of the twelve tribes of Israel and the twelve disciples of Jesus. Every week the members of the Catholic Church could watch the Cardinals perform and show their spiritual strengths. Each week people could call in and vote off one cardinal. Commercial time would be sold at premium prices.

The Church needs to modernize a bit. I like the smoke signals. They should keep those, but why do they have to be black and white?

155

That's so 1950s. And besides, if I were of African descent I'd be pissed off. It's the whole white versus black, good versus bad thing all over again. If someday we get an African pope, I mean a really black pope, he'll understand the need for change. We need colored smoke bombs; red for stop and green for go. The Vatican can do this. I know they can.

Pope John Paul II was a great man, three dimensional. I can see him as both good pope and bad pope. His papacy forever will be associated with the collapse of the Soviet Union. He denounced the American insurgence into Iraq. He also denounced the use of condoms, thereby contributing to the demise of many Africans by HIV. All in all, it can be said he is a man loved by God. You can pray to Pope John Paul II. He is in heaven and will listen.

Is he a saint? That not only is an interesting question; it turns out to be a little amusing. Pope John Paul II was more mystical than most popes, and he saw sainthood in many who otherwise would have been overlooked. He liberalized the rules of canonization to make it easier for holy people to reach sainthood. Here is an excerpt from the June 2005 edition of *Vanity Fair,* an article by John Cornwell: *John Paul created more than 1,000 blesseds and saints by the turn of the millennium; in other words, he made more saints than all the other Popes put together since the start of the formal process.* Pope John Paul II made it easy enough to become a saint that he himself is almost a shoo-in. It used to require two documented miracles for a person to become a saint. John Paul II reduced this to a requirement of just one miracle, so if you want to be facetious about it and why not, you can say it was a miracle he got away with making it so easy to become a saint. That could be his miracle. Voila! We have a saint.

There are other miraculous things about this popular pope. Already mentioned was the downfall of the Soviet Empire. He also was the first Slavic pope in history. I think he's a saint, even though he was too conservative for my tastes, and I disagree with him on some things. He's a saint. I've made my decision.

The Church has its problems, and it's not clear to me that it realizes fully what those problems are. If it is to retain believers it will need to update according to accumulated scientific knowledge of our world. Science never has nor ever will challenge God. It merely challenges our concepts of God, and we should welcome that. So relax. God is safe. You don't need to throw him a life-saver.

The Church needs to change according to the teachings of its own Jesus who, when asked what was the greatest commandment answered,

"Love the Lord your God with all your heart and with all your mind and with all your soul. And the second is like it. Love your neighbor as yourself." It may be the only way to show God your love for him. At least it's your best way. Love every single one of your fellow humans. Give generously to those in need. Welcome into your society and bless those who have lifestyles and beliefs different from your own.

The Church's success will be determined by its ability to maintain beautiful tradition while adjusting long held doctrine to accommodate new understandings of what science has taught us about heart-felt and sensible love.

90. THE POPE APOLOGIZES

At Starbucks I met another man named Tom who resembled me also in that he had white hair and was drinking coffee. He impressed me as being very well read, and he could talk about many things ranging from current events to Shakespeare to the 1864 presidential election of Lincoln over his challenger and former general, McClellan. The interesting thing here was that while Lincoln wanted to stay the course in the Civil War, to preserve the Union, his challenger encouraged peace by letting the South go. Let the Confederacy be its own nation. Divide us.

It interests me when I meet people who are better read than I, who arrive at different perspectives than mine about the world. Of all the things Tom said, the one that has stayed with me is the one having to do with the need for the United States to balance against the imperialistic goals of terrorists who identify themselves with Islam. "Because nobody else will," is what Tom said. The counterbalance will not come from Europe, where religion has continued to lose its influence. Tom said, "Secularism is no match for Islam."

Then there was the uproar about Pope Benedict having cited a medieval text that called any religion evil that tried to spread itself by use of violence. Muslims around the world protested violently, even set fire to churches. Clever irony! The Pope apologized for the misunderstanding by Muslims and mentioned his own suffering about the terrible violence that ensued. Muslims protested his apology because it didn't go far enough. On one picket sign was written, *The Pope's suffering is equivocal.* Muslims burned the pope in effigy.

Then according to my secret operative in the Vatican, Pope Benedict started to like the idea of making apologies. He apologized for Notre Dame having lost its football game to Michigan.

Then he apologized for the poor officiating that altered the outcome of the football game between the Oregon Ducks and the Oklahoma Sooners, and he mentioned his own suffering that the officials' lives actually were threatened by disgruntled fans.

Then he apologized for the rapidly melting permafrost in Siberia. He did not take responsibility for global warming, but because of global warming the permanently frozen ground has been melting five times faster than scientists previously thought, releasing prehistoric mammoth methane into the atmosphere and causing ... well, a stink. So he apologized that Siberia smells like one great big fart. "There," he said. Nobody will complain about that." We hope not because if somebody in Siberia burns the pope in effigy, it will begin a flaming torch that never goes out, forever fueled by the melting permafrost.

91. THE PROBLEM WITH CHRISTIANITY

Stan the Rev wrote to me: Religion develops when people discover they have similar beliefs about the divine. They covenant and worship together, and that is good. However, when a religion becomes arrogant, and to protect itself states that people must believe their particular way because they are the only ones who have the truth, then it becomes problematic.

Let me briefly consider the Christian Church as I know and understand it, from the Lutheran and the Methodist points of view. Both denominations are very Catholic, holding for the most part to the doctrines of the Holy Roman Catholic Church.

The Holy Roman Emperor Constantine brought together the leaders of the Christian Church in 325 C.E. at the city of Nicea. The conservative elements of the Church were those who most influenced the outcome of that meeting, and that served Constantine well, not because they were right in their theology but because their brand of Christianity was most usable by Constantine to control the populace and institutions of the Empire. The product of that conference was the Nicene Creed which states the Christian belief system as we now know it. Constantine made Christianity the state religion and used it as a tool in the building of an empire. He used it to control the populace.

The Church would save itself by relinquishing its overemphasis on the Fall/Redemption theology which became the dominant theology when promoted by Augustine. Augustine was wrong.

Augustine's writings were and still are very influential in the Church. He wrote that there was a revolt in heaven against God, lead by Satan, in which God's angels triumphed and kicked the rebels out. He also wrote about when war is justified and laid out six criteria in which it is alright to make war. This particularly annoys me since it is contrary to what Jesus taught, and it was used by the Church to justify the crusades. It is what many so-called Christian nations have used to justify going to war.

No other major world religion believes in original sin, not Judaism, Hinduism, Islam or Buddhism. It is interesting that the Bible gives no indication that Jesus, a practicing Jew, ever believed in the original sin or Fall/Redemption theology. For the first several hundred years until Augustine, the Christian Church didn't believe in it either.

The very nature of the Fall/Redemption theology encourages separateness and judgmental attitudes, as in winners over losers, the saved over the damned.

The Christian Church struggles today because it is caught up in an outdated cosmology that the world is by its nature a sinful place. Much of the rest of the world has grown up spiritually and questions these teachings of Christianity as being irrelevant at best, and at worst wrong or superstitious.

There is a difference between having a belief in the teachings of Jesus, and calling oneself Christian. There are many who claim to be Christian who are not Christian at all. They claim to worship Christ, but they worship their doctrines instead, the doctrines that teach them that they are by nature sinful and unclean. This leads them to mistrust the world and even themselves.

Why doesn't the Church change? The answer is tangled in the Fall/Redemption theology of Augustine. Many in the Church don't embrace change or growth because they continue to consider all people in the world sinful, and societies they consider chaotic. That leads to an assumption that any change proposed by people must be wrong or evil. All this is to say the Church has lost touch with Jesus, whose message was about change. Some years ago a frustrated bishop commented, "Wherever Jesus went there was a revolution; wherever I go people serve tea."

Why then am I an ordained minister in the United Methodist Church? I choose to work for change on the inside because the Church does teach the stories of Christ in whom I believe. I challenge people to grow in their faith, to dare to be challenged and to challenge me. Some welcome what I have to say while others are appalled. That's life.

There is hope. When the Church embraces, as other religions do, the original blessings of the world and the universe, of our lives and the blessings we have from Hashem (God), then we will understand, just as much of the rest of the world already understands, that the Church is guilty of fostering a mentality and a way of life that divides peoples. It encourages self righteousness, even to the extent of violence or abandonment. Only when the Christian Church realizes this and changes will it become what it was meant to be, a leader in the development of a world in which everyone knows what it means to say, "Thy will be done on earth as it is in heaven."

I am hopeful.

Love,

Stan

92. CONSTANTINE

During the evenings I spent reading about Constantine, the Holy Roman Emperor who established Christianity as the preferred state religion, I found myself wondering if, as a child, Constantine used a magnifying glass to burn caterpillars and other helpless creatures, or was his cruelty reserved for application only later in life and only against human subjects of his empire.

Riding on the bus I asked Fearless Leader what the Catholic Church had taught him about Constantine. He looked puzzled. "Nothing," he said. "I think he brought back a lot of relics to his mother."

Shush now. Lean in closer; I've got to whisper. Constantine embarrasses the Catholic Church. He should embarrass the rest of us as well, but we are oblivious to our heritage in a way that maybe the Catholic Church envies. Ignorance is bliss.

Before Christianity, the Roman religion was a conglomeration of fragments collected over the years from other civilizations. Greek religion had a heavy influence, but there were contributions from the Etruscans and from other Latin tribes that preceded the ascendancy of Rome. Popular traditions and holidays persisted even after nobody could remember what they were about. A festival was held every year on July 25, to honor the goddess Furrina, but nobody could remember exactly who she was. It was just a very nice time to have a party. Romans celebrated at least one religious holiday every month. Toga! Toga!

Superstition ran rampant in Rome, and everybody tried to make special contracts or bargains with the gods of their choice. There were structured government traditions, but also there was considerable tolerance for individual families to make their own deals and traditions with their own gods, at the discretion of the man of the family. Roman religion did not have a coherent central belief that precluded other religions, and so foreign religions were acceptable and frequently found fertile root in Roman society. Early on, before they were made guilty by association with Christians, Jews were free to worship in Rome. The cult of the Persian sun god, Mythras, was popular among soldiers. Greek stoicism gained influence and suggested there may be just one god. Romans were okay with all this.

Christianity was a different matter. During the first century, at a time when little was known about it, rumors about Christianity included suspicions of cannibalism, incest and child sacrifice. Even after Romans learned Christians were a moral lot, still there was the problem of the Christian claim that Jesus was king. This, along with their refusal to worship Caesar, demonstrated to Roman authorities that they were not loyal to their rulers. Also Christian insistence that there was only one path to salvation made them appear intolerant of the other religions of the empire. They were party poopers. Sort of like now, the most loudly boisterous of the staunchly intolerant Christians irritated a lot of people.

The Roman Empire was not as friendly a place as the United States. Although hoodlums in both civilizations perpetrated ugly crimes against humanity, in Rome the government embraced this practice as well, more like Nazi Germany during the holocaust. Germany perfunctorily conducted its state sponsored murder, and the persecution of Christians in Rome also started out that way. It was punishment by the authorities for disobedience. Later it was made a spectacle.

Christians were persecuted heavily from 165 to 180 Common Era, under the reign of Marcus Aurelius. That was a long but temporary thing. After about 260, for awhile Christians enjoyed toleration and were able to establish roots within and across the empire. Christianity acquired influence among the influential, and increasing numbers of Christians held high positions in society.

Christian power came to be seen as a threat by Augustus Diocletian, and in 303, he and his Caesar Galerius launched a vicious purge of Christians. If you are not familiar with Roman rank, Caesars were subordinate to the Augusti.

Constantine was born either in 272, 273, or some time around 285. His mother, Helena, was an inn keeper's daughter, and his father was Constantius Chlorus, a man who was given considerable respect and who was appointed to the level of Caesar in 293.

Constantine himself became an officer of promise for Galerius during the years of the great Galerian purge of Christians.

Two Augusti, Diocletian and Maximian, abdicated their thrones in 305, and Galerius felt confident that he would become the next dominant Augustus. However, Constantine's father, Constantius Chlorus, was more popular with the people and had more senior rank than Galerius, and that put Constantine into a somewhat dire position. Luckily for Constantine, Galerius was high enough on himself that he willingly released Constantine to join his father's army which at that time was campaigning in Britain. When Constantine's father died of illness in 306, the troops hailed Constantine as Augustus. Galerius was pissed, but he also was compelled to acknowledge the strong public support for Constantine. He granted the upstart a rank of Caesar.

Constantine married Fausta, daughter of Maximian, one of the former Augusti who had abdicated and who now returned once again to power in Rome. Maximian elevated Constantine to rank of Augustus, a very nice wedding present if you ask me. Upon this turn of events, all the other Augusti and all the Caesars were beside themselves with displeasure, and at the Conference of Carnuntum, in 308, they demanded that Constantine relinquish his title of Augustus. Constantine answered, "No thank you," and he went his merry way. So all the Augusti and all the Caesars decided instead that it was easier to force Constantine's father in law, Maximian, to abdicate. Maximian thought that wasn't fair.

Soon after that meeting, while Constantine was having a good time fighting marauding Germans, he got news that Maximian had turned against him and was trying to become Augustus again by unseating Constantine. Maximian's troops in Gaul were not adequately prepared and were no match for Constantine's army which laid siege to the city of Massilia, where Maximian was staying. The city surrendered, and Maximian either committed suicide or was executed in 310.

Galerius died in 311, and the absence of any dominant command of the empire was enough to spur Caesars into fighting each other to determine who would be the next boss of the empire. This was when Constantine saw the light of Christianity.

In 312, he invaded Italy against his foe, Maxentius, who had about four times as many troops as Constantine, but Constantine's were better trained and much better disciplined. One night before a battle Constantine dreamed he saw the *Chi-Ro*, a symbol of Christ, shining above the sun. The *Chi-Ro* looks like the letter *P with a smaller x* on its leg. Constantine had his soldiers paint the symbol on their shields and then defeated Maxentius in the Battle at Milvian Bridge. After that Constantine proclaimed himself emperor of the Christians.

He was welcomed into Rome as the senior Augustus of three emperors. He ordered an end to the repression of Christianity.

The other two emperors warred against each other, and the victor was Licinius. Then there were only two emperors, and they appeared to be trying to get along with each other, Licinius ruling in the East and Constantine in the West. Licinius even married Constantine's sister. However, let's just say the two emperors continued to argue a lot, and the blood of their armies flowed.

Constantine remained tolerant of the persistently popular Pagan religion, but he started little by little actually to learn about the Christian faith he had chosen to defend. He did not as yet choose to be baptized. There were disputes within the Church, and Constantine did what he could to resolve them. He gathered into meetings all the elders of different factions of the Church, and they peacefully debated. Then he brutally enforced their decisions. He himself persecuted people who were not the right kind of Christians.

As Constantine got more and more involved in the building of his brand of Christianity, Licinius in the East got more and more annoyed with his brother in law, and increased his suppression of Christians in his part of the world. Constantine went to war, defeated Licinius in 324, and became sole emperor of the Roman Empire. Licinius was imprisoned and then executed.

Then Constantine pretty much had things his own way. He outlawed pagan sacrifices and robbed Pagan treasuries to fund construction of Christian churches. By law, sons were forced to work the same careers as their fathers. Constantine taxed heavily, and those who could not pay were beaten or tortured. He harshly prohibited sexual immorality. Rapists were burned. If the victim had been raped while away from home, she also was punished because young women had no business wandering outside the safety of their homes. Any woman who eloped with her lover was burned alive. Any chaperone who assisted a young lady to elope, had molten lead poured into her mouth.

It was with this as a backdrop that the religious council of bishops was congregated at Nicaea in 325. The Nicene Creed was written and became the only permissible creed of Roman Christianity. The branch of Christianity called Arianism was branded heresy, and Constantine eradicated it.

Later in life Constantine planned to be baptized in the river Jordan, just as Jesus had been. I like to think that it was an act of God that he never made it there to enjoy this last bit of supreme arrogance. He died in 337 and was baptized on his deathbed. The baptismal waters washed away his sins and all was forgiven.

Constantine was without question a great man who unified the Roman Empire and gave Christianity a leg up in its religious dominance of the western hemisphere, but the Christianity that survived his brutality had neither the diversity nor the innocence of itself before him. Stan the Rev has observed, "Constantine used Christianity to consolidate his power, and Christianity used Constantine to do the same." They were a match made in, you tell me, heaven or hell.

I cannot help imagining that at his reception in the afterlife, socializing with Jesus and Mother Mary, Moses, Abraham, Buddha, Confucius and a lot of other good people, Constantine must have felt pretty small.

Back in my naïve teen years and early twenties, I thought the *Chi-Ro* was the niftiest of Christian medals, and I wore it around my neck. Now I relegate the symbol to a locked, cavernous prison in the farthest, Siberian reaches of my mind, and the key is thrown away. *Chi-Ro's* cell mate is named *Swastika*.

There is an important difference, though, between the *Chi-Ro* and the *Swastika*. While Hitler lost, Constantine triumphed and forever changed the landscape of western history and religion.

93. ORIGINAL SIN

Much but not all of what I have read about Saint Augustine and concepts of original sin, was extracted from the Catholic Encyclopedia via the internet. Although other parts of that compendium of useful information, particularly the one entitled, *The Teaching of Saint Augustine of Hippo*, were academically outstanding, the article written by the same author, *The Life of Saint Augustine of Hippo*, I found to be verbose, biased, and heavily laden with judgmental editorial comment. Looking past all that, there was the old fashioned and quaint diction. Repeatedly the word *farther* was used when the more fitting word would have been *further*. Take note readers, in modern usage *farther* connotes a greater or more remote distance in space or time. In other situations the word *further* is better, connoting more or additional consideration of something other than temporal or spatial dimension. Patiently getting beyond these distractions, I found many amusing things in the online Catholic Encyclopedia.

Yes, that was a snooty paragraph I just wrote, but I did it because Saint Augustine himself was a literary master, and before being ordained a priest of the Catholic Church he was a teacher of grammar. Although his and my takes on the concept of original sin are very different, opposite poles of a piece of chocolate decadence, we are blood brothers on the topic of good writing. Put 'er there, Augustine. Imagine us shaking hands.

Augustine's father was pagan until shortly before he died, when Augustine's mother, the highly regarded Saint Monica, finally persuaded him to convert to Christianity. According to the Catholic Encyclopedia this gave Augustine's father a *holy death*. Good for him. Throughout his life he was a generous and charitable man, and he deserved as much.

Augustine did not accept baptism as a child or young adult, but he received a Christian education and excelled. At the age of sixteen he was ready for scholarly studies at Carthage, but he had to wait a year while his parents saved enough money to send him.

The encyclopedia informed me that during this year of idleness, Augustine's interests turned hedonistic, by which I presume he liked beautiful cars and fast women. When later that year he got to experience the distractions of the big city, Carthage, it was more of the same. He ended up having to tell his mother he had fathered a son out of wedlock. The encyclopedia implied that Augustine referred to this bastard youngster as his "son of sin," and here is my chance to lay on that ugly phrase my own little judgmental editorial comment. The sin wasn't the events leading up to the child born out of wedlock. The sin was to call the precious baby a "child of sin." That was blasphemy against the Holy Spirit dwelling within the boy.

Augustine felt guilty about it, and likely he absorbed himself in a search for answers as to why he had behaved so irresponsibly. For almost a decade he studied the teachings of Eastern philosophers, the Manichaeans, who proposed the idea that all people have within them an eternally evil nature. For awhile Augustine imagined this Manichaen philosophy to be more scientifically based than Christianity, until he at last met their leader, Faustus, and found him to be an intellectual vagrant.

His next philosophical absorption was with Platonism, and that philosophical school carried with him into his many years of Christian faith. He finally came to an understanding that we all are inherently sinful, and our only path for salvation is via Jesus Christ.

It commonly is thought that the concept of original sin, as a Christian concept, began with Augustine, but that is not so. Others before him had written and talked about it. Augustine's prominence on this topic came about because of his passionate adherence to a quest for explanation of his own meanderings earlier in life. He philosophically explored original sin and wrote voluminously about it.

Religious argument has persisted through the centuries, and when reading the many differences of opinion, the fine gradations and subtleties of interpretation, I got the distinct notion that it has been a debate of many lawyer-look-alikes over the precise meanings of scripture. You see, it's all about how you interpret and extrapolate excerpts from the

Bible, and here is the crazy thing; the foundation of the argument for original sin is the story of Adam and Eve, a perhaps allegorical item of literature written by an ancient poet aspiring to get published. Well, lucky him. He got a huge contract with the Christian Church that declared his story was the work of God. I'd like to get to know his agent.

Here are the basic elements of the argument for original sin. Adam sinned by his disobedience. That sin bought mortality upon him, meaning perhaps that had he not sinned he might have been granted eternal life. This was not by any means a certain gift though. From Genesis 3:22-23, *The Lord God said, "The man has now become like one of us, knowing good and evil. He must not be allowed to reach out his hand and take also from the tree of life and eat, and live forever." So the Lord God banished him from the Garden of Eden* .... Apparently, until Adam and Eve defiled themselves by breaking his command and becoming knowledgeable, God was willing to let Adam and Eve find and eat from the tree of eternal life. It was their sullying of themselves that must have made them unacceptable for eternal life.

Adam's disobedience brought upon himself the stain of being by nature a sinful being. His sinfulness was passed on to the rest of humankind by a process either like genetic inheritance, or a more mystical concept that each of us actually was Adam and each of us actually did break the rules. This last mystical concept is at odds with the Catholic Church's denunciation of the concept of a universal soul.

So here is where I lose you who are literal in you interpretation of the Bible. I'm disappointed that you cannot take the next step with me that the concept of original sin does not fit the scientific, psychological data now available. It is a matter of diction, and I hope you also are listening to me, Augustine, because this will soothe your soul. Of course you now already know this because you've gone to heaven and learned it there. If we use as a definition for sin any behavior that separates a person from God, then it would be absurd to think we are born inherently sinful. God made us. Why would he make us to be inherently separate from him? How could he do that? Since he made us, the behavior would be his. He would be the sinful one.

God didn't make us sinful. He made us imperfect. The two words have different meanings. God made us imperfect for a reason, and we ought to accept our imperfections as a gift of grace, for it is by acknowledgement of our imperfect nature that we learn to forgive, not just others but also ourselves. Our imperfection brings us closer to God. It doesn't separate us.

Because it interferes with our ability to forgive when we think of ourselves and others as inherently separate from God, the concept of original sin is contrary to the teachings of Jesus. This makes it anti-Christ.

FOURTEEN

Obsessions

94. GRAND GUIGNOL

It troubled me that so many people enthusiastically anticipated attending a movie that advertised itself with brutal violence as its featured uniqueness. Don't mistake my meaning. This is not a criticism of Mel Gibson or his film, *The Passion of Christ,* released in late winter of 2004. I understand the allure of such a project and do not object to its having been made. My comment is directed at society, and again don't mistake me. I'm not surprised, just troubled.

I have not seen this movie, but I've read a lot about it and so far have not found anything spiritually or theologically new or intriguing about it. Maybe it has a claim for cinematic achievement, maybe. It is said to adhere to an earlier interpretation of the four canonical gospels, a grouping of literature that is inherently inconsistent and has been critically scrutinized by historical and theological scholars alike.

I'm disappointed that so much effort was put into a movie that doesn't have much to teach me. Already I am fully aware of the ruthlessness and brutality of Pontius Pilate, a personality trait that I understand was not brought out in the film. Again, the film was based on an earlier interpretation of the gospels, gentler in its depiction of Roman authority. I'm also aware of the horrific brutality of Roman crucifixion.

William Arnold had a nice critical review of the film in the February 25, 2004, edition of the *Seattle Post-Intelligencer.* He thought two hours of violence did not capture the reality of Jesus' life, and he also didn't think the movie was completely realistic in another way. If its intent was to be realistic it would have shown Jesus totally naked on the cross with loss of control of his bowel and bladder. Mr. Arnold wrote that Mel Gibson didn't want realism; he wanted some Grand Guignol.

Mr. Arnold also pointed out a discrepancy of the Christian Right condemning such pandering violence in movies, but somehow from this film they took away a profoundly spiritual experience.

Mr. Arnold thought this movie was best suited to adolescent boys who go in for such gore.

I read the review and decided that *The Passion of Christ* was a horror film, a genre of which I'm not fond. To use religion as a reason to pay money and see a brutal murder would be morbid, so I passed on it. As a society, our continued interest in such things shows how little society has progressed from the spectacle of gladiatorial games.

I suspect the Jesus I know would not be enthusiastic about our using his story to turn up the volume on the societal violence dial. I bet he doesn't get a kick out of being used that way.

There came to be a lot of discussion about this movie stirring up anti-Semitic feelings. Well, not among enlightened folk, but there were a couple of people out there who were not enlightened. And yes, those two morons said that the Jews killed Jesus. Whether or not you choose to blame Mel for the anti-Semitic feelings that might be inspired by the film, he was being faithful to the canonical gospels.

Why did Matthew, Mark, Luke and John put anti-Semitic remarks in their books? Weren't all but one of them Jews themselves? Luke was a Greek physician. Writing in a Roman occupied world, the authors of these books did not want to have happen to them what happened to Jesus. So they took as much blame away from Pontius Pilate and his Roman thugs as possible. The books also were written at a time when the early Church was trying to sell the concept of Christianity to the Roman People. Also, several hundred years later, when decisions were being made as to which of the fifty or so gospel stories should be included in the Bible, yes, you already guessed it; the leaders of the committee were Roman.

Without exactly meaning to, Mel Gibson showed us exactly why the canonical gospels are subtly anti-Semitic, and maybe, just maybe, that was the most important spiritual value of this movie.

There remains the lingering question. What is *Grand Guignol?* The term means *big puppet show* and was the theater created in 1897, by Oscar Metenier in Paris. The building he purchased for this once had been a chapel, and two large angels hung above the orchestra, stirring greater emotional response from the audience. These angels of heaven passively observed with seeming indifference, the insanely cruel torture humanity inflicted upon itself, enacted on the stage beneath them. *Guignol* was the name of the bloodthirsty main character of the puppet show.

Metenier's early productions boldly depicted lives of the disenfranchised elements of society, those of vagrants, street kids, prostitutes, criminals. This embarrassed the privileged class, and the police frequently censored it, even shut it down.

Max Maurey soon succeeded Metenier as director, and from 1898 to 1914 he turned the Theatre du Grand Guignol into a center of horrific spectacle. The theater's popularity had mostly to do with its audacity in crossing boundaries of decorum. From an earlier purpose of social commentary, it ventured into fantastic horror, showing such things as a nanny strangling children, a woman having her eye gouged out, people being scalped, disemboweled, raped, guillotined, hanged, burned, cut into pieces.

People from all levels of society attended, and while some may have acknowledged acquaintances in the back alley where they escaped to vomit, others kept their faces covered to avoid being recognized. Not everyone wanted the world to know they had been there. Crowned heads of Europe attended as well as pimps and thieves. There were no differences between us in our appreciation of the gruesome.

World War II put an end to the Theatre du Grand Guignol. Prior to horrors of the holocaust, scenes depicted on stage were regarded as terrible flights of the imagination, but after society confronted the reality of such things, people no longer craved to see the pretend of it. The theater closed. Do you suppose the Nazis acquired some of their ideas from this theater?

My God, people, Haven't we read or seen enough going on still in the world? Do we need to see more of it? Do we need the images floating in our minds, clawing their way to the surface, perhaps to be expressed? Do we need to see our beloved Jesus brutally murdered?

95. SAVING FACE

In November of 2004, a story came out in the Miami Herald describing how there was on eBay an auction of a grilled cheese sandwich made ten years earlier, which resembled Mary, mother of Jesus. The lady selling it had taken a bite out of it back then, and as she set it down on the plate she saw Mother Mary. She decided to save face, protectively placing it in a plastic box.

The sandwich never got any mold on it, and in this one small way Mary Mother of God resembles a Hostess Twinkee. Of course we all know that Twinkees don't grow mold because they contain chemical preservatives, and I guess it would be appropriate that in the twenty-first century we would revere a chemically preserved Mary as well.

When I heard this story I searched eBay and learned that bidding had reached $22,000. Then the item was removed because of suspicion it was a hoax. When the lady reassured authorities that this was the real deal, it was placed back on auction. The second time around bidding reached $5,100, but the item then mysteriously disappeared. Nobody could bid on it any longer, but it was not in the list of items recently sold. Spooky!

I got on the phone to my secret operatives in high places, and they gave me two different stories. One was that somebody suddenly bid $100 million. If so, my guess was that the somebody was Jesus himself. He's famous for being able to motivate large sums of money at crucial times, and who could blame him? This was his mom.

The other story was that a quirky millionaire with a sense of humor paid $5,100, mainly because he was curious about what it would be like to eat the Virgin Mary. Burp.

Holy Mary, Mother of God, pray for us sinners now and at the hour of our lunch. Amen.

On November 24, 2004, the mystery was solved, and in the spirit of full public disclosure I must admit that my secret operatives in high places were completely wrong. They were nincompoops.

Heather Langan of Bloomberg News wrote the answers for us in her article describing, *$28,000 FOR MOTHER OF ALL SANDWICHES. A grilled-cheese sandwich said to bear the image of the Virgin Mary has been sold for $28,000.*

Golden Palace.com, an online casino based in St. Johns, Antigua, bought the Mother Mary sandwich and announced it would take it on tour, along with other icons, to raise money for charity.

That was that, or so I thought it would be. It turned out to be an economic windfall for many who took advantage of it. Soon there was cookware that would reproduce this "Mother of all sandwiches." By the way, would that make Jesus the brother of all sandwiches? This is just weird.

For awhile, all up and down I-5, at every truck stop you could order a Mother Mary Grilled Cheese Sandwich Special. It was a relative bargain at just $82.99 a plate. Sliced pickles and a handful of fries came with it for free, your choice of beverage.

What is it about us that we keep mixing food and religion? On March 10, 2006, a report came that the same casino had spent another $10,000 to claim a pretzel that looked like Mary holding the baby Jesus. Well, it looked like that if you really wanted it to look like that. As a matter of fact, don't all pretzels if you look at them kind of squinty-eyed?

Fearless Leader suggested we should make and sell pretzel holders for the dashboards of cars. This could become lucrative. With a good imagination you could have any pretzel-body you want, protecting your vehicle from hazards of the road. Depending on your spirituality you could put Arnold Schwarzenegger up there. Good choice! Gandhi would be too passive for today's traffic, although the Gandhi approach probably would be the best way for reacting to another's road rage. Stop eating until the other guy quits yelling at you. Then if you're hungry enough, you could eat the Gandhi pretzel. They could put one in every bag.

It could be like animal cookies only they'd be pretzels in shapes that adults enjoy, like the large bosomed silhouette lady on the mud flaps of trucks.

The Catholic Church has changed, we think. If Fearless Leader and I had been caught talking this way about these things during the Middle Ages, we would have been burned at the stake. Hey, maybe we were. That could explain all those scary dreams. Or maybe it's wish fulfillment; maybe I want to be my own pretzel.

Fearless Leader was brought up Catholic; he is Catholic. But he also is Jewish by ancestry, and this religious combination makes it tough on him for culinary decisions. It's not that he would melt if he ate meat on Friday, or if he ate ham or meat with cheese. Maybe he'd get a stomach ache from those things, but he wouldn't melt. The real problem confronting him is that because of his dietary restrictions he has less chance than the rest of us to see the Blessed Virgin in his food. He's dealing with it.

96. RAIN

Torrential rains have deluged our Puget Sound Region to the degree many of our hearts have turned somber. This morning I could hear the pounding rain on our roof over the din of shower spray, and when I looked out the window, there was my cheerfulness floating on a tiny papyrus raft down the gutter toward the storm sewer. Of course I was disappointed to see it leaving, but the deepest cut was that my cheerfulness did not appear to be as sorry as I felt about our separation. It was, you know, cheerful. So as we waved to each other I thought that really I should run out and fetch my cheerfulness even though I was still naked. But I didn't, still possessing that one fluid ounce of decorum. If I had it to do over, maybe I would have chased after it anyway. At five o'clock in the morning, any chance observer would have understood. I could have gotten away with it.

At times like this I feel with greater emotional sensitivity the up-heavals of human sentiment that otherwise might not reach my aware-ness. Have you noticed a profound up-tick in the loudness with which people around the globe profess their hatred and intolerance for one another? Is it the hatred itself that is stronger, or is it just that the sabers rattle louder?

This is not only in the obvious places such as Iraq, Iran and Pales-tine. It is everywhere. Once I thought the homogenous population of Norway, home of the Nobel Peace Prize, was immune to such rhetoric, they who withstood and prevailed against Nazi occupation during World War II, but even there racism is strong.

During the last few decades there has been a large immigration of Pakistanis into Norway, this country with a state religion of Lutheran Christianity, and also with a tremendous social conscience that has found it appropriate to spend public money also on places for Muslim wor-ship. Some Norwegians have resented this.

My eighteen year old son is my operative in that beautiful country, and he shared with me a couple of jokes that may hold interest for you. Think about the image Norwegians have about our beloved United States in this first one. When the United States blows up Pakistan, how many Pakistanis will be killed? None, because they all live in Norway.

The second is so racist it is difficult for me to write, but I will share it to make the point. What is the difference between the movie charac-ter, E.T., and a Pakistani? E.T. is better looking. E.T didn't bring his family with him. E.T. at least tried to learn the language. E.T. went home.

Then I learned that a little boy came up to my six year old daugh-ter, Stella, and poked her in the forehead. He said, "If a Chinese person pokes you in the forehead like this and tells you that you'll have bad luck, then you'll have bad luck for the rest of your life unless you beat him up before the next day."

My cheerfulness laments on its little papyrus raft in the sewer.

Is it that our hatred is worse? Or is it just that the sabers are rattled more loudly? Does it even matter which? Scientific study of psychology and sociology informs us that the sounding-off of such intolerance tends to be self-reinforcing. It grows stronger, wickeder and unabashedly com-monplace.

What is the sociological dynamic that feeds this satanic fire? Some who are religious believe in a very real battle being fought between good and evil for the souls of us all. Is there an assault on us by demons of the universe?

Is it the demon in each and every one of us that is selfish and finds its strength in teaming with others who are like us, against those who are not? Why is it that we become obsessed with the differences between peoples? Why aren't we obsessed with the similarities? Why aren't we obsessed with the need of each of us for love?

There is a battle. Is it a battle with the demon within us as well as the demon we see in others? Outwardly our country is at war with a foe called terrorism, but the real war is against racism in all its forms, even our own racism.

Agnos tapped me on the shoulder. "If we were being invaded by demons from outer space, what would they look like?"

I shrugged my shoulders.

He asked, "Have you looked in the mirror lately?"

97. HAIR

We could talk about men and middle age, about hair and lack of hair, solutions for same. Yes, why don't we do that.

On the back of the bus, Fearless Leader mentioned he had been visited by an old acquaintance who was a bit ... um, interesting. This was a fifty-five year old man who claimed not to be aging at all. He showed a photograph of his younger and balding brother and commented on how much younger he himself looked.

Fearless Leader made little headway explaining to this man that baldness doesn't really, in itself, make a man look old. Fearless Leader has better manners than to point out that this man himself had nose hairs exceeding the acceptable confines of his nostrils. Yes, you look young Mr. Nose hair man.

One characteristic of middle aged men is that we tend to have too little hair where we want it and too much hair where we don't want it. Include our ears on that. Nasal hair trimmers are great until the batteries slow down or the blades get dull, and the whirling little bastards pull the hairs out fifteen at a time. It can bring tears to your eyes.

So Fearless Leader and I got the idea for nasal hair transplants. A good plastic surgeon could take the hairs from where we don't want them in our noses, and put them where we do want them, on our scalps. If the left nose hairs get put on the left scalp and the right hairs on the right, then the procedure also provides a permanent, natural part. A bad surgeon would get the sides mixed up, and a guy's hairstyling always would be a mess.

Then one night my son, Christoffer, pointed out to me that in Tokyo people can purchase toupees for their dogs. Why on Earth would they want to do that? Maybe so that their dogs can resemble Donald Trump whose natural hair only looks like a toupee. Then, while Japanese dogs are on a walk, they can bark at each other, saying in dogspeak, "You're fired."

One last thing about hair. I remember a cosmetologist, a beautician, who wanted to be a cosmologist, a scientific philosopher who thinks about the universe as an ordered whole. His name was Cosmo. His favorite cosmologist was Carl Sagan who used to talk about "billions and billions of stars." While cutting my hair Cosmo would do Carl Sagan impersonations, saying things like, "billions and billions of hairs."

Finally I had to give up Cosmo. There's only so much of that I could take. "Billions and billions of hairs," on my head. "Billions and billions of hairs," on the floor. "Billions and billions of hairs," in my nose. Enough!

98. GOD MADE ME DO IT

On October 19, 2004, the Boston Red Sox historically erased an earlier three to zip deficit against the New York Yankees. Pitcher Curt Schilling said it had been God out there pitching, not him. Accepting this as a frank statement of humility, I've got to respond that God has some very nice pitches in his repertoire, and his control is magnificent. You would expect nothing less from the Grand Architect of the Universe.

One of my secret operatives in high places, this time the high place being the upper deck along first base line, told me he was pretty sure that it was not God out there pitching that night. He said he saw God being a spectator. He saw God in line for a brew and some garlic fries. I asked if he was sure it was God, and he said, "Yeah, it was Him alright. I know."

So many people these days know God. They know what's inside the mind of God. Did you hear or read that some Muslims in the Middle East had been praying for the hurricanes that devastated Florida during the summer of 2004? They seemed to be pretty deep into the mind of God. Since Florida was the deciding state in the 2000 presidential elections, maybe the Muslim God wanted to pay them back. Wait. I thought the Muslim God was the same God as the Christian God. There's only one God, right? Bush talks with God.

This whole thing makes God look indecisive. First one way, then another. He's a flip-flopper.

Is God a Bo-sox fan? I venture to say that with this flip-flopping, probably he is neutral on the outcome of sporting contests. He just likes us all to give it our best. That's part of the mystery of God and his ways. God can have it both ways. He can eat his cake and have it too. It must be nice to be God.

To tell you the truth, it irritates Agnos when people claim to know the mind of God. He likes the idea of people working as vessels of God's love for man, and he also likes it when they keep quiet about it. God's own attention should be reward enough. But that's just him.

It's the same as whenever somebody receives a huge acclaim. So often they say that they are "humbled" by the honor. Sure I believe that; don't I? Agnos says, "No."

Back on October 20, 2004, in the series deciding finale between Boston and New York, I remember wondering who would be the vessel through whom God would pitch that night. I wanted it to be Wakefield because I liked God's knuckle ball. It wasn't, but the Sox won anyway.

99. MARY JUANA

At the top of the first page of the Seattle Post Intelligencer on April 21, 2006, the headline read: *FDA rejects medicinal use of marijuana. Agency contradicts scientists, jumps into a political struggle.* Then the article went on and on and on, and in typical frustrating fashion it required effort and search to find anything to substantiate legitimate claims why marijuana should be rejected. In my search of the article, these were the two reasons: Marijuana hasn't been shown to be of any use, and the second was like the domino theory used back in the sixties to justify the Viet Nam War. Then it was to stop communism from spreading. Now it is to stop patients from smoking marijuana because the next thing you know they'll want methamphetamine.

Huh?

What's so bad about Mary Juana? Dope smoking minds want to know.

For years doctors have hinted quietly to our patients that they may possibly want to try smoking marijuana, always including the qualifier, "If you tell anybody I told you this, I'll deny I ever met you."

Marijuana probably is the most effective medicine we have to reduce muscle spasms in persons with multiple sclerosis or spinal cord injury. It is a wonderful medicine to improve the appetite and reduce the nausea of chemotherapy patients and others. It often reduces nerve pain that responds poorly to the opioids, those narcotic medicines like oxycodone or morphine.

In 1998, voters in the state of Washington approved an initiative that legalized medical marijuana here. Eleven states have legalized this drug.

U.S. Representative Mark Souder, a Republican from the state of Indiana, said he believed that efforts to legalize medicinal uses of marijuana are "a front" for efforts to legalize all uses of marijuana.

You may ask yourself, "So what? So what if people happen to use it recreationally? They did back in the thirties during the years of U.S. prohibition of alcohol, and it seemed to make the Great Depression a little happier, didn't it?"

As a little aside, do you remember who really did well during that age of not being able to buy legal alcohol? Why yes of course! It was the bootlegger gangsters. What great stories we have now to tell about Al Capone the crook, Elliott Ness the cop, and all those other guys.

When I think about legalized recreational use of marijuana, I worry just a little about what kind of pizzas I'll have to eat in the future. Awhile ago my wife and I were certain we somehow had been afflicted with bad pizza karma. Every time we got a pizza delivered to our house, it was the wrong pizza or the toppings had all slid to one side. So one evening we decided to go out to a pizza restaurant, and I remember waiting for about fifty minutes with my irritation growing about how long the kitchen was taking. Finally I returned to the counter and asked why our order was taking so long. They answered, "What order?" I'm fairly certain that for awhile every pizza cook in our vicinity was stoned on marijuana. This is the hideous and scary truth about Mary Juana.

Also there's the problem of driving. When I was in medical school I heard this story about a friend of a friend who was stopped by the police on the interstate highway. Through the rolled down window the officer seemed to be wearing a contemptuous face. "Do you know how fast you were driving?"

The driver really had no idea at all. "Seventy miles an hour?" he asked sheepishly.

The policeman just stared at him.

"Eighty miles an hour?"

The officer shouted, "You were going five miles per hour."

Enough of that story.

This most recent statement by the FDA contradicted a 1999 review by the Institute of Medicine, a division of the National Academy of Sciences, which found marijuana to be moderately well suited for particular conditions such as chemotherapy induced nausea and vomiting, and AIDS wasting. Dr. John Benson, co-chairman of the Institute of Medicine committee that examined the research, said that the federal government "loves to ignore our report."

Dr. Jerry Avorn, a professor at Harvard Medical School said, "This is yet another example of the FDA making pronouncements that seem to be driven more by ideology than by science." I wonder. I wonder.

I say, "I wonder about that. Ideology? Or is it that somebody is paying somebody else to keep this drug illegal because somebody will lose a lot of big business profits if this drug goes legal. Oh, excuse me. I don't know that such suspicions have any credibility at all. I just can't stop thinking about Al Capone and Elliott Ness."

What about the effectiveness of this drug? Government approved studies have allowed use only of the government approved marijuana that is grown in Mississippi, but critics have described that crop as having poor quality. Professor Ash Roachenbong of Nofoolin U. said, "You see there are different species of plants. There is Mary Juana, and then there is this government crap, oops I mean crop, that we call Marita Juanita. Serious patients and researchers are saying, 'We don't need no scrawny governmental Marita Juanita.' That's the problem in a nutshell. Here, would you like some pistachios?"

So now I guess I'll tell my patients that if marijuana does become legal, don't buy the Federal brand. My patients will have better results if they purchase their medicine from Gus, the guy who lives two blocks down the street in the house where the lawn gets mowed only once a year.

FIFTEEN

Nature

100. MOUNT RAINIER

My sons and I, and our friend Jack, enjoy our annual trek on Mount Rainier along the skyline trail at Paradise. It may be the one day I feel most alive. The awesome grandeur of this great mountain used to be startling, but although its magnificence endures, that is not what now surprises me. I have come to expect it, and so the mountain's majesty has become familiar, a part of me. What once seemed proof of God's existence now has become a meaningful, memorable part of who I am.

The little things surprise me. Yesterday I was delighted that glacial melt ran directly down one of the paths, and we walked a short distance in the stream bed. The water was no more than a quarter inch deep, so we didn't get wet. It was just different, and in a small, irregular way, supremely satisfying.

People surprise me always, on and off the mountain.

Yesterday we had luck with animals. Marmots whistled at us, and we didn't even have to show our legs; good thing for me. One fat, lazy marmot regarded the on-path route easier than the natural way, and it waddled past us within touching distance.

At Panorama Point, chipmunks as tame as household pets coerce visitors to feed them nuts, but we really mustn't. They may have peanut allergies.

This annual Mount Rainier tradition has its smaller associated traditions. On our drive to the mountain we always stop at the same gas station in Ashford to use the bathroom and to purchase caffeinated pop. There's a specific spot along the early trail where we stop to catch our breath, and we make sounds like we're burping and farting. About an hour or so into our hike we stop and eat a Hostess Twinkie. A year ago my sons and Jack started a new tradition for which I am truly grateful. It's called *stop and wait for Dad to catch up*. Thank you boys.

Now whenever I eat a Twinkie I think about Mother Mary because like a Mother Mary grilled cheese sandwich on white bread, Twinkies never spoil. So there I was hiking up the trail, every now and then looking ahead to see the rest of my party, fuzzy in the distance, and I was thinking about Mother Mary. I asked myself if Mother Mary might ever have been reincarnated. Does God decide to retire some souls from reincarnation, just like sports teams retire the numbers of their favorite superstars? That made sense to me as I struggled up the mountain with pain in my legs and with my heart racing. I thought about my favorite numbers. Forty-two tops my list now for awhile, Jackie Robinson, 42.

The mountain gradually has become more of a challenge for me. It is a beloved quest of which I'll never let go. Yesterday I told Christoffer and Joshua that in ten or twenty years they will be carrying me up the mountain on a stretcher. They thought I was kidding, and that's okay. Little by little, step by step, the sincerity of my request will sink in.

101. KATRINA

Once I named a pet catfish Katrina, so to me that seemed an appropriate name for a storm that demolished a city famous for serving Cajun style, blackened relatives of my pet who itself died a natural death and got thrown into the garbage. I had no problem with the naming of this storm.

As this behemoth pounded the gulf coast my curiosity was aroused by the journalistic use of anthropomorphic terms. Writers ascribed to this awful and awesome event the human emotions of fury and wrath. This irritated me at first because I value accurate use of our versatile language, and this storm was not a creature of wrath or fury. Chalk those words up to easy and unskilled poetic license.

My irritation increased when I read a newspaper article about a far right wing group claiming this storm was a torrent sent by God to punish the debauchery of New Orleans. Without using such fancy diction this group ascribed to the storm a human emotion of moral indignation and gave it empowerment by a cruel Almighty.

The article was written by a left wing journalist who saved me from my own moral indignation by pointing out that the storm destroyed Trent Lott's house as well. The writer's sarcastic perspective therefore was that this hurricane was God's wrath directed at Trent Lott's house. Everything else was collateral damage. God needed smart bombs, like the U.S. military. He needed the capability for *surgical strikes* in his outpourings of rage against us inadequate and flawed creatures of his own making. The clumsy breadth of this destructive stroke reminded us that we indeed were made in his image.

I was impressed also by our need and ability to blame. This natural catastrophe came without an evil chaperon. There was no Osama Bin Laden. We had to be more creative, but we found culprits. Left wing editorials pointed out that our federal administration cut funding for the building of the New Orleans levee. In the September 2nd issue of the Wall Street Journal, page B2, was an article describing the scrutiny applied after the levee failure, to the Army Corps of Engineers, for having substituted a less expensive and less sound architectural design for the building of part of it. Left wingers also blamed President Bush for decisions ignoring the implications of global warming, blaming him for the excessive warmth of gulf waters that fed this hurricane to its vastly swelled and enormous proportion.

My response to these accusations simply was that global warming has been the product of decades, and decisions get made without the benefit of prophetic visions of the future.

Starving victims were criticized for looting stores for food and water, blamed for violence against each other. In our caring smugness we purported that if we were put into the same circumstances we would have behaved better. Victims were blamed even for having settled foolishly in such a dangerous place. They had asked for disaster.

Such capacity to blame is distinctly human.

Along with others I wondered about the grievously slow delivery of help.

We looked with horrified fascination at the pictures and videos, listened attentively to the reports of sorrow. For awhile I thought about writing an article entitled *The Allure of Hell,* but then DK from the Heartland sent me a few sayings from the Gospel of Thomas. No, you won't find these in your Bible. They aren't there. They were perhaps too controversial, too inexplicable for the early Church that collated the Bible under the heavy handed influence of Constantine.

I read them, and I especially liked saying 72, in which a man wanted Jesus to intercede in a quarrel he was having with his brothers. *"Tell my brothers to divide my father's possessions with me."* Jesus answered, *"Mister, who made me a divider?"* He turned to his disciples and said to them, *"I'm not a divider, am I?"* What was Jesus saying about sharing? What was he saying about envy? What was he saying about how the truthful meaning of our lives is not tied to material things?

I was reminded about how we are all one, and I returned once again to read John 17:21-23, in which Jesus prays *that all of them may be one, Father, just as you are in me and I am in you. May they also be in us so that the world may believe that you have sent me. I have given them the glory that you gave me, that they may be one as we are one: I in them and you in me. May they be brought to complete unity to let the world know that you sent me and have loved them even as you have loved me.*

When we looked at the scenes of the storm's destruction, even the sorrow and even the violence, we observed what heaven can be. If you ran from it and hid, you took yourself out of the kingdom. But if you now involve yourself with everything that is humanity, whether it is good or bad, happy or sorrowful, then you knock at the door that will open for you.

Our fascination with the horrific tales of Katrina should not be called the allure of hell. It is the allure of Father's kingdom. It is humanity, within which we want to be included.

Once again I present you the words of John Donne: *No man is an island, entire of itself; every man is a piece of the continent, a part of the main; if a clod be washed away by the sea, Europe is the less, as well as if a promontory were, as well as if a manor of thy friend's or of thine own were; any man's death diminishes me, because I am involved in mankind; and therefore never send to know for whom the bell tolls; it tolls for thee.*

102. METAPHYSICAL NONSENSE

Often ideas come to me from many different and widespread places. They coalesce and congeal in my mind like a blood clot on my prefrontal cortex. Then I get excited and have to run to the computer to share them.

I was reminded of this method of creativity by the wonderful artistic imagination of my then five year old daughter, Stella, who showed me her many drawings. One picture was a circle with nine different legs sticking out of it in all directions, every leg wearing a shoe. "That's the world with many feet," she explained. She drew a picture of many shoes tangled together by their laces. Another was a picture of a turtle wearing a wig. Another was a giant watching his newly washed shirt drying on a clothesline. My imagination is nothing compared to hers.

Maybe you've become bored with the craziness of how people explain the occurrences of super-killer hurricanes, but I'm still intrigued, and if I continue to find humor in the craziness of the imagined things some of us believe, hopefully you'll be entertained. I heard a new one.

The idea started reasonably enough, and interestingly. The lady told me that hurricanes will be getting stronger and stronger not because of global warming and the increasing temperature of gulf waters, but rather because of the cyclical pattern and currently increasing wobble of the Earth's rotation on a cosmologic scale. Wow! This was interesting.

I told her that I had read before about this wobble, but I never had heard it linked to the production of more powerful hurricanes. She seemed to miss the question implied by that, and told me something else instead.

"Yes," she said, "and God doesn't protect us from these natural events anymore like he used to."

I asked, "So you don't think God cruelly punishes us with these hurricanes, but he's decided to let us experience the consequence of these natural events."

"That's right."

You would have been proud of the way I didn't even blink. I did not let her notice the inflamed appearance of my consciousness that she had slapped. What I said was, "At least that is not cruel," when what I was thinking was that here we had a passive-aggressive cruelty attributed to our hero in the heavens. Mercy me!

First God made us in his image, and then we made him in our image. This is spiritual and metaphysical give and take. If you're not amused by this, it is either because you're bored or enraged. Either way I'm now going to pull out of my hat some ideas of a widely different sort.

As I was going to the bathroom I noticed urine dried on the toilet, and I began to think about how animals mark their territory with urine. At least dogs do. On a primitive level maybe that is what people do when we spray a bit wide of the target. We are marking the toilet seat as our territory, and it works. People won't sit there until Lysol is applied. The toilet is ours until then. Some of us post-void-dribblers also lay claim to our underpants and our pajamas this way. Yes they are ours for good after we do that. Nobody else wants them.

Does God mark his territory? Please take me seriously here. We really don't know what divine pee would look like, do we? All we know or think we know is that there would be a lot of it, and it would happen with great force. Ladies and gentlemen, I present to you the metaphysical concept of God marking the United States' gulf coast as his territory. There must be something about it that he likes.

You may think this is blasphemous, but you'd be mistaken. I'm not making fun of the Grand Master. I'm making fun of us. We're a

hoot. What I'm saying is no more crazy, no more insulting or disre-
spectful than the crap of people saying God either directly or passive-
aggressively participates in the use of natural forces to punish. Oh,
speaking of crap, I'm pretty sure dogs don't use that form of expression
as a way of marking territory. Thank you, God.

103. LOGO CHANGE

Our nation is polarized now in so many different ways, blue-red,
right-left ... yes that is the one way we are so very polarized that it
seems like many ways. For awhile it seemed that if such a referendum
were legal, the West (left) coast of the United States, along with the
upper Midwest and North-eastern states, would be willing to secede
from the union, sort of a reverse Civil War scenario. Since Idaho, Mon-
tana and the Dakotas separate the West from its political simpaticos in
other parts of the nation, maybe the West would have to be its own
separate country, Washoregofornia, or Califoregington. Those are mouth-
fuls. Maybe secessionists could satisfy themselves with a simpler name,
like Calorietown. That makes a pleasing image.

Or maybe Canada could annex these secessionist states. It would
embarrass Canada, put them into an awkward position, but they would
understand. That would keep the blue states united, The United Blue
States of Canada.

The day I wrote those above two paragraphs and sent them out
over the internet, was the day my computer started behaving irascibly,
and I just knew I'd been bugged and scrutinized by powers that be. It's
a good thing I'd been clean as a whistle. As a matter of fact I whistled a lot
then and still do. The sound bothers me when I walk in the wind. Doctors
have no idea how to help me get rid of it. Sometimes it is a buzzing noise
like when we were kids and blew across a blade of quack grass held
taught between our thumbs. People get annoyed with me when I make
those sounds, but I can't help it. It's a lot like when I write.

Truth be told, there are no blue and red states. We have various
shades of purple, some more violet and others maroon. Burgundy is a
lovely color, but politically I'd have a hard time living there.

Maybe it's time for Democrats and Republicans to change their
logos. Elephants and donkeys don't any longer seem to fit the bitterness of our passions. I read a story about an event in nature that may
represent better the way we are. In Florida over the years, many people
have released pet pythons into the Everglades. Naturalists have expressed
concern that the python may threaten the role of alligator as the un-
challenged king of the food chain. A thirteen foot python managed to

swallow a six foot alligator, whole. But the python unknowingly had failed to kill the alligator first, and the alligator clawed its way out of the snake. I believe both animals died.

Republicans and Democrats may decide who is going to be the alligator and who will be the python. One of them of course represents the long established predator, and the other represents the alien challenger to the throne of predation. The unavoidable allegorical symbolism is that in the end, both animals die. Maybe that's how it should be. Maybe then the gentle manatee can be king of the Everglades and live in peace … except for the motor boat propellers tearing them apart. Maybe the manatee and motor boat could be our logos? No, I don't think we should go with those.

104. WEEDS I HAVE KNOWN AND LOVED

I love Spring and Summer, but they don't love me. More specifically, Spring and Summer in Seattle don't love me. I never had allergies until I moved here, and now my life is lived in episodes separated by sneezing. It's like living in a television program that has bad commercials. I know of a guy who moved away because of the allergies. He told me that everybody has allergies in Seattle, and his hypothesis has yet to be disproved.

It's not just the allergies. It also is the impossible challenge of yard maintenance for the average working person. If you have time it's different, but I don't have time. Spring is filled with rain, and if the day or two of sunshine each week never land on a weekend, the grass in the yard gets longer; the weeds in the garden get uglier. Mine have started smoking cigarettes and whistle at my wife when she walks by. This is a problem.

I've kept up with the front yard because it's small. My back yard looks like a meadow surrounded by a jungle, no exaggeration.

This brings me to a digression about Seattle's nick-name, Emerald City. Many of us here are distressed with this name. It's way too Dorothy and Toto. We used to be called Jet City, and that was okay when Boeing was the only dominating industry here. But Boeing management moved to Chicago, and Seattle has matured. It's home to Microsoft, Weyerhaeuser and Starbucks. It is the birthplace of grunge music, Heart, Pearl Jam, Nirvana, Jimi Hendrix. We've got it together here. So we can't fall back to the good old name of Jet City. It no longer fits.

Fearless Leader has told me that Anchorage, Alaska, "has a back yard feel to it. Seattle is like a front yard." I like that name. Seattle, Front Yard of the Northwest. I'm the only one I know who likes it.

So my own front yard is like Seattle, and my back yard is like ... well, more like the Olympic peninsula in Washington State. This and Vancouver are the location of the world's only temperate rain forest. That's what my back yard looks like.

In my front yard I dig out weeds with a dull hunting knife, works like a charm. In the back yard I need a spade and sometimes a pick axe. Some weeds are taller than my eleven year old son. What am I saying? They're taller than I am. The neighborhood kids come over to watch. They bring lunches, and every time I bring down a weed they shout, "Timber!"

There is a vigorous wood behind our house, and it constantly invades my yard. This is war. Insurgents mainly are maple and alder trees, black berries, horse tails, thistles and wild peas.

I wrote this piece on the first day of the Memorial Day weekend, a time when we remember those who have died in wars, when we also remember others we have loved. There are those people in my life I miss, and my love and memories attend them. In the lightness and honesty of this article, however, it also is a weekend for memory of the very personal encounters I have had in dispatching weeds I have known and loved.

105. KAPE

My good friend Tom Sproger wrote to me:

I have the answers to your weed problem. You too can be weed free. Join KAPE today! KAPE stands for Kill 'em And Pave 'Em. I am thinking of starting a new chapter of KAPE in Seattle, and you are invited to become a member. The first fifty to join get free decoder rings.

There are two parts to our KAPE answer to your weedie woes. The first is chemicals. Commit weedicide. Better living through chemistry. Kill them suckers dead. Oh I know, the Greenies and doctors warn us about environmental and health concerns using chemicals, about lung disease, brain damage (too late already) and things too fierce to mention, but we don't let them scare us. Our motto is, *Let us spray*. Think of how you can rid yourself of those pesky weeds once and for all, and your neighbors too if you aren't careful to guard against overspray.

The second step is concrete. Yes, that's right, good old Portland Cement or any brand of your choosing. First you kill the weeds. Then you pave over them. Add to the décor with green indoor-outdoor carpeting or green paint. You'll never have to pull a weed or mow your lawn again.

In fact, not only is KAPE a social organization, but there is talk among members, both of them, of starting a political party. Our campaign for the next election would be based on the KAPE anti-weed platform. KAPE would field an array of candidates who advocate killing weeds. After all, as our leader often has said, "Weeds don't vote; weed pullers do." Don't you just love progress?

106. RESPONSE TO KAPE

I was eager as can be when you wrote me about KAPE. I was excited about becoming a member, but just as I was about to put into the mailbox my completed application form, a worry suddenly came to mind. Isn't this just exactly what the weed insurgents want? Isn't this the ultimate objective of botanic terrorists, to corrupt our thinking so much that we become willing to forfeit our rights and the peaceful democracy of our back yards, to make them into cold, hard police states?

We must ask ourselves if this is the future we want for our children. We have lived in pluralistic back yard societies where peaceful plants have the right to life, liberty and the pursuit of happiness. When evil, punk weeds start threatening us with suicide buddings, yes we often feel a gut instinct just to level the land, to flatten it and make it a lifeless wasteland. But we must remember not all plants in the back yard are bad. Some contribute productively to the welfare of society. We must protect the civil rights of rhododendrons, azaleas, lilies, hydrangeas and the like.

But I do appreciate your letter, and thank you for your comments. There's one last thing. Could you please tell me a little bit more about the decoder ring?

107. NORTHERN GREENY

My good friend DK from the heartland wrote.

When I read about the concrete lawn, I hoped the letter was in jest. Yes, you can call me a green. Before all grass lawns are eliminated, I would need to express my viewpoint. Weeds are okay. Just do your best to keep them short. Maybe a tiny squirt of weed killer will do. Just because many will buckle to the fashion setters and will use stronger and stronger pesticides, weed killers and fertilizers in order to comply with the community standard, doesn't mean we have to yield to the onerous pressure that our lawns need to be immaculate. We don't need to have our yards as short or weed free as the golf greens demanded by the PGA committee.

If we lose our diversity this world will die. We have enough parking lots without making our yards the same. Why should one care what others think of one's yard, house, children, spouse, clothes, looks, manners, athletic abilities, children's athletic abilities, smarts, wit, job performance, money making abilities, sexiness, love making abilities, coolness, composure, religious preferences, or any trait or ability?

I know. I know. I buckle too. I live in a neighborhood that has an Association. I think it is relatively easy to be in violation of the Association. My son now has the lawn mowing responsibilities (lucky me), and last year August-September he let the grass grow for about three or four weeks. Now I'm talking about Minnesota climate. The weather was cooler, the days shorter, so the grass was growing slowly. It wasn't too long by my standard. I received a letter that we were in violation of the Association rules.

It didn't help my cause that the neighbor in front of me was the ex-secretary and the neighbor behind me was the ex-president. They might have had it in for me for a number of years. My lawn maintenance could be called borderline. As Peter Pan told Captain Hook, "You're next Hook! This time you've gone too far!" Last year I guess I went too far. I shouldn't thumb my nose at the Association.

I buckled under the pressure and addressed all the violations in one weekend; call me a chicken. But I didn't like it, and I do worry that our Mother Earth is becoming a cesspool of chemicals. It is bound to lead to our eventual destruction; I have no doubts.

By the way, in the end the weeds will win. Our concrete cities will die and Nature will take over. It's happened before to many civilizations and will happen again.

108. RESPONSE TO GREENY

I'm sure you are right. An environmentally friendly herbicide is white vinegar applied on a hot, sunny day. The other day I was trying to do this, and one of the weeds grabbed a shovel out of my hand and swung it at me. When I ducked, the weed squirted me in the face with my own bottle of white vinegar. They're taking over alright. We must brace ourselves.

109. FROGS

At our house there are frogs. They are an early and certain sign of Spring, beginning earnestly their noisy croaking on March first, every year like clockwork. The evening din grows louder for weeks before subsiding. Still in May we are in the midst of choruses.

Out of the wetlands they venture up into our yard, and early in the Spring they are fairly large, about the size of my thumb. They are cute unless there are four of five of them clinging to the front door. Once one got into the house, and it took us several days to discover what was making the intermittent noise in our living room. It was under the moss of a potted plant.

I think these are frog scouts, and the assertive behavior is a sales ploy. They sell frog scout cookies. These tiny wafers are not so delectable, made with fly parts and mosquito larvae. The cookies are nicely crisp, but don't chew them; you'll gag. They are small enough you can swallow them whole, and that's the way to do it.

I hope the money I have paid for frog scout cookies has gone to a good cause, but I doubt it. Later in the summer our yard gets assaulted by tiny little frogs less than the size of a dime, hundreds of them. They are the newly born. I'm certain that the frog scout proceeds went to pay for little frog motel rooms.

One way not to feel guilty for refusing to purchase a few boxes of frog scout cookies is to give generously to some other charity. It's just like with people. Instead of giving fifty cents to a bum who likely will buy liquor with it, make sure to give money to a food bank or the United Way or Doctors Without Borders, or some other notable charity.

In the case of frogs, I tell them that I have stopped washing my car in the drive way, so no detergent gets into the storm water drained into their ponds. Detergent would ruin their protective slime layer. When I explain this to them they look puzzled, but that's okay. It helps me to feel better about not buying frog scout cookies, and that's what matters to me.

110. JUST A BLUR

I wore my glasses to work today, first time in months. I think it was because I wanted to see the slide show at grand rounds. It wasn't because I wanted to make a fashion statement. Actually I think mostly I wore them because I was tired of them staring back at me from the kitchen counter.

Einstein's theory of relativity tells us that the speed of time plus the speed of movement always equals the speed of light. That means that when you go really fast, time for you goes slower, but you don't notice it as much as others. As a matter of fact you may even think you are staying still and all those others are moving really fast. Maybe to you it looks like their time has slowed down. They are staying young while you are getting old. So everybody disagrees. Who's correct? That's relative. I think it has to do with gravity. Maybe it has to do with who's better grounded.

I also have a theory about the speed of time, and it has to do with being over forty years old. Everybody says that the older we get, time seems to pass by faster and faster. I don't believe this has to do with our moving slower and slower through space, even though admittedly we do move slower and slower through space when we're past the age of forty.

Very honestly and truly this has been studied, although I'm sorry I don't remember and can't tell you in which journal I read this. In the study they put older people and younger people in rooms devoid of any clue to the passage of time. No windows, no clocks, no radio, no television. I think they gave them a package of potato chips and a game of monopoly. Participants were asked to comment on how much time they thought elapsed.

The older people thought time was going faster than the younger ones. Maybe the younger people were more bored than their elders. In the monopoly games the older people more often owned Boardwalk, and the younger people more often did the bored walk. Next time they do this study they should use electronic games.

There's another explanation. As we get older any segment of time, such as an hour or a day, is a smaller percentage of our entire life, so it seems shorter. Time seems to go by faster.

It was not until I was over forty that my vision started to dwindle. Finally at about 46 I yielded to my need for glasses. Ophthalmologists explain that presbyopia has to do with thickening and stiffening of the lens, and doesn't that sound like scientific jibber-jabber?

What really happens is that time goes faster and faster as we get older, and by our late forties everything is flying past so rapidly it's all just a blur.

111. IN MY GARAGE

There are animals in my garage. This discovery was made while I was cleaning the place, spiffing it up for a garage sale. Not mammals, thank God, no, but the bugs have organized and aren't behaving like they used to. They've been reading either the United States Constitution or the Communist Manifesto, one or the other.

We hadn't heard the music earlier, mainly because bug bugles are so tiny, but when you get close to them you can hear it. I told friends about this, and they snooted at me, "Bugs don't play musical instruments." That's how I came to realize the animals in my garage have gotten out of hand.

They've organized into orderly little militias, training together in groups, but marching has been a problem. Some of the bugs have eight legs and some of the bugs have six legs, and so they struggle with staying in step with each other. They yell a lot. Sometimes it isn't so quiet in the garage, and it surprises me we haven't noticed it sooner. Maybe the racket of our own kids just drowns it out. Yes that's it.

One of these days the bugs may split, the sixes going one way and the eights going another, and they're going to fight. I just know this is going to happen. There will be a bug Armageddon in my garage. Maybe the water heater will explode.

Smart money is on the eights to win. Have you seen them? It's not just their eight legs. They also have eight eyes and eight ugly tattoos that say, *BORN TO DIE*. They're a scary bunch.

The other day I swept many of them out of the garage, and a short time later there was a bug up on a soap box preaching that God destroyed their cities because of their bug-sinfulness. Really and truly, he was up on a soap box, Tide with Downy mixed in. He was up there preaching away, and it pissed me off, so I stepped on him.

What worries me the most is the bug air force. Their planes have yellow and black stripes, and they're irritable little shits. One day they were building a tiny hangar on the underside of a piece of trim wood just outside the garage door, and I decided it didn't belong there. So I knocked it down with a broom. Negligently I failed to warn my Joshua about this, and he got stung three times. Then, as I wanted to make at least something educational out of this experience, I told Josh, "See, they won't sting you unless you bother them."

I found their bug-science reading room. This miniscule library was in a turned over flower pot. Under it I found dozens of stacks of little tiny pages. There was an old ant sitting on a bottle cap with four of its legs crossed, and with the other two it was holding what looked like the tiniest newspaper you can imagine. It was too small for me to read, especially in the darkness of the garage, so I took this newspaper reading ant out into the sunlight and read the newspaper headlines with a magnifying glass. I read, *We've Had Enough of the Evil Giant Sticking His Nose Where It Doesn't Belong.* I guess it's good for a guy to know where he stands on any given issue.

So I was there with the magnifying glass a little too long, and the ant with his newspaper kind of burned up. Just then I saw a person's shadow, and I looked to see the neighbor lady. She studied me for a moment and shook her head. Sometimes it is clear that no matter what you say to explain, you'll just dig a deeper hole for yourself. At these times it's better just to shut up.

112. FLAME RETARDANT FISH

There was an article in the Seattle Post Intelligencer about the unacceptably high levels of flame retardant chemicals in the fish of Lake Washington, the hazardous waste likely having got there from treated and trashed furniture I suppose, and although biologists reported this as undesirable, the fish weren't complaining. Maybe they thought it would mean fewer fishermen angling for their dinners.

It might go the other way, although you couldn't say the idea would backfire on the fish. They're flame retardant. People may decide there could be benefit from eating such fish. Preparing the fish for dinner is only a small task. Of course you can't seer them on the grill, but they still can be baked or boiled or steamed.

The study hasn't been done yet, but eating such fish may reduce the incidence of spontaneous human combustion. Firemen may make a regular diet of them for protection on the job.

Most interesting to me has been an upstart punk cult that eats flame retardant fish not just on Fridays but on every day of the week. The idea is to rob the devil of a good time. Let's say you go to hell, but you can't really burn because you've become flame retardant. Of course it would be quite boring standing around in the flames for all eternity. And even though you wouldn't burn, it still would be hot as a kiln. But you know; it's a dry kind of heat.

SIXTEEN

Precessions

113. RESURRECTION

This short conversation happened when Joshua was nine and Stella was four, right after we had recited the Apostle's Creed at bedtime.

Dad: Do you know what we mean when we say resurrection of the body? It's the most incredible thing in Christianity.

Joshua: It means that after Jesus died, he came back to life again.

Dad: That's right, and do you know what's even more incredible than that? After you die, you will come back to life too.

Stella: How does Jesus do that, Dad?

Dad: We don't know, Stella, but he does.

Stella: Maybe Jesus is a zombie.

114. PRECESSIONS

The word *precessions* has three meanings, all of them applicable here. It means activities that precede the main event. This chapter will scrape your skin a little in preparation for the next chapter, *Provocations.*

The word *precession* also is a term in the science of physics, having to do with the slow movement in circles of the axis of a spinning body. For example the earth's axis does not remain resolutely stable. The poles of its axis move in a circle. You have seen this also with a spinning top, its axis wobbling ever more as the rate of spin slows. In this and the next chapter I will point out how Christian beliefs spin about an axis that wobbles and therefore cannot be called resolute. This is not a criticism of God or of Jesus or of God's or Jesus' will. This is a heartfelt criticism of Christian beliefs. As a Christian myself, I find it appropriate and necessary to point this out to my fellows. Also, and you may scoff at this if you like, God told me to do it. Agnos is scoffing.

The word *precession* also is found in the astronomical term *precession of the equinoxes*. This refers to the slow westward migration of the earth's rotation, meaning that exactly one year ago this moment, you were a little farther east than you are now. It takes 26,000 years for the earth's rotation to spin, in this way, backward an entire day. Change, we never know quite what to do about it. Also, it is this meaning that ties the word *precession* to Easter, which is assigned to the first Sunday following the first full moon after the Spring equinox.

Agnos said, "You're taking a word that's pretty much a technical term used by physicists, and you're applying it to your spiritual argument."

"Yes, I guess I am."

"You're twisting the meanings a little. Aren't you sort of forcing the metaphors?" He smiled. "I hate to do this to you, but I've found a fourth meaning for you. *Precession of the perihelion* refers to the effect of the sun's gravity to twist space and hence the orbit of planets. This effect on Mercury's orbit was one of the ways used to confirm Einstein's theory of general relativity. So maybe you're using that meaning too, twisting. Aren't you twisting meanings?"

"Maybe a better way of looking at it is to ponder what it is that twists the trajectory of our own lives. What is the massive gravity that changes the shape of the time and space through which we as souls travel, which pushes each and every one of us off balance? I like that meaning. We cannot confidently continue, passively to follow an orbit we might have thought was clearly carved out for us. The enormous force of that nucleus, around which everything else gets busy, pushes us in directions different from what we expected. If there is a benevolent God, won't he try to shake you loose from blind, unthinking and hurtful piety for a mistaken belief?"

115. PALM SUNDAY

Palm Sunday launches the holiest week of the Christian year, one that is harrowing for me and deep with spiritual meaning different than what you're used to hearing from the usual Christian crowd. During this week I become absorbed with the question of whether Jesus needed to die to save our sins, and to me the answer comes back, no. And I listen to the arguments of fellow Christians, and they ring hollow for me, and many of them sound ignorant. Most Christians talk about Atonement but have no clue about the problems associated with that concept and justifying Jesus' death to skeptics like me. So I have had to find my own way, helped by others, helped by Agnos. In this and the next chapter, *Provocations,* you will read a different story, one of Jesus the courageous hero rather than Jesus the sacrificial lamb. This is merely an alternative. I expect you to believe honestly what you believe.

We assume that God is good and loving, but in this world of his making there are evil and hatred as well.

We assume that we are here to learn or nurture our spiritual essence, but maybe life is simpler than that. Maybe we are here to experience, whether or not we learn.

One thing about the agnostic lynchpins of my belief, consistent with modern physics as well as with the Gospels of John and Thomas, is that we do not escape from the lives of other people. I am Thomas the physician and amateur theologian. I am less aware during this particular life time that I also am the mother caught in the genocide of Darfur, bound fast and forced to watch as her children were thrown into boiling water. I am the assholes who perpetrated this horror.

And in this holy week of Christianity, I am the Roman soldier pounding nails into the hands and feet of Jesus. I am that part of Jesus that God has made me, right now dying on the cross.

116. FOR I DID NOT EXIST

Through no craving or effort of my own,
for I did not exist,
I was made.
I spend my days searching
for a reason
which I'm told may or may not be.
Those shallow of spirit
tell me I must believe
this way or that way.
They disturb my quest
by filling my mind with answers
that are not answers.
But they are part
of the answer,
and so I listen.
For they are as I am
and we together
are part of the whole.
And the reason is the whole
for which I search,

for which I yearn.
And if this whole, this reason,
judges me,
it judges itself.
For I am a part of it,
the reason I am,
the whole that made me.

117. PINHEAD?

All religions could learn a lesson from the quest undertaken by modern physicists for the grand unification theory, the search for the forces of nature made explainable by one encompassing mathematical concept.

Christians have a heaven for those who believe on the word of Christ. Jews have a Jewish heaven. Muslims have a Muslim heaven. Buddhists and Hindus have a spiritual journey of transcendence.

If there is a God who created this universe, then he is God of us all. Lutherans believe that what a person believes is itself a gift from God. It is curious then, that God would make a person who does not believe and then refuse to welcome that person into his eternal home.

Some of you will interpret me as blasphemous in this piece I'm about to write because I shed an appreciative light on atheists, also because I call God a pinhead. But look, this is a story about how we bumblers, Agnos and I, are trying to work through this with honesty and common sense. We're not really calling God a pinhead. We are saying that the way some of us believe about God makes him look like a pinhead.

The ultimate survival of Christianity will depend on its recognition that the message of Jesus is for all souls, even those who don't believe it. The message truly is *GOOD NEWS*, not a life or death ultimatum.

There are at least three different theologies having to do with the way in which Jesus connects to the salvation of humanity. The first explanation is that he was punished in our place. He died for our sins. The second is that by first descending into hell and then arising again from the dead he broke ground, so to speak, making it possible for the rest of us also to overcome death. The third is that Jesus told us the message God wanted us to hear, that he loves us and will save us. I'm sure there are many more explanations than just these three.

There are ways to construct a metaphysical system in which it makes at least a little sense that Jesus could pay the penalty for all the rest of us. If he did in fact understand the two major determinants of behavior and personality, those being genetics and environmental influences, then Jesus would have realized that people become what they are and behave the way they do because of factors outside of their control. How could people be held accountable for things they have done or left undone because of the way God made them? They can't. Purely and simply and clearly, the crap that goes on in this world is God's fault. He made us this way. If Jesus is God, then it is right that he be held accountable. Does this seem ludicrous to you?

How about this explanation? If Jesus is the embodiment of the relationship between each of us, for he said that wherever two or more of us are gathered in his name, there he also would be; if he is the embodiment of our relationships, then he has been directly involved in the actions and consequences of all living things of all time. That would make Jesus even more directly responsible for the evils of the world. Does this sound right to you?

Let me tell you why it is not right. It is not right because revenge is an emotion that is unworthy of God, at least a God I would worship. Did God make us imperfect just so that he could deny some unbelieving people, of his making, the salvation he gives to others? Did he make us imperfect so that he could inflict pain and suffering on himself, Jesus? This is pretty cornball theology if you ask me.

In ways of parenting we think of punishment as a way to improve the behavior of our children. Scientific study shows that punishment doesn't work. It is called negative reinforcement, and that name is fitting because it does indeed reinforce the behavior for which it is given. In other words if, as a consequence of a child's behavior, you give a lot of attention, any sort of attention, that child becomes more likely to repeat that behavior. The most effective way to mold good behavior is to give a lot of positive reinforcement, praise and prizes, for the doing of desirable things.

So it also doesn't make sense that God might have punished Jesus as a way of teaching us to be better. Science tells us that approach doesn't work. All this hoopla about sinfulness doesn't make the sin go away. In fact we enjoy it. We roll around in the mud of sinfulness, lamenting and repenting, so that we can be showered over and over again by the attentions of the Almighty, even if those attentions are punishment. Our repetitious rolling in the mud and showering it off is self reinforcing. We do it over and over again basically because we think it focuses God's attention on us.

This theology makes God out to be either stupid or cruel or both. It is primitive theology and obsolete. It is the phlogiston of spirituality and is fit for the scrap heap. Thank you, God, for having pointed that out to me.

By the way, if you have a hard time relinquishing this insulting image of God, I'm sure he understands and won't take offense. Don't worry that he may punish you either. He would regard that as barbaric.

The second theological construct is the one that says Jesus overcame death first so that now the rest of us also can. We can follow in his footsteps. Although this also is funny thinking, at least it doesn't make God look cruel or stupid. It does make him look foolishly and elaborately wasteful of his own effort. If he wants to save us, he'll save us. How complicated does he need to make it? How hokey?

On the other hand, it seems too simple that God might have decided to come into the world just to deliver the message that he loves us and will save us, but there is no question that this was a message people needed to hear, both then and now.

Does one need to believe Jesus' message to get into heaven? No, God's not that petty.

"How do you know he's not?" Agnos interrupted.

"Listen Agnos, God actually has a special affection for atheists who are good."

"Oh he does, does he?"

"Certainly. When atheists do good things, it's for the right reason. They do it simply because it's right to do good things. God gets annoyed with people who are good just because they want to go to heaven."

"I thought you don't like it when people pretend to know the mind of God. I see some inconsistency here."

"Okay so maybe God is a pinhead. Maybe he made us all imperfect just so that he can punish us for acting on our God-given natural urges. Maybe he made all of us capable of thinking for ourselves imperfectly, just so that he can withhold salvation from those of us who don't believe in him. That's just the kind of ruthless and narrow minded god I want to worship, one whose self esteem is so low he has to create morons so he can feel big about punishing them."

"My oh my, you're getting sarcastic now." Agnos smiled. He loves to get me riled. "Well sarcasm does have its place. There is another explanation you know. Maybe God doesn't exist at all. Then we could assign all this nonsensical theology to the goofiness of people. God could take whatever goofy form they want."

"But what if God does exist? What then?"

"Then your points are well taken. If that is so, then either God loves and will save each and every one of us, or he's a pinhead."

After awhile Agnos announced, "You have another problem with your idea of Jesus being just a messenger of God's love. If you are to believe the Bible, Jesus placed importance on the crucifixion. Listen to this. Agnos read from Matthew 16, starting with verse 21. Jesus began to tell his disciples what his destiny would be, that he would travel to Jerusalem, suffer at the hands of the elders, chief priests and scribes. He would be put to death. On the third day he would be raised to life again. *Peter took him aside and began to rebuke him. "Never Lord!" he said. "This shall never happen to you!" Jesus turned and said to Peter, "Get behind me, Satan! You are a stumbling block to me; you do not have in mind the things of God, but the things of men."*

Agnos looked up and smiled smugly. "What do you think about that?"

It did not take long at all to understand how this passage fits. I told Agnos, Read the next two verses."

Then Jesus said to his disciples, "If anyone would come after me, he must deny himself and take up his cross and follow me. For whoever wants to save his life will lose it, but whoever loses his life for me will find it."

This time when Agnos looked up it was I who smugly smiled. I said, "Jesus told us that to follow him means we must do the right thing no matter what the personal consequence. We are not to step away from the path he puts us on. We are to follow it to its end, even if the consequence is brutal crucifixion and death. It is not that his own crucifixion was necessary for us to be saved. His admonishment of Peter was to tell him not to stand as an obstacle to completion of God's assignment for him."

Agnos asked, "So what is the assignment God has given you?"

"To write this book," I answered quietly.

"Where will it take you?"

"I don't know."

Agnos went away with his Bible, and then a little while later he came back and said, "There's more to it than that. Just before the crucifixion all the disciples were so afraid of the authorities that they denied they even knew Jesus. They were cowards. Then after the crucifixion, when Jesus appeared to them in bodily form, they were transformed into courageous martyrs who went to their deaths willingly because they were completely convinced of Jesus' message."

"What are you getting at?" I asked.

"If you want to believe the Bible, then the reason God came into the world as Jesus and maneuvered his way to a death by crucifixion, and then finally came alive again in bodily form; simply was so that people would believe. God wanted people to believe they would be saved because then they could feel confident about heaven even while they were still on earth, but he realized that nobody would believe the message unless he proved it, point blank, no questions left unanswered. And according to the Bible, he did it."

I smiled at Agnos. "So my thoughtful friend, are you also coming to believe this?"

"Oh hell, I don't know."

118. BRAINSTORMING JOHN 3:16

I got some flack for that one. My brother, who theologically is profoundly better versed than my meanderings, told me I needed to examine what my agenda was. I told him *agape*, God's love for man. Also, I was searching for some reasonable explanation for Atonement, man's reconciliation with God and what Jesus' death on the cross had to do with it. All the explanations I had found were not acceptable to me. So I was searching. Oh yes, and agape.

Let's move on. I have struggled with what once had been my favorite Bible verse. *For God so loved the world that he gave his only begotten son to die for us, that whoever believes in him will not perish but have everlasting life.* What a gorgeous piece of literature. What a coercive politico-religious strategy.

Dear God, I don't want to leave behind my friends: Sohail who is Hindu; Shamsi and Danish who are Muslim; Rochelle, Tom, Marci, Steve and Bruce who are Jewish; Sven who is Buddhist; Ernie, Chris and Lacey who are atheists; Eloise who is native American spiritual. And so God, I challenge you.

When my children go to bed we say the Lord's prayer and the Apostle's Creed, but when I go to bed I pray, "God, enter me so that I may understand you. Jesus, enter me so that I may be like you."

There was a time when frequently I would awaken in the middle of the night, look at the clock, and in digits clear as could be it told me 3:16, which I interpreted as meaning my once favorite Bible verse, John 3:16, a verse I no longer can accept as it is written in the Bible. It demands belief in Jesus as a condition for salvation, and that is just another form of works righteousness. I can't believe God makes that a condition for salvation.

I've heard theological apology that says just because those who believe are saved doesn't mean that the others are damned. The problem with this apology is that when reading the Bible, nobody comes away with the apology's allowance for disbelief, and I have a problem with that.

Just before Easter of 2006, it happened again. I was awakened by a low frequency humming very like one of the large bull frogs in the pond next to our house, but the sound was in my head. I looked at the clock. 3:16. I prayed, "God you know that I love you, that I am absolutely convinced of you and your love for me. You keep showing me this verse, and you know I cannot accept it the way it is written. How am I to interpret it? His answer as best as I could make it out at the time was, "For I so loved you that I came into the world and suffered life and death in order to tell you that if you believe what I teach, then you will know that heaven is yours, now and forever."

This meant to me that at this moment we are in God's kingdom. It may even be heaven, though it is not always comfortable. The physical aspects of this world are interesting, difficult and instructive. But my spirit at this time, and at all times, is with God and in his eternity. My knowledge of this is the peace that passes understanding.

I shared this piece with DK from the Heartland. Dan wrote me a wonderful response that I then edited heavily, and so the following is pleasantly a literary and spiritual co-mingling of Dan's and my mind.

For God so loved the world that he gave his only begotten son, that whoever believes in him shall not perish but have eternal life.

For spirit so loved the physical creation that it gave us itself in flesh, that whoever believes that this has happened will know that they are cherished and will find ultimate meaning.

For the very fabric of the universe was so enthralled by itself made physical, that it found a way to participate, that whoever trusts that this is so will not languish but be joyous in being a part of all that is.

For the gods so loved humanity that they allowed their message of love to be comprehended, that whoever finds true compassion in himself will remove selfish desires and will participate in peace on earth.

For doctors so loved their patients that they worked diligently, that whoever comes to their clinics shall transcend illness and have more meaningful lives.

For mothers so loved humanity that they gave their children to the world, that whoever finds joy in them shall be lifted from their doldrums and know that love is eternal.

For the seasons of seasons so loved the earthly cycles that they gave The Four Seasons to the earth, that whoever lives in harmony with this music should witness heaven in the earth.

For patriots so loved this nation that they gave themselves in war and peace, that whoever upholds the Constitution and the Bill of Rights shall be satisfied with true harmony of the Republic.

For Newton and Einstein so loved searching for truth that they soared like eagles of effort and creative thought, that whoever comprehends their mathematics shall leave the dark ages and make an improved world.

For MOM and POP so loved all their children that they gave their only SON, Savior Of Naughties, that whoever incorporates his message, that all you need is love, shall eliminate hatred and bigotry and achieve heaven on earth.

For heaven so loved the earth that it kissed the horizon and the sun rose.

119. PASSOVER

This fragment account of the Passion story was written sometime around 2006 CE, and because of its remoteness from actual events, it is not regarded as historically reliable.

Passover is the celebration of God's having delivered the Jews out of enslavement by the Egyptians. The breaking of Pharaoh's hold on them resulted from the final plague, that of the angel of death passing over and killing the first born sons of households whose doors were not painted with lamb's blood.

The literary parallel to Christ's crucifixion is extraordinary. The Christian story is that we are delivered out of our slavery to sin by the death of God's only son, whom we call the lamb, and we drink into the households of our own bodies the blood this lamb shed.

For the Romans occupying Jerusalem, Passover was a challenging time as concerned maintaining peaceful control of the population. It celebrated delivery out of the hands of oppressors, and so social discord and even military uprising was commonplace during this holiday.

Pilate was ruthless, perfunctory, and by the time of the Passion of Christ he was experienced and well prepared for control of the Jews. He governed by forceful and occasionally brutal suppression.

At the temple Jesus made a scene by casting out the money changers, condemning the commerce of the temple that paid the priests, and by contract the government as well. It even is possible that he tore away the curtain surrounding the Holy of Holies. Jesus was a troublemaker, and he started a small riot. He escaped immediate arrest probably because of the chaotic crowd, but Pilate took into custody many of the people who had been there.

These captives were held hostage, with the very real intent to crucify them if the perpetrator of the riot was not given up. You, dear gentle reader, were one of the hostages taken by Pilate. I saw you there.

You were one of us. We were to be scourged by leather whips into which were tied pieces of bone and metal, and then when our flesh was stripped from our backs we were to be nailed to trees and left to die.

This had not been part of Jesus' plan, but now it was on his plate. What could he do? If he went himself to the Romans, they would take him and crucify him along with the rest of us. He likely could not himself have made it undetected to the Priests because of the throngs of celebrants on streets during the holiday.

So, to the priests he sent Judas, the only one of his disciples who would do it. He himself went to a lonely spot, the Garden of Gethsemane, to await his capture. Judas was to bargain with the priests and the priests with Pilate for the release of the hostages in exchange for Jesus.

In the Garden Jesus prayed that God would enact some miracle, "If it be your will, Father, let this cup pass over me, let this angel of death pass over us." In the specter of impending torture and brutal death, Jesus gave himself up, scared but willing.

As a serious scientist I do not find it difficult at all to believe in the bodily resurrection of Jesus into life again after death. My differences with the church have to do with the theological meaning of that death and resurrection. I often wonder if we would have had a better understanding and consensus on the meaning of his message, his life and death and his resurrection if Jesus had had more time preaching before this all happened. Maybe it was God's will instead for us to argue about it. Maybe there is no one single meaning, but several, and we can arrive at the various meanings only through the mystery of unanswered questions.

120. NEVER GOING TO LET YOU GO

Every now and then my children and I play a game in which I hold on to them as they try unsuccessfully to escape, and I sing, "I'm never going to let you go; no, no, no; never going to let you go. Never going to let you, never going to let you, never going to let you go, No!" They laugh and look for the button somewhere on my person that will let them go. But even if I let them go, they come back to me and are caught again by me singing the same song, over and over again. This is like our relationship with God.

121. BELIEVE IT OR NOT

My God includes all of you in his heaven. His love is that great.

Abraham Lincoln signed the Emancipation Proclamation on January first, 1863. He had been to New Year's Day celebrations all morning, had been shaking thousands of hands, and excitement surged through him. At 2:00 P.M. he returned to his office to sign the document, but his hand trembled. He put his pen down and said, "I never in my life felt more certain that I was doing right, than I do in signing this paper. If my name ever goes into history it will be for this act, and my whole soul is in it. If my hand trembles when I sign the Proclamation, all who examine the document hereafter will say, 'He hesitated.'"

If you want to read about this moment, look at the January 2006 issue of the *Smithsonian*, in which it was written, *The signature proved to be unusually bold, clear, and firm, even for him.*

Abraham Lincoln signed a document welcoming African Americans into freedom, into the human family of the United States.

So what does that have to do with me? Here I am challenging the most beloved biblical verse of Christendom, welcoming even nonbelievers into the kingdom of God. *For God so loved the world that he gave his only begotten son to die for us, that whoever believes in him will not perish but have everlasting life.* If you look at the phrase critically with a strictly mathematical logic, John 3:16 welcomes believers but does not exclude nonbelievers.

On the Monday morning after Easter one of my patients, a lovely, very Muslim woman, returned to see me. At that moment I knew I had written my opinion correctly, and I understood well the words of Abraham Lincoln, "I never in my life felt more certain that I was doing right."

I will show you in essays to come that Jesus is not just for the Christian crowd. God chooses different ways to show himself to different peoples because what speaks most clearly to one culture may not be as readily understood by another, but the event of Jesus in our world has meaning for all of you, whether you believe it or not, and I can explain it to you.

Oh, by the way, I need to continue reminding myself of my agenda. Remember, it's agape, God's love for man. That is our destination. Maybe to get there I'll need to deliver a slap across the face of the antichrist. You who love your fellow man have nothing to fear from this beast, but you will be more effective in your ability to love if you learn how to identify it, even when it is inside of you.

Some poems are really short.

122. NOT WHAT I TAUGHT YOU
You divide my body against me.
This is not what I taught you to do.

123. WITNESSED

I saw souls descending from above
and some of them ascending from below,
and they came together but still were separated
as though there were a fence between them.
All of the souls had faces.
Those from below yearned and reached for those from above.
They shouted and pleaded for the fence to be broken,
but they needed help from the others.
And the souls from above were like sheep being shepherded,
and they blandly answered, "It's in the hands of God."

The voice as quiet and reliable as thought said,
"Everybody who has ears listen.
You are my hands.
Tear down the fence between yourselves."

124. NURTURE THEM

Broken bodies and sorrowful souls
come to you.
They are fretful and frightened.
You are their heaven given.
Nurture them.

SEVENTEEN

Provocations

125. PAUL TILLICH

Agnos told me, "Sometimes you are just a little bit weird."

"But just a little bit, right?" I answered.

"Like I said, sometimes you're just a little bit weird," He smiled. "Other times maybe not just a little bit. Today you look a little boobish, theologically speaking I mean. Did theological scholars call you a boob again?"

"Sort of."

"Yeah well, I could have predicted that."

"You did."

"Oh yes." Agnos laughed, "So I'm the prophet and you fulfilled prophecy. What did you learn from the theologians?"

"Mainly I think I learned that they are busy. Instead of writing to me from their own minds, they sent me stuff to read or references to read, and I read them."

"Did you enjoy them?"

"Yes, but they weren't very funny."

"Theology not funny? Go figure. So what did you learn from the theology masters?"

"Well Agnos, I really don't mind much when theologians anthropomorphize God. It lends a mythological air to the old man, and that's not really how I think of God, but it's okay because our science isn't advanced enough to explain the creator of our universe and how his involvement with us continues. So I can live with God delivered to me as a mythological character, but I have difficulty when emotions are ascribed to God that not only are human but also are less than noble."

"You mean like when God tested Abraham by commanding him to sacrifice Isaac?"

"Don't get me started."

"So how about this guy, Paul Tillich. Did he ascribe less than noble emotions to God?"

"He's a curious one. Paul Tillich didn't at all like the application of mythological characteristics to God. He wanted to explain God in a way that better fit the mind of modern, scientific man."

"So he avoided an emotional God altogether?"

"No, that's the curious thing about him. He ended up doing just what maybe he wanted to avoid. He sounded a lot like Sigmund Freud.

"Paul Tillich lived for 79 years, between August 20, 1886, and October 22, 1965. He's described as a German-American theologian and Christian existential philosopher. He was Lutheran. Lutherans tend to be independent and creative. Have you noticed?"

"Yes, you're Lutheran aren't you?"

"I started out that way. Maybe my writings distance me a bit. But if you lump me with those other guys who found problems with the status quo, then yes I guess you could say I'm like them. They pissed people off, too."

"Paul Tillich pissed people off?"

"No, not so much. Martin Luther did. He managed to get Pope Leo X of the Catholic Church to excommunicate him on January 3, 1521, and then he said some nasty things about the Jews."

"No!"

"Yes, well you know, nobody's perfect. Oh there was that one guy, but we killed him."

"Okay, so what did Paul Tillich have to say about God and why it is important to believe in him?"

"Tillich made a distinction between that which exists and that which is essence. This is the Plato versus Aristotle thing again. Remember that? Vitalism or mechanism, what is the true world? Is it the world we can see and touch and measure? Or is it the world of spirit? Tillich taught that the world of existence is what we see here in our every day life. But then there is the world of essence, beyond time and space.

"Tillich said that we all suffer from the anxiety of our potential of non-being. We are afraid of our own non-existence, our death. So then he asked the question, what causes us *to be* in the first place? If we only exist, then we are finite beings. What can sustain finite beings is *being* itself, or the *ground of being*. Tillich called this God."

"So God is the essence within us that is eternal."

"I think that's the point, except Tillich said God is beyond even essence. Essence is the power of being, and it cannot be grasped by the

conscious mind. It's beyond the realm of thought. That's why we benefit from religious tradition. It gives us a way of understanding it."

"This is deep."

"Well we're only part way there. The next point is that here we are
doing all this existing in the world, and since existence is completely
separate from essence, we are separate from God."

"We are?"

That's what Tillich says is sin. To exist is to be alienated."

"We can't help it then? So this is a modern, updated version of
original sin. Okay. So what did Tillich say about Jesus?"

"He said Jesus was a finite man like the rest of us, but essence fully
showed itself in him. He was and is the *New Being*. He is the revelation
of God. Tillich believed Jesus was the emblem of the highest goal of
man, what God wants men to become. We are to make ourselves progressively Christ-like."

"You've said yourself that you want to be Christ-like. So what's
your problem with Tillich?"

"Before I get to that, let me tell you one more thing because this is
pretty cool. Tillich said, 'God does not exist. He is being itself beyond
essence and existence. Therefore to argue that God exists is to deny
him.'"

"Huh?"

"We cannot think of God as a being which exists in time and space
because that constrains him, makes him finite. We must think of God
as beyond being, above finitude and limitation. He is the power or
essence of being itself. We aren't able to comprehend that, so that is
why we need the metaphors and symbols of religion. But we need to
recognize that this is what religion is, and therefore it is inherently
finite and corrupt."

Agnos leaned back a bit. "You know what this reminds me of?
Homeopathic medicines."

"What?"

"Let's say you want to make an antidote to a poison. What you do
is you take some of that poison and put it into a diluent such as alcohol. Then you take one drop of that potion, and you dilute it with one
hundred drops of alcohol. Then you succuss it."

"You succuss it?"

"It gets shaken vigorously and maybe in a very special way. I don't
know, maybe three big shakes, then two small ones, then really fast for
a count of ten."

"You're teasing me now."

"Yes, of course I am. The idea is to get the essence of the poison to leave the existing chemical of the poison. Do you see the resemblance now to Paul Tillichism? So this poison diluted 1:100 is called 1C. A drop of it is diluted again with one hundred drops of alcohol and is again succussed."

"To shake the living essence out of it."

"Exactly, you're understanding the process. The result of that is a potion of one part poison, ten thousand parts alcohol, and full of the poison's essence. That's called 2C. Then you do it again. 3C is a dilution of one to one million, and so on. Sometimes they dilute it so much that there no longer is any existing poison in the medicine. It is then all essence. It is the essence of poison."

"So what's the point to this very dilute poison?"

"It's safe."

"That's the point? It's safe?"

"Well yes, of course. You wouldn't want to hurt anyone would you?"

"But how does it work?"

"The idea is that such a tiny dose will mobilize the body's defenses."

"Even if the poison is so dilute that it doesn't exist?"

"Yes well, I guess then it mobilizes the defenses of the person's essence."

"Okay, so in order for homeopathic medicines to work, we would need an essence on which they could work."

Agnos sighed. "I guess I should have told you that part. Homeopathic medicines don't work, except maybe in some cases about thirty percent of the time. But I wouldn't think the success rate is even that high with something like a rattlesnake bite. Don't treat rattlesnake bites with a homeopathic medicine. You'll want your money back."

"So what's the thirty percent figure all about?"

"Psychology. Placebo effect. If a medicine doesn't do better than that, you've got to wonder. Hey, remember we were talking about Paul Tillich. Do you think his theology also is about psychology? He puts the whole structure into a form more acceptable to modern man, so by placebo effect alone, thirty percent of us will feel better."

"Agnos, you have a way about you."

"What does Tillich say about why it's necessary to believe in God?"

"I'm still looking for that. There's a lot to read, but I will share with you what was written to me by the theologian who turned me on to Paul Tillich. My brother Stan said, 'God's/Christ's Spirit is already within us. Most major religions accept Jesus as a prophet of God, as the example to follow. It is only the Trinitarian Christians who interpret the gospel of John to mean that in order to be saved you must believe that Jesus is the only divine Son of God. All spiritual people are in touch with God, regardless of their religious beliefs. With one exception, it isn't whether or not you are a Christian but how you live your life according to God's love for you and your neighbor. My Buddhist friend quoted the Dahli Lama as saying, *My religion is living loving kindness.* The one exception is those who don't believe God exists. Since they are ultimately spiritual beings here on this earth to learn, by denying God they deny their own true essence. Does this mean that they are damned for all eternity? Absolutely not. It only means that when they die and transcend this physical plane they will need help to understand what they had spent a lifetime denying. All they need to do is ask for that help and they will receive it. Of course what I'm sharing with you is not orthodox Christianity. God meets each of us according to our need. I don't share with everyone how God has engaged me because I am more interested in how others are spiritually connected. I've learned that each of us must follow our own path, and when we arbitrarily judge that our path is better than someone else's, we do harm to that person and to ourselves.'"

Agnos raised an eyebrow. "So that's a loving and forgiving person who wrote all that. He didn't mention people like me who just don't know and don't profess to know. Is this expression of his belief also what you believe, Mr. T the splogger?"

"Agnos my dear friend, it is almost what I believe. God must have had a reason to make some spirits live lives in which they do not believe. They are learning something different from those who do believe. And that goes for you too, my agnostic friend. The placebo effect of believing is this. If you believe, then you don't have to wait for the Kingdom of Heaven. You know already that it is inside you.

"I once told you that I would show you how to identify the antichrist. This theologian has written one of the ways, only one mind you, but it is one of the ways. When we arbitrarily judge that our path is better than someone else's, we do harm to that person and to ourselves."

Agnos smiled, "So there you have it, the essential Paul Tillich."

126. GERHARD O. FORDE

"Nobody objected to what I wrote! Somebody should have objected."

"Objected about what?" Agnos yawned.

"In my last essay about Paul Tillich I said that it was characteristic of the antichrist to say that his own path is better than someone else's."

"So what of it? I think most people agree with you."

"But do they agree because they have thought it through, or just because this is easy for them? I wasn't going for 'Yeah sure, whatever.' I expected at least some Christians to object because of John 14:6. The disciple, Thomas, had just asked how we can know the way to God's house. *Jesus answered, "I am the way and the truth and the life. No one comes to the Father except through me. If you really knew me, you would know my Father as well. From now on you do know him and have seen him."* Christians should have stepped up to the plate to tell me what Christians always say, that Jesus is the one way. So if Jesus is the Christ, and he says there is only one way and he's it, how can it be the spirit of the antichrist who says there is one path that is better than the others? How could Jesus be both Christ and antichrist?"

Agnos lifted his eyebrows. "You got me boss."

"The solution to this seeming discordance is that Jesus was talking about the Holy Spirit. We come to Father by way of the Holy Spirit, and each of us has the Holy Spirit within. Jesus put a lot of importance on the Holy Spirit. In Mark 3:29 he said, *'Whoever blasphemes against the Holy Spirit never has forgiveness, but is guilty of an eternal sin.'* So it was Jesus himself who gave us this rule. We are to respect and even nurture the Holy Spirit in others, even if their Holy Spirit takes them in a direction we do not understand. I'll be talking more about the Holy Spirit in a later essay.

"For now I'm still exploring the questions of why God changed his mind about giving us eternal life, and why did Jesus have to die for it, and why is it so important whether or not we believe it. I was provided ideas of another great theologian, Gerhard O. Forde. Some have described him as having stood at the forefront of Lutheran thought."

"Another Lutheran. What's with you and Lutherans?"

"I'm dealing with what people send me. I guess I've got a lot of Lutheran contacts."

"So maybe we should take this with a grain of salt?" asked Agnos.

"Lutheran salt, yes." I smiled.

"Tell me what Gerhard O. Forde had to say."

"First of all it was no small potatoes when we murdered the Son of God. Forde wrote that we'd like to forget about that, but we shouldn't. We'd like to hide from our responsibility for that murder by claiming God required it of us, that it was a step we had to take in order for him to forgive us. In Forde's words, 'We exonerate ourselves, so to speak, by blaming the necessity for the cross on God.'"

"So, Forde said that God didn't need Jesus to die in order to forgive our sins."

"Right."

"That's nice of him."

"Yes, if God demanded this as some sort of payment then it would make him look like a vindictive tyrant or at least caught up in some crazy scheme of honor. God wouldn't look very merciful if that were the case.

"Forde also argued against the idea that God might have sent his Son to a shameful and painful death in order to provide an event so powerful it would entice us to be reconciled to him as a God of mercy and charity. Forde didn't like this explanation because it again ignored our own responsibility for having killed Jesus. He wrote that he wants us to own up to that."

"We are some bad-assed creatures, huh?"

"We certainly are capable of bad-assed things."

"I don't feel as bad-assed as all that."

"You're supposed to. You killed God."

"I did? Guilt by association, I say." Agnos recoiled.

"By some metaphysical means you've got to come to grips with the concept that what one human has done, you also have done. We are together, one in God."

"When did I sign on the dotted line? I want to know how I got connected with this hoodlum gang. To tell you the truth, I want no part of it."

"That's Forde's point. You want no part of it, but you can't escape it."

"Why?"

"Because God made you connected to the rest of us. You're not alone."

"Christianity depends on this?"

"Maybe."

"So if I'm guilty by association, I must be saved by association too. It's either me and Pope Benedict together, or neither one of us, right?"

"And Charles Manson and Adolph Hitler and Attila the Hun."

"I'm not sure I like my chances with them."

"There's something to this Holy Spirit; I mean it. You've got some good guys in your corner too, like Gandhi."

"Was he Christian?"

"He studied Christianity and the other major world religions. He himself remained pretty much Hindu. He led a campaign for, among other things, brotherhood among communities of differing religions and ethnicity."

"I think I like my chances better with Pope Benedict."

"And Pat Robertson and Jerry Fallwell, right?"

"Um, how about that other way Jesus might save us? You know, the way in which he sort of cuts a new path, blazes a new trail for us to follow. I'm kind of liking that way better all of a sudden."

"Forde described this other way as Jesus defeating the evil demons who would keep us from eternal life. But this doesn't explain why Jesus had to die. We still are stuck with that question, and we're still stuck with the question of why God changed his mind about us and why we have to believe. Forde asked the same question I asked earlier but in different words. I asked, 'If God is God, why can't he just save us?' Forde asked, 'If he is God, could he not have spared his Son the agony?' Forde wrote that with these various ways we commonly have used to explain the Jesus connection, *God's reputation is endangered, not enhanced. Why should a God, who is by nature merciful, demand satisfaction?*"

"Because he's a gangster?" Agnos chuckled.

"Agnos, I think you're getting Forde's point. And I agree with him up to this point. We deserve better answers than what have been provided so far."

"So what answers did Forde suggest?"

"To the question of why doesn't God just save us, Forde answered simply, he does."

"He forgives us just like that?"

"Yes."

"Well I'll be. Simple as that. He sounds like you."

"Yes, except Forde says we don't accept God's forgiveness."

"We don't? What's wrong with us that we don't accept such a nice thing as that?"

"The brutal fact, according to Forde, is that we don't really want unconditional forgiveness. Unconditional forgiveness would turn our world upside down, so when Jesus came around telling us what unconditional forgiveness would mean, we threw a tantrum and slaughtered him."

"Is this really the reason why Jesus got killed?"

"Sort of. He created a riot in the temple during Passover celebration, remember, and it was all about putting an end to the money making ways of the priests and the government. And he said God would forgive people even if they didn't spend the money to sacrifice animals. So sort of, yes. Jesus was a serious threat to the commerce of big wigs, and Forde has a point."

"But once again I'd like to say that given a choice of whether or not I would kill the Son of God, I think I'd go for the forgiveness instead."

"But we didn't."

"But I'm not them."

"Maybe by means of nuances in the fabric of time and space, weirded out by Einstein's theory of relativity and by the non-locality surprises of quantum mechanics, you are them."

"It's a stretch."

"Let's go on. Forde said that God knew he was a problem for us. We kept insisting that he would judge us conditionally, and that he would have mercy on only those of us for whom he decided to have mercy. We perceived him as a God of wrath, very different from what he really was. Therefore to show his pure mercy and love, he decided to get out of the way for us. He decided to die so that we no longer would have to fear a God who was wrathful, even if that wrathful God was of our own making, our perception only."

"Wait a minute. Remember awhile ago Stan the Rev pointed out that even before Jesus, the Jews did not believe God was a wrathful God. He said that Jesus was not the one who gave us a loving God. The Jewish people already understood that God was loving. *But you are a God ready to forgive, gracious and merciful, slow to anger and abounding in steadfast love, and you did not forsake us.* Nehemiah 9:17. Then also there is the 23rd Psalm in which David sang, *Even though I walk through the valley of the shadow of death, I will fear no evil, for you are with me; your rod and your staff, they comfort me. You prepare a table before me in the presence of my enemies. You anoint my head with oil; my cup overflows. Surely goodness and love will follow me all the days of my life, and I will dwell in the house of the Lord forever.*

"I guess we must have started thinking of God as wrathful at the same time we began thinking he would be merciful to some people and not to others, when we ascribed to him the characteristics of ourselves. According to Forde it is our placing of conditions and qualifications on our love and forgiveness that continues to crucify Christ."

"I'm confused about the timing here. Just when does all this stuff happen?"

"Agnos, everybody is confused by the timing. Don't get caught up in it because there's one more point made by Forde to which I want your response. He wrote, *When … we actually believe God's unconditional forgiveness; then God can say, 'Now I am satisfied!' … Christ's work therefore satisfies* (our perception of God's wrath) *because it alone creates believers … . Christ actualizes the will of God to have mercy unconditionally.*"

Agnos sat back, stroked his chin and remarked, "Codependency. But before I say that, please remind me about what that means. What is codependency?"

"Codependency is a dysfunctional relationship in which maintenance of the maladaptive behavior of one individual depends on interplay with the maladaptive behavior of another."

"Yep, that's what it is alright, codependency. This is a theology that makes sense to me, a dysfunctional relationship between the maladaptive behavior of God and the maladaptive behavior of humankind. This explains a lot about the world. It speaks to me."

"Agnos, are you teasing me again?"

"You're damned tootin' right I am."

127. PROVOCATIONS

I was going to write some very interesting things when Agnos interrupted me. From feedback given by some of you readers, it became clear to me that Christians confuse Atonement with salvation, that everybody confuses the battle between Christ and antichrist with the struggle of good against evil, and finally that some people actually think John 3:17-18 explains and justifies John 3:16. None of these things is so, and I was going to write about it when Agnos butted in.

"I saw a great t-shirt today that reminded me of you. It said, 'I know Jack Shit.'"

"I know Jack Shit?"

"That's right. You say all this about God, and you talk with him and all that, but the truth is that you only believe this stuff. You have no incontrovertible evidence. The closest science will come is to say none of this is testable. It's not verifiable. It's outside the realm of science. You say you know God, but really you know Jack Shit."

"Is Jack Shit your new name for God?"

"Hey! Blasphemy dude."

"Here's the deal," I started to explain. "We can live in the scientific, mechanistic world of Aristotle or we can live in the philosophical, vitalistic world of Plato. I'm fairly comfortable moving back and forth between the two. If I spend a lot of time in the theological world, it's because I see so much harm in the world caused by religious fanatics who put their beliefs before the welfare of others. These people close their minds to science. The only chance I know of getting to them is to use their own weapon, the Bible, along with logical reasoning, to show the error of their ways."

"So you admit you know Jack Shit?"

"Jack Shit? Who's he? I don't think I know Jack Shit."

Then Agnos said, "You should share with your readers that wonderful book written by your friend, Dan Kurtti. I like his book."

Okay, so here it is in its entirety.

128. THE MAN FROM GALILEE
By Dan Kurtti
Poke Him in the Eye Publishing Company
Minneapolis, Minnesota

PREFACE

In this book I have tried to boil down the essence of the historical Jesus. There has been much written about him, starting a couple of centuries ago, but interest in the historical Jesus increased significantly about twenty to thirty years ago. Perhaps the most famous work has been done by the *Jesus Seminar*. I eagerly anticipated their book concerning the authentic sayings of Jesus, but I was upset that some of my favorite sayings were written in gray or even black, meaning that the seminar thought it unlikely Jesus actually said those things. How could they have been so blind? Don't they understand who Jesus really was?

I also have read several books by authors that I would categorize as Jesus debunkers. These authors believe Jesus was entirely a fictitious character. These writers make some very good points, but don't they understand that where there is smoke, there is fire? To me it would make sense that such strong enthusiasm by Christians, two and three generations after his death, would have been the result of the actions and words of an actual person, not a fictional character. Would the first generation Christians risk their very lives for anything less? I know how comic book enthusiasts love Superman or Batman, but are they willing to risk their lives over their favorite characters?

So I decided to do my own search into the historical Jesus. I had to wade through a lot of chaff to get to the wheat. It was very itchy along the way, but I think I found the authentic Jesus. I had to omit any statements in the New Testament that were references to the pagan christs. I also deleted any statements that appeared to be propaganda by the early Christians, any statements that just appeared to be too far-fetched, and anything that appeared to be too biased by the New Testament authors. The result is this book.

After much research I have come to the conclusion that Jesus felt actions were more important that words. I think he probably did not say too much. I think he lived the famous declaration in the Tao Te Ching, Chapter 56, *Those who know don't talk. Those who talk don't know.* (Stephen Mitchell's translation, 1988).

So what about all the words that he allegedly said in the New Testament and the Gnostic literature? I think these sayings came after his death, not before! My conclusion may be difficult to understand, but my detailed discussion and explanation would need to be in a forth-coming book, not this one. I wanted to keep this book very short and simple. Briefly, I think he taught his disciples meditation and astral projection techniques. These came in handy when his disciples were lonely after his death and needed comfort. So they talked to him in the after world. They also were very curious to know what may await them after they died. Jesus answered all of their questions and patiently provided consolation. The bottom line is: Jesus didn't say much when alive and was very chatty after his death.

ACKNOWLEDGEMENTS

I am eternally grateful in having a wonderful wife, Yuko. She has inspired me to greater heights and has been a source of strength during the lows. I am thankful in having two wonderful children, Kenny and Amanda. To watch them grow up into intelligent and caring adults has been the greatest thrill in my life.

I would like to thank Mrs. Gasman, my first grade teacher, and yes that was her real name. She saw the potential in my academic career about three or four weeks into the first grade, and I think it provoked an early drive in me to succeed. I am also very appreciative of the pastor of my communion, Pastor Gerlich. He was a calm, gentle person and was patient with our class. But he was a traditionalist, and I was inspired to look elsewhere rather than in the church. In the long run my unorthodox seeking has made the search for meaning all the more rewarding.

Finally I would like to thank Tom Curtis, my dear friend. I think of him as a brother. We met more than 25 years ago in Okinawa as Navy physicians. I always will remember our stimulating conversations when jogging or eating meals at the officers club. I think this was the greatest impetus for my seeking what life is all about. Now, thanks to email, we have had many interesting and intriguing conversations about religion, Jesus, cosmology, politics and just exchanging humorous stories.

Chapter One
MAN FROM GALILEE
There was once a man from Galilee who healed many and taught others to love their enemies.

Chapter Two
LOOK WITHIN
One day he was asked when the kingdom of God would come. The man replied, "The kingdom is inside you, and it is outside you."

Chapter Three
PUT TO DEATH
The man thought he was the Messiah and was put to death when he got into trouble with the Jewish and Roman authorities.

Chapter Four
AFTER HIS DEATH (OPTIONAL)
He taught his disciples meditation and techniques of astral projection and had many interesting experiences with them after his death.

INDEX

APPENDIX: AUTHOR'S COMMENTS

I'm glad you enjoyed *The Man From Galilee.* I think I like it best of different things I've written in recent months. When I was writing it I couldn't stop chuckling myself.

What would surprise the average reader is that we don't know even Jesus' name! Actually I should say, we don't know the real name of the man from Galilee. Careful reading of Matthew may lead one to consider that the name Jesus might have been a political ploy. Matthew 1:21-23: *She will give birth to a son, and you are to give him the name Jesus, because he will save his people from their sins. All this took place to fulfill what the Lord had said through the prophet: "The virgin will be with child and will give birth to a son, and they will call him Immanuel"—which means, "God is with us."*

This is why I don't write the name Jesus in the main part of the book, only in the Preface. It is only when I talk to others that I use the name Jesus so I can share with them a common denominator during discussion.

It is possible that he was given that name after his death. He may have been a fairly unknown healer and teacher when alive, only known to a small circle of friends. If we were to learn his real name we might be surprised.

While the Preface of the book has some sarcasm, it also is honest. I truly wonder if most of what we know about Jesus is his after death communications with his friends and disciples.

One more point about the authors of the historical Jesus. It seems that the Jesus they portray is really the Jesus that they want to believe existed, and the proof they give is slanted because of that. In a way, it is like dream interpretation. It becomes very personal, filling personal needs. The Jesus written down in the books is the projection of their inner dreams and conflicts. That is why there are so many versions of who he was.

In fact his disciples probably had their own different versions even when they interacted with him day by day. Their versions probably separated significantly from each other after his death. There was no longer the physical man to straighten out their errors about him. No wonder the second and third generation Christians warred with each other. This became vicious by the time of the Council of Nicea.

129. HOOPLA

The preceding two pieces upset some people. I started by making provocative statements and then immediately set them aside as topics for later. These were: 1. Christians confuse Atonement with salvation. 2. Everybody confuses the battle between Christ and antichrist with the struggle of good against evil. 3. Some people actually think John 3:17-18 explains and justifies John 3:16. I wrote that none of these things was so. Rightfully people burned by these statements would complain that no argument was made to support them. Just wait. It's coming.

Then I shared with you Dan Kurtti's spoof of the Jesus Seminar, also a spoof of the tendency authors have to spend more time and energy on the explanations than on the piece of literature itself. I so enjoyed his little book. Let me tell you that Dan is very well read and very spiritual. More about that in just a bit.

A minister whom I esteem and love, wrote me this. *After quite a lot of money spent and several years of study and experience, I really hate to say this, but in my opinion, what you have written here only shows how truly ignorant you both are about God and Jesua ben Joseph. We know a great deal about the Jews and the Christians of the first four centuries of the Common Era. So what you have written is basic jibberish. I think both of you need to do some serious soul searching and possibly get some therapy.*

This rang in my head like name calling. For days I was saying in my conscience, "Hey Dan, we are ignoramuses who need psychotherapy." And I said to myself, "Dan and I both are searchers after the truth. The books he has read on spirituality likely number in the hundreds. The books I have read on the topic probably aspire to one hundred. The point isn't that one person reads more than another. The point is that Jesus said, "Seek and you shall find. Knock and the door will be opened to you." So I guess we can be ignoramuses needing therapy, who walk through the door opened for us.

To seek, to share, to spill our guts; that is what this is all about.

My theological friend and brother sent me more clarification of his concern that Dan and I possibly might have damaged our readers. Our attempts at humor have not been funny, and I personally have taken scripture out of context, much the way fundamentalists do. The difference between them and me is simply that my agenda is liberal.

I certainly can say what needs to be said without taking anything out of context. The message to be delivered simply is agape, God's love. It is a love of unification and inclusiveness, not one of division. If you will do just this one thing for yourself, for me, for Jesus; whenever you read anything within or without the Bible, please interpret it through the decoder ring of Jesus' instruction to, "Love the Lord your God with all your heart, with all your mind and with all your soul; and ... love your neighbor as yourself." If you do this the rest will follow. Oh yes, here is my agenda. My neighbors include Muslims, Jews, Hindus, Buddhists, Native Americans and Atheists. One God for all.

130. ATONEMENT

Frustrated after her most recent debilitating flare of multiple sclerosis, my patient complained and then declared, "Oh I know, inexplicable things happen like ... God."

Do you ever wonder who should forgive who? Or do you believe there is a God-given reason for every horrible event this life has to offer?

Even if something can be learned from every thing that happens, that is not the same as ascribing causality. Do things happen just because we will learn from them? Every event has a cause, but is that cause a mindful and intended act of God for our edification? Or is the cause of each event more compatible with chaos theory? Does it just happen? Does our resultant edification arise only out of our curiosity and study?

Questions such as these are pertinent to the consideration of Atonement.

Atonement is a process by which individuals of a broken relationship are reconciled. There are a variety of specific definitions of atonement, and you may choose whichever you want.

An old edition of Webster's New World Dictionary defines it simply as, *satisfaction given for wrongdoing, injury; amends; expiation.* It gives another definition, *the effect of Jesus' sufferings and death in redeeming mankind and bringing about the reconciliation of God to man.*

The American Heritage Dictionary gives more examples of different religions. In the Hebrew Scriptures it is, *man's reconciliation with God after having transgressed the covenant.* Spelled with a capital A, Atonement means, *the redemptive life and death of Christ.* In Christian Science it means, *the radical obedience and purification, exemplified in the life of Jesus, by which humanity finds man's oneness with God.*

Among the simple definitions, the one I like most is also found in the American Heritage Dictionary and is described as an archaic use of the word. It means simply, *reconciliation; concord.*

Psychology literature is busy with this word, atonement.

Imagine two young men, and just for fun let's call them Cain and

Abel. Cain cheats Abel in a game of poker and takes all of Abel's money away from him. Because of this Abel cannot pay what he owes to his cocaine supplier, and the supplier breaks Abel's legs with a baseball bat. This story isn't exactly what you might have read in Genesis, but just play along with me.

A complete process of atonement requires several steps. Cain must realize that a wrong has been committed. He must admit he played a role in the commission of that wrong. He must acknowledge Abel was hurt by the wrong. Cain must understand the appropriateness of making amends for the wrong and, to the extent he can, he must make those amends. It is this step of atonement that most appropriately is called expiation, the making of amends. You see, expiation and atonement are synonyms, but only sort of. Finally, and this may be the hardest step of all, Cain must honestly promise never to do it again.

This final step is what I call the definition of the phrase, *I'm sorry*. My own children squirm irritably when, after they have told me they're sorry, I ask them, "What is the meaning of sorry?"

They know what I want them to say, "I won't do it again," but usually they don't say that. At least they're honest. Instead they whine, "Da-a-a-a-ad!" In this instance the word Dad has two syllables, and in the process of atonement it substitutes for the promise never to do it again. It has similarities to honest, selfish prayer.

From the other side of all this, Abel's role in atonement is to recognize and understand the origins of his injury, acknowledge Cain's attempts at expiation, and finally Abel must forgive Cain.

Let's add one more thing because it is of supreme theological interest. Cain must accept Abel's forgiveness.

Then there is atonement.

The only problem is that Abel's legs are still broken. To the extent he can, Cain will run errands and chauffer Abel around to his various drug deals. Oh yes, Cain also will pay off the brutal supplier along with the 50% penalty for late payment. Atonement isn't always such an easy process. So maybe that's the first point to be made. If atonement is going to be worth all this, you really have got to want the relationship to continue. Otherwise isn't it easier just to blow it off?

For example I met a woman who once was a thirteen year old Jewish girl when Nazis first occupied France, and when this woman let it be known to me that she of course had been raped, I asked her by whom. Her answer was, "Everyone."

Did this woman have to forgive her many assailants? Why should she? She didn't want a continued relationship with them. Why not let

God forgive them? God is better at such things, and God also is good at forgiving those of us who cannot forgive. Give it to the Master of Forgiveness.

Could she benefit herself by forgiving them? Would it comfort her own torment? Ah, think about that.

And think about this too. Forgiveness of yourself is most important if you want to continue your relationship with you. After I had told one man this, he objected by telling me it made no sense for us to forgive ourselves. He preferred the idea of allowing ourselves to be comfortable in the knowledge of God's forgiveness. I will tell you that the only difference between his way of thinking and mine is syntax of expression. Otherwise they are the same thing, and you soon will understand this better. When we say, "Forgive us our sins as we forgive others," what are we saying? It could be that we are saying, "We are your hands with which we will tear down the fence between us."

We don't always know that we've committed a wrong, and this is the single best argument I know for incorporating an omniscient being into the process of atonement.

Imagine a woman, Alice, who decides that rather than paying $35 a month to sponsor a child via World Vision, instead she spends that on payments for her new high definition television. What if, because of that decision, a child doesn't get malaria prophylaxis and dies? Alice has no clue that her behavior contributed to the demise of another person. The full process of atonement cannot occur. Does it matter? Does Alice feel a need to reconcile a relationship she never had? Is this a situation in which the rightness or wrongness of action falls outside the realm of atonement?

What if you believe Jesus' admonishment to love your neighbor as yourself, and you believe his likening that to loving God with all of yourself? Then this becomes a matter of atonement in your relationship with God, the omniscient creator who knows and feels the spirit of all he has created.

But what if you don't have or want a relationship with God? What if you don't believe in God? We'll come to that later.

For the time being let's just say Alice thought she was humming along quite sweetly in her own divine relationship with the Creator of the Universe, and all of a sudden he was giving her the silent treatment. She didn't know why, but he was as sullen as her husband when his football team loses ignominiously. This of course would be a God with human frailty, and so maybe the true God wouldn't actually get so sullen.

An omniscient and infinitely forgiving God could come to the rescue. A God who knows our wrongdoings better than we do can still forgive us, even when we do not fulfill our own steps of atonement. In other words, God's forgiveness would be freely given, would maintain Alice's relationship with him even when she was helpless in her own role of atonement.

Father came to me. "You have sinned."

"Yes," I answered.

"Tell me about your sin."

"Father you know how I have sinned even better than I do. Please forgive me."

"You are forgiven, but that's a lazy answer. I hoped for more from you."

"Oh yes, okay. I'm sorry."

"What does sorry mean?"

"Da-a-a-ad."

Is forgiveness enough? Can reconciliation occur even without the fulfillment of all steps of atonement? It seems at least sometimes that is necessary. Sometimes forgiveness occurs without the accompaniment of the other steps, and so is forgiveness all by itself enough to reconcile relationships? Does it depend on the ability of the forgiver, and does the Master of Forgiveness indeed have infinite ability to forgive? Will he reconcile based on his forgiveness alone?

Or does he require us to accept his forgiveness, even if the forgiveness is given for a sin we don't even know we've committed. Maybe he gives carte blanche forgiveness in exchange for our carte blanche acceptance in a process to which, at its deepest and most meaningful levels, we are oblivious. What I mean is that if we are unaware of our wrongdoing we cannot examine the behavior, and if we do not examine it then we cannot learn from it and grow. Or maybe God forgives for a simpler reason; he just plain wants to. Maybe he wants to just because he loves us. Maybe he wants our relationship never to be divided, never lacking reconciliation. Maybe!

So what if you don't believe in God? If God regarded disbelief as a sin, wouldn't he forgive you? Since he made you that way in the first place, maybe it is more likely that he would not regard your disbelief as a sin. Isn't it more likely he gave you that role of disbelief because you and the rest of us have something to learn from it? Maybe it's a situation that actually has a God-given purpose. Or maybe not. Maybe it's just one of those things, a composite of genetics and environment, and we'll learn from it only if we're curious and studious enough.

What would Jesus' role be if God just plain forgives?

Christianity is based on Jesus' death paying the price of our sins for us, the penalty being death. It's not that you yourself have committed a crime that warrants death, but you're lumped in with the rest of humankind, and let's face it, humans have done some despicable things. This substitution of Jesus for the rest of us makes some sense if he himself actually is responsible for all the sins of the world. An argument could be made that if God created us all the way we are, then God is responsible; and if God is responsible and Jesus is God, then it makes sense that he should pay the price. Maybe the Christian ethic is about man forgiving God. I've asked some Christians, and they don't think so.

Or maybe Jesus is what science fiction stories call an empath, a person who can take on the pain and suffering of others. Then his death would be a mechanism to extinguish pain and suffering. Alas, but there still are pain and suffering in the world, so that can't be it.

Gerhard O. Forde also expressed his reluctance to reconcile his own sense of decency with the thought of Jesus dying to provide "satisfaction" for a God who resembles a gang-land boss. Forde's way out of the quandary was to devise a story of God acknowledging that he's a problem for humankind, then committing suicide by way of crucifixion to get out of humankind's way. I bet if you did a survey of Christians on it, they'd have a problem with Forde's explanation as well.

Nobody ever has explained, well enough to persuade me, how the brutalization and murder of Jesus expiates. Nothing about his suffering and death on the cross makes amends for wrongdoing. Belief that this paid the price of humanity's sin is based on an archaic notion of justice by punishment and revenge. This is un-Christ-like.

Each of you has my sincere request for an answer to this question. How does the death of God's son expiate?

If Jesus is not the sacrificial lamb, does this mean the cross loses its meaning? No, but the meaning changes. The cross symbolizes the intersection of God and humanity, with Jesus at its center. Jesus is the result of God's decision to participate in his creation, to become the nucleus of life both in earth and eternity. Also the cross symbolizes God's gift to us of the Holy Spirit. How cool is that!

What then of the Lord's Supper? Does it lose meaning? No. Jesus' body was broken, and his blood was shed, and they were broken and shed so that others could live. His role, not of sacrificial lamb, was more heroic than that. Father did not demand his death. We humans, as the authoritative, policing Roman force in Jerusalem, tortured and murdered Jesus because we perceived him to be a threat to the peacefulness of our precious way of life, our occupation of the city, and more abstractly our occupation of God's kingdom. He challenged us to change our world, and we killed him for it. We did. It was our archaic system of justice by punishment that killed him. We are the ones who demanded satisfaction, not God.

We also were the potential victims saved by Jesus. We were the hostages taken by Pontius Pilate with hopes of drawing Jesus out and into his control, to punish him for the riot he caused at the temple. Were it not for Jesus we would have been crucified. He took our place.

It is hard to understand that we were they, and they are us, but that is the message. We have been entangled with one another since the Big Bang, and the science of quantum mechanics is only the beginning of our understanding of what we were taught two millennia ago. You don't have to believe this. Whether or not you believe, won't change it. By not believing you won't escape it.

With this way of understanding, Jesus' death was atonement in an archaic system of one human satisfying another human's ignorant and evil need. The concept of Christ then, is that of God entering the world and saying, "You cannot kill each other without also killing me."

So we killed God, and the meaning of the resurrection is that no matter how hard we try, really we cannot kill God. Ultimately we cannot suppress the Word. It will spring back up here, there and everywhere, like weeds.

Did it end with Jesus? Throughout history, has God as Christ entered our domain and heroically sacrificed himself for the salvation of those who would be victimized, allowing himself to be killed by ignorant and evil humans? Over and over? Is Christ the love of God manifested in human behavior? When we drink the wine and eat the bread, do we bring into ourselves the broken body and shed blood of Christ through the ages?

Here's a little side commentary. As science continues to break down the barriers in our understanding of what makes man different from the animals, a Christian can always answer the question with, "God decided to come into this world as a human." Puts some responsibility on us then, doesn't it? We are God's chosen species to nurture his garden, and what we do reflects on him.

To be fair, a mathematician would say that the difference between humans and animals is mathematics. Birds have all they can do to count up to just three. Paul Davies says that man is the only animal that not only observes the world but also can learn to understand it.

I launched this discussion of atonement and Atonement because my earlier statement was challenged, the one in which I wrote that Christians confuse atonement with salvation. What I meant was that Christians have been so thoroughly schooled that the two are inseparably linked that of course in their minds it follows that the only way we can be saved is if our relationship with God is reconciled. But these are two different things, reconciliation and salvation.

So I'm asking not only the question of whether forgiveness alone is sufficient to reconcile a relationship, and I've implied that it is if the forgiver is as good at forgiving as God. But the next major question is whether reconciliation is necessary for salvation. These are two different things and worthy of separate theological consideration.

Are we or are we not eternal? As a spiritual scientist I can understand either a "yes" or a "no" answer to this question because by current technology it cannot be tested. I have trouble answering it as "yes, sometimes" or "no, sometimes." "It all depends on whether you believe ... ."

Whether living creatures are or are not eternal is bound up in the structure of the universe, both within and without the construct of space and time. It does not seem likely that one person's psychology would transmute the very fabric of the cosmos, either for everybody or for just himself. It just doesn't make sense, unless that one person is God, perhaps Jesus, and in a single act the entire cosmos gets changed.

You may remember what I wrote about space and time being a continuum, or field, as physicists have up until now believed. Or maybe it's not. Maybe the fabric of the universe is composed of tiny packets of spacetime which flow in a sea of something else, a concept for which there is mounting interest. And is that *something else*, within which time-space packets flow, eternity? Then eternity would be within us all. How neat! And that may give a foothold for physicists to begin understanding how the non-locality features of quantum mechanics connect entangled particles instantly, not bound by the restrictions of time-space, seemingly faster than the speed of light, an inexplicable observation, truly and definitely so, but impossible given our adherence to the field concept of spacetime and the proven theory of relativity. The explanation we have for this so far is that entangled particles, no matter how far apart they are, even light-years, actually are two parts of the same entity, and they are not at all separated in—let's call it the fifth dimension. We are connected, you and I, by our entangled particles. Hello neighbor.

So it is sensible, both by theological and by science logic, to entertain a belief that we all are eternal. But to think some of us are eternal and some of us not, at least by scientific logic, is hard to reconcile with what we already know about the available evidence. Maybe we'll just forgive the divisiveness of the *some-saved* theology and move on.

If not supported by scientific logic, what about theo-logic? Does theo-logic make sense of the argument that we are saved based on our belief system? I've already answered this, but I'll answer it again. Theo-logic tells us that God made us the way we are. A scientist says this same thing by observing that we are the product of our genetics and environment. If God makes some of us believers and some of us disbe-lievers, wouldn't he be a crumb-bum to save the one and not the other?

The answer given to this question by at least some traditional theo-logians is that we are not necessarily to understand the logic or the justice of God, and they can cite verses that show God to be vindictive, divisive and violent. This is a mystery of God, they tell us, and since we are to put the biblical word of God above us, this mystery is for us to accept however blind that acceptance must be.

To this answer I object. If we are to worship this mysterious God, then it is appropriate for us to demand from our understanding of him, clarity of his morality. And if you ask him, he will tell you so. "The other is like it; love your neighbor as yourself."

Also if you believe in reincarnation, then the persistence of evil and ignorance in the world despite wonderful thinkers like Lincoln, Gandhi and Madison, and despite the teachings of Jesus, is evidence that God has saved even the ignorant people who do evil.

The evidence strongly suggests that if there is a God, and if God is benevolent, then he wants the world to be changed by coercion and conversion of evil into good, not by destruction and casting away of the person. By the way, how sinful is the wanting to destroy another per-son you perceive as evil, or to send him to hell?

So there you have it. In summary, without challenging the divinity of Jesus and so remaining faithfully within the realm of Christianity, this treatise supports the concepts that God's forgiveness all by itself is enough to reconcile his relationship with humankind, that reconcilia-tion and salvation are two separate theological considerations, and that with or without reconciliation God either saves or dispenses us each the same, whatever we believe.

I believe we are of eternal spirit, and by his choice not our own.

131. CAVEAT AGNOS

Agnos said, "There is one consideration that should gnaw at you. Some people may argue that consistent with Heisenberg's uncertainty principle, quantum mechanics tells us that how we observe the past from our point of perspective in the present determines which of an infinite variety of pasts actually happened. That is to say, observation from the present determines what the past was. Paul Davies goes a step further, theorizing that even the laws of physics might have been different in the past if we were to have observed them differently from the present.

"Since there might have been an infinite variety of pasts, only one of which we've chosen to be ours, there also would be an infinite variety of presents, only one of which we are aware.

"The same can be applied to the future, and if this is the case then there will be very different places to go, and this truly may be determined by whether our belief and behavior center on love for all our fellow living creatures, as Jesus instructed, or whether our belief and behavior focus on a concept that salvation depends on a belief in the slaughter and resurrection of Jesus.

"Also, the direction of our future may be determined by whether our belief and behavior require that we go there together, or alone, or only with those others who are like us."

I thought about this awhile, and then answered. "Heisenberg's uncertainty principle applies to the infinitesimal. The past history of the universe is enormous, and there are so many of us now who have observed the past to be the way it is, that it is fixed and stable. At least for our own experienced world, it is determined. Likewise our future will be so overwhelmingly the product of us all, the observations of everyone, that there is no question about whether we will be alone or together. The future is ours to share with everybody else."

I took this to Father, and he said, "If it troubles you to write about the structure of it all, the interplay of heaven and earth, then keep it simple. I am pleased if people just treat each other as they would themselves be treated."

"But Father," I protested. "What they believe matters to their behavior."

"Then don't be troubled. There are many at work on this. You are not alone."

132. THE CRAPPY SPIRIT

The second of my three provocations was that nearly everybody confuses the battle of Christ versus antichrist with the battle between good and evil. Let me say very simply that the antichrist is more effective when working with subtlety than when working overtly. Seldom will you see antichrist behavior as blatantly evil as the Nazi holocaust.

If Christ is the love of God manifested in human behavior, then the antichrist must be behavior that is counter to the love of God. If God's love is characterized by courage and selflessness, such as that of Jesus when he chose torture and death on the cross, then we should expect the antichrist to use the behavioral tools of fear and greed. Certainly there are other tools that can be used by this crappy spirit, but lately fear and greed have been used a lot. They are favorites of the Crappy Spirit.

The Crappy Spirit lives in us all, in the nooks and crannies of our souls, places we vacate when we don't encourage the Holy Spirit to swell like yeast and take complete control of us. The Crappy Spirit is an opportunist and will nestle into our vacancies. Pray for God to enter and fill you entirely. "Make me like yourself, fearless and selfless."

The Crappy Spirit will make some of you greedy and some of you fearful. And the greedy will use threats to extort from the fearful. One of them is the perpetrator and one is the victim, and both are injured by their behavioral manifestation of the Crappy Spirit.

Don't be greedy or fearful. If you make your decisions based on either fear or greed, your decisions will lead you where you do not want to go, away from what the Holy Spirit tells you. Love others as you love yourself.

The Crappy Spirit loves the good guys and eschews the bad guys, but the Holy Spirit sees only the Holy Spirit, and loves.

It was the Holy Spirit who said through FDR's voice, "We have nothing to fear but fear itself." It was the Holy Spirit who said through Douglas McArthur's voice, "Always do the right thing no matter what the personal consequence." It was the Holy Spirit who said through Gandhi's voice, "We must be the change we want to see in the world."

It is the Crappy Spirit who says, "Be afraid. Be very afraid."

Now we see all these negative, pejorative political ads on television, and it's clear to me that the political candidates themselves are not such mean spirited people as these ads would lead us to believe. But they use these ads because they work. Studies show that they work. Why do they work? Because society is infected with the Crappy Spirit.

When you cast your vote in an election, do not be guided by fear or greed. Be guided by courage and selflessness. Do onto others as you would have them do onto you.

Make the Crappy Spirit hit the fan.

133. TAKING THE GLOVES OFF

It may surprise you that it embarrasses me to write so much about spirituality. I know that many or most of you enjoy it more when I just write funny, and that is also when I most enjoy writing. So why do I keep writing about spirituality?

I read a wonderful book written by Paul Davies, *The Mind of God, the Scientific Basis for a Rational World.* I must read it again. There is so much in it. From this book I learned that advanced logic proves that ultimately, answers to questions about existence cannot be ascertained by rational thought arising from minds within the system that is being considered. In other words, we can ascertain answers to questions about a scientific experiment because the experiment is separate from us. We are outside of it. But if our questions are about the universe, why we are here, these questions cannot be answered by science and mathematics because we ourselves are contained within the system being studied.

If we truly yearn for these kinds of answers, they must come from a source outside of the system about which our inquiries are being made. The only exception to this is if the universe is complete all by itself. If there is nothing like a God outside of the universe, then the answers may indeed be available to us. Otherwise no.

On page 226 of his book, Dr. Davies begins his discussion on mystical knowledge. *Most scientists have a deep mistrust of mysticism.* But then he writes, *In fact, many of the world's finest thinkers, including some notable scientists such as Einstein, Pauli, Schrodinger, Heisenberg, Eddington, and Jeans, have also espoused mysticism.* Science is our most reliable means of substantiating theories, the things we justifiably suspect. But science may not always be available to answer some of the questions we want to ask, like *Why?* For that we may have to rely on some sort of communication from an entity beyond our technological capacity.

Father speaks to different people in different ways. "What's all this shit about a Crappy Spirit?"

"Um, eh, well, that was a nickname I gave to the antichrist because I wanted to demystify it and make it less frightening."

"But you made it sound as though it were some sort of dark force alternative to the Holy Spirit. Is that what you believe?"

"No it's not. How could it be? The Holy Spirit is you and your eternity that enters us and fills every part of us that is not of this physical world of time and space. There is no room for a dark force spirit as an alternative to the Holy Spirit. The Holy Spirit is whole and constant in each of us. It is the entity to which we refer when we say we are one."

"Why then did you write it the way you did in your piece, *The Crappy Spirit?*"

"It was a mistake. I hurried the piece because I wanted to send it out before Election Day."

"Ah yes," he nodded. "Time is a troublesome thing. Did you know that if you take the *I* and the *ME* out of the word *TIME* you are left with only a *T*, a cross, the symbol of the eternity I gave you."

"That is what my earthly father used to tell me."

"It is what I used to tell you. Pretty nice trick of the English Language, don't you think? It doesn't work so well in Vietnamese. So tell me next, if the Holy Spirit does not have a dark force adversary, and if the antichrist exists, what is the antichrist's adversary? The answer is obvious. Don't think this is a trick question."

"The adversary of the antichrist is the Christ."

"Yes. I want you now to write about what is Christ and what is antichrist and what is Holy Spirit."

"This will upset a lot of people."

"Yes, it will upset a lot of people. You're familiar enough with that, aren't you?"

"I am, but this will be heresy on a larger scale."

"Yes it will. You will do this for me."

That was the end of that conversation. Later as I was crawling into bed, not even close to sleep and with my mind on completely unrelated topics, my thoughts were interrupted by a voice within my soul. "I love you." And the voice was an amalgam of my earthly father and earthly mother, both of whom have passed.

"I love you, too."

For awhile now I think I will choose as my favorite Bible verses, those that mention the unpardonable sin, Matthew 12:31-32, and Luke 12:10. They are so very duplicitous.

Matthew 12:31-32 tells us that Jesus said, *"And so I tell you, every sin and blasphemy will be forgiven men, but the blasphemy against the Spirit will not be forgiven. Anyone who speaks a word against the Son of Man will be forgiven, but anyone who speaks against the Holy Spirit will not be forgiven, either in this age or in the age to come."*

Luke 12:10 tells us that Jesus said, *"And everyone who speaks a word against the Son of Man will be forgiven, but anyone who blasphemes against the Holy Spirit will not be forgiven."*

Wanting to find these verses in the Bible, I looked them up in an online Bible Concordance, and of course I was given a short sermon on them as well. The very reasonable sermon nevertheless burned my shorts, so I thought I'd share it with you and then explain the burn holes in my pants.

The website sermon told me that the *unpardonable sin,* described in the Bible as *blasphemy against the Holy Spirit,* can't really be done by people now because it was a very specific sin of the Pharisees claiming Jesus was empowered to do miracles by a demon rather than by the Holy Spirit. So Jesus denounced them for their rejection of him.

The website sermon continued to say that the unforgivable are only those who had *no Godly regrets.* It pointed out that Peter denied Jesus three times, yet Jesus forgave him. At least Peter hadn't ascribed Jesus' miracles to the power of the devil. So Peter was forgivable.

The website sermon told me that I can't commit the unpardonable sin today *because it's impossible for me now to attribute to Satan those miracles that were performed by Jesus Christ.* To that I have a question. Can't I? Can't I do that? It's not that I want to mind you. I love Jesus and believe that his miracles were holy, but I point this out to you to show that the website sermon was beginning to sound fabricated to fit someone's own personal agenda.

Finally the website sermon reversed itself and said that in fact we can commit the unpardonable sin, but the sermonizer changed how a person happens to do that. Instead of what Jesus said, the website sermonizer said that, *when people reject Jesus Christ and His gift of eternal life, they are in a sense committing the unpardonable sin of unbelief.* Let me make sure you understand that this is the website sermonizer talking, not Jesus. The sermonizer told me that if I reject a belief in Jesus all the way up until the day I die, then I will not be pardoned and will spend an eternity in hell, apart from God. However, if I repent my sins and ask Jesus into my life as my Lord and Savior, then Mr. Website sermonizer says I will be saved by grace through faith. Have you read enough?

In the words of logic you see, the sermonizer says that it's not God's act that is the *independent variable,* but yours. If you do the independent act of faith, then God's action automatically follows as an act dependent upon your behavior. Talk about blasphemy!

Of course the argument against this is that God offers eternal life to everyone, and then we either accept it or not. This ascribes to The Almighty a passive-aggressive personality absolving him of responsibility for his neglectful cruelty. Yes, this view is even more insulting of Father, even more blasphemous, one thing more for him to forgive. He puts up with a lot.

Before I go on, I wish first to say a short prayer: Father, help me to explain accurately the battle shown here between Christ and antichrist.

If the Holy Spirit is in one of us it is in all of us. If we say that one person goes to heaven because he believes, and another person goes to hell because he does not believe, then we deny the Holy Spirit in that other person.

It is by our faith that we derive the psychological benefit of knowing God loves and will save us. But it is by God's grace alone that we are saved. We are saved by God's love, not by our faith.

This shows the duplicity of these verses. Jesus is written to have said, " ... *anyone who speaks against the Holy Spirit will not be forgiven, either in this age or in the age to come.*" Does this mean that all the religious people in the world, who say that people go to hell if they don't believe, are themselves committing the unpardonable sin of denying the Holy Spirit within the nonbelievers? Wow! What an unexpected turn of events!

But what of Jesus himself, who said that these witless nincompoops will not be forgiven? Is Jesus himself committing the unpardonable sin of denying the Holy Spirit within the religious nincompoops? Ah, Jesus suddenly becomes a more three dimensional character, and quite honestly I love him all the more because of it. Learn to love an imperfect Jesus, and you will be a step closer to understanding God.

Why would Jesus, Son of God, make such an obvious error of logic? Excuse me, not obvious. It seems nobody is talking who might have recognized this earlier. Why would Jesus make this blunder?

One reason might be that he didn't. Matthew and Luke were written after Mark, and Mark doesn't talk about this event. So maybe these are add-on verses of the early oral tradition, espousing somebody else's agenda, not that of Jesus.

Another reason might be that Jesus was both complete man and complete God. It is the complete man part of him that could get in the way, sometimes saying stuff like this. Oh dear. Now people will think I'm blaspheming against the Son, a sin forgivable by God but not by the religiously faithful. Woe is me. I'll be an outcast.

Jesus was more than the Christ, and the Christ is more than Jesus. The beauty of Jesus, in part, is that he was frail and mistaken and sinful like the rest of us, and some of the things he said were wrong. He also was the Christ, and some of the things he said were on target, truly the *Word of God.* How are we to know? *"The second one is like it. Love others as you love yourself."* Everything in the Bible needs to be filtered through that simple statement of the Christ.

Father, please be with me on this one. My beloved Jesus is both Christ and antichrist, and as such he perfectly presents us with our

135. TATTERED SHIRT

I had a purple shirt that I couldn't throw away; I loved it so much. It was royal purple, the perfect color for those of us with white hair, but its cuffs were frayed and buttons were either broken or lost. Nobody forced me to throw away my purple shirt, and it took me a long time, but finally I did. I still love it.

Now I have a green T-shirt that has worn so thin it is difficult to put on or take off without tearing a little bit larger the hole just below the neck line. It's a perfect green color. Elliot Evergreen would be proud of it. Nobody has told me to throw it away, but they're hinting. One of these days I'll throw it away, but I'll still love it.

I will not tell you to stop wearing your tattered shirt. It will be up to you when or if you throw it away, and whether you do or don't, I still love you.

EIGHTEEN

Solutions and Resolutions

136. MARCIA'S CHALLENGE

My friend Marcia wrote to me. Marcia means *warlike one*, and it implies a fiery willfulness to struggle against common wisdom that makes no sense. The name is in a way like my own, Thomas, the same name as the doubting disciple. My friend Marcia also is close to the earth and seeks understanding from clues in nature. This is what she wrote.

Each of the atoms in your being has made countless journeys before it came to you. Each carbon atom traveled repeatedly through the carbon cycle and has spent its time in rocks, plants, atmosphere, and in the bodies of other animals before coming to rest temporarily in you. Each water molecule has been part of an ocean, of clouds, raindrops and rivers before coming to rest temporarily in you. Each of us is a unique assemblage of atoms and molecules, but the convention is brief. Death will release all the particles to resume their eternal meanderings through cycles of nature.

The cyclic nature of the earth and other bodies in the universe is the closest I can come to the idea of God. My wristwatch is round, with two moving hands, and I liken it to the earth with the hands reminding me of sun and moon moving at different speeds around it, that old egocentric, geocentric illusion that the earth is center of all. I never cared for digital watches. The cyclic feeling gets replaced by a linear, indefinite notion. The modern generation thinks more linearly in a fashion dictated by digital images, but I find more comfort in the rotation of seasons and heavenly bodies, so I'll hang onto my old watch.

Religions, as a group, possibly have done more to harm mankind than good. They often display a zeal that is used as justification for war. Think of the Christian crusaders and the Islamic fundamentalists. *Imagine no religion*. I like that line in John Lennon's song. I don't understand where the intense need for religion comes from. Is it our mistaken feeling of superiority over other beings that leads us to believe death can't possibly be the end of things for us, even though it might be true for other animals? And if there really is a God, what kind of personality does he/she/it have, that believes it is okay for innocent beings to suffer in the terrible ways they do? Do I want to be acquainted with this kind of entity? There's something very disturbing about it. Random suffering is something I can understand, but suffering allowed to happen that could be prevented by a greater power, makes me think that God must have a dark side. And if indeed man is created in his image, then that would explain a lot.

137. THE BODY AS A MEANS OF REDEMPTION

Before explaining the process of redemption, let me describe the parallel between God and human. In this treatise the mind of God, or divine mind, will be written *Mind,* and the mind of humans will be written *mind.* The mind may change at the death of the human, but will continue to exist in some manner. The equivalence of the physical universe, which is the body of God, is the individual body for humans. Occasionally the physical universe will be called *Body* in the rest of this discussion. Therefore we have the relationships of God/Mind/Body to human/mind/body. The physical universe is not only the known universe, and the unknown universe still not detected by technology, but also all of the other parallel and alternative universes that we cannot detect no matter how powerful or sophisticated our instruments become. While God lives in the Body, He/She/It also transcends it, just as the human lives in the body but also transcends it.

Why did the Body come to be? There are various theories, including the idea of the universe being a random event. I have pondered this question without coming to any particular answer, but in recent years I have thought it may relate to an act of redemption. In other words, God created the universe for self redemption. We are only along for the ride. While we have some form of free will, it probably is more limited than we would like.

I speculate that something happened in the Mind that could be corrected only by creation of the Body. An analogy would be a dream that becomes out of control and can be corrected only by waking up. God was having a nightmare and needed to wake up. This process of his own salvation was instituted by development of a physical universe with certain rules that would not be violated. For example, the law of gravity provided attraction between two material bodies.

The Body provided a way of structured suffering. Some people may recoil at this and say, "How dare you suggest that God wants us to suffer. Are you suggesting that the whole point of the universe is suffering?" No. There are multiple purposes for the universe, but I think suffering is one of them, and it may be an essential purpose. Furthermore, whenever we suffer, God suffers. As the mind is a part of the Mind, God suffers when we do. In our relationships, when one of the partners suffers, so does God. So God will escape suffering only when there is not any exploitation in a relationship. Every time someone is raped, beaten, robbed, lied to, judged, humiliated, neglected, persecuted, or forced into any state of suffering, then God suffers.

There is more to our lives than just suffering. Besides depression, grieving, hatred, apathy, pain, etc, there also are joy, love, pleasure, sense of accomplishment, etc. As we experience all these thoughts and emotions, so does God.

The attempt to control our own destiny makes matters still more difficult. At times we seem to have about as much control of our destiny as a cork bobbing up and down in an ocean. Genetics and environment seem to control us as though we are puppets on strings. Furthermore we are aware of only our conscious motives. How about the vast forces acting on us through the unconscious? We truly do not need anyone else to sabotage us, as the forces of our unconscious mind can do a good job all by themselves. A person's will can be free only if all the forces influencing it are clearly understood. Is free will an illusion?

Should we just give up? If a person has limited free will and limited resources to change his or her own thinking patterns, is the answer to suffering just to admit, *it is God's Will?* Worse is the answer of blaming the victim. *This evil person deserved it.* If a city is ravaged by a natural disaster, are people just expressing their own helplessness by attributing this to a type of cleansing by God in preparation for some supernatural event such as the second coming of Christ?

While at least to some degree the suffering of one person can be handled by that person in a stoic manner, this doesn't mean we should use that same stoicism with the suffering of another. I think that although the universe was created with suffering at its root, the redemptive act is not the act of suffering but how one responds to the suffering.

What does *human* actually mean? The religion, Eckankar, defines *HU* as the ancient song of God, or even as an ancient name for God. *Man* is the root of some words such as *manual. Man* can mean *hands.* Therefore *HU-man* boils down to *God's hands.* We as humans are the hands of God. Our role is daunting. As we think, feel and act, the will of God is being done for better or for worse. So with limited free will, driven largely by unconscious motives influenced by our genetics and environment, as bobbing corks in an ocean, we are God's agents of redemption in this world of suffering.

How would this predicament be corrected? The answer is love. If one message comes through loud and clear in Jesus' teaching, it is to love one another. *"Love others as much as you love yourself."* Also see Matthew 5:43-45: *"You have heard that it was said, 'Love your neighbor and hate your enemy.' But I tell you: Love your enemies and pray for those who persecute you, that you may be sons of your Father in heaven. He causes his sun to rise on the evil and the good, and sends rain on the righteous and the unrighteous."*

Jesus keeps saying that love is the greatest commandment. Love God. Love your neighbor. Love your enemy. When you treat everyone compassionately, God does not suffer. Redemption ultimately will follow when the cycle of suffering is broken. Creation has allowed suffering in all its many ways, but in every situation compassionate love is the solution.

How can we love others when we cannot love even ourselves? Behind every judgment we make of someone else there is a projection of a self-loathing thought. We damn others so that we do not have to examine our own unacceptable thoughts. So the situation may seem hopeless. Suffering is in the root of the world and we seem to have little in our abilities to do anything about it.

Except we have help. See John 14:15-20: Jesus said to his disciples, *"If you love me, you will obey what I command. And I will ask the Father, and he will give you another Counselor to be with you forever—the Spirit of truth. The world cannot accept him, because it neither sees him nor knows him. But you know him, for he lives with you and will be in you. I will not leave you as orphans; I will come to you. Before long, the world will not see me anymore, but you will see me. Because I live, you also will live. On that day you will realize that I am in my Father, and you are in me, and I am in you."*

Do you object that it is too simplistic to believe that all suffering will be alleviated by acts of compassion? Maybe you challenge, *How about physical pain, cancer, injury and other painful conditions? Will cancer pain go away just with a compassionate act?* This point is well taken, but how would we know it wouldn't be taken away? And as a matter of fact, with the compassionate efforts of scientific research these things are indeed being taken away. One step at a time, it took eons to get us to where we are today. Maybe it will take eons longer for the Mind to be saved from its own torment.

138. QUANTUM TRINITY

What we believe is important not because our salvation depends on it, but because it determines whether we see ourselves as united with or separated from the rest of humanity, with or from the rest of the body of God. Does our God love all people or only some?

A necessary step in the spiritual evolution of humankind demands realization that every single person is cherished by God with attentiveness equal to any other. This realization also values that any person's path to understanding God, or not understanding, is as valid as any other. We were not all made with the same curiosity or interests, and isn't it wonderful.

This concept may be extended not just to other people but to all living things, and of necessity we are responsible as the species on this earth that is best equipped for stewardship of God's garden.

An ultimate objective of peace throughout the world cannot be attained without unity, and to be spiritually worthy a religion must nurture the cohesiveness of all peoples. Can a Christian theology be constructed that accomplishes this laudable goal? This is where belief is important. If all people in the world truly believed in peace, we would have peace. If all people in the world regarded everyone else as a member of God's body, we would have peace.

John 3:16 has been called a mini-Bible, eloquently encompassing all of what current Christianity is about. *For God so loved the world that he gave his only son, that whoever believes in him will not perish but have everlasting life.* Let me point out that it was not Jesus who said this. It was written by someone, we know not who, and put into the Gospel of John, whoever this particular John was.

Jesus taught us that the most important commandment is "to love the Lord your God with all your heart, with all your mind and with all your soul, and the second is like it. Love your neighbor as yourself." He taught us that the way to show love for God is to obey this second command. Love others as you love yourself. This is the Christianity of Jesus, and there is no qualifier placed on whether your neighbor is Christian, Jew, Muslim, Hindu, Buddhist, atheist or any other religion, gay or straight, man or woman. We love our neighbors as though they are ourselves, and we respect that we ourselves are saved only if they also are.

Let us explore a reasonable metaphysical structure for who Jesus was and is, from a Christian perspective. God revealed himself differently to other peoples of the world, and they may not believe Christian concepts. However, remember that for it to be a worthy religion in the spiritual evolution of humankind, Christianity must include all of humankind, even those who don't believe. I will construct for you a simple and noble explanation of Jesus, but no less incredible, by which I mean unbelievable, than what you have heard from others. You are welcome to believe this if it makes sense to you, but if you believe it you will see clearly that it does not allow you to separate yourself spiritually from the rest of life in this world. You may not divide the body of God against him. If my story anthropomorphizes God, at least it will not be in a way that seems contrived or written like a hideous plot in a soap opera. Here goes.

Imagine a place without time and without space. You may call this by various names. It may be called the universe before creation. Or it may be called pure light. Or if you are willing to allow that this place has a consciousness, you may call it God. God existed beyond time and space. If you want you may call this place eternity.

Within this place was created the universe of time and space, the universe that we are now able to perceive in every day life. We can say that God created this universe of time and space within himself, which is to say that whatever it was that existed before time and space; it was involved in its appearance. In this sense the word *before* is difficult to understand because time did not exist, so this term means basically that the place before time and space simply was necessary for the creation to happen. Paul Tillich would call it the Essence of Being.

Many but not all scientific minds may balk at the idea of this place having consciousness, but this is the direction my story will go, and it is the same direction that many religions go. Certainly if this story is to provide a structure for a sensible Christian theology, then the Creator is a thinking entity.

The Almighty Creator of time and space studied his work of art, and in one moment he observed it all from beginning to end. Given the considerations of Einstein's theory of special relativity, God could do this without breaking the rules of physics, strange as it seems, because he could observe the time and space universe from every vantage point at once.

As wonderful as it appeared to God, living things disturbed him with their natural inclination to harm and even eat other living things. The ascendant species, humankind, most creatively afflicted cruelty upon itself and others. "I created this?" God must have wondered.

At our current understanding, it is not possible for us to know whether God intended from the beginning for living things to share with him the eternity beyond time and space, but borrowing from the story of Adam and Eve, my story will accept that he did not. What had been created in the universe of time and space would belong in the universe of time and space. There it would stay.

But this cruel nature of living things puzzled God enough that he decided to learn for himself what it was like to be alive. He became a man, and to make it a fair experiment he became a man without knowledge that he was the incarnation of God. In his first go around, and you'll understand this later, Jesus had no idea he was essentially different than the other people around him. He had the Holy Spirit within him, God, and the others did not. But he did not know it.

He thought he was of shameful origin, called Mary's son, meaning Mary's bastard. His step father, a good and religious man, cared for Mary and her son, but his devotion for them in large part grew out of a need for a wife to care for his children from another woman who had died. Joseph was kind but aloof. His skill as a carpenter was given to his own seed, his own son(s), and Jesus learned as an apprentice not so much from Joseph, but from Joseph's sons who were more involved with and friendly toward him. Jesus' skill as a carpenter was not sufficient.

In those days a man without a trade was not trusted. These were the people who often became thieves and joined together in gangs that troubled society. Jesus likely was mistrusted more and more as he entered young adulthood.

He took a different path though, very likely because of Mary his mother. He would ask of her, "Who is my father?"

"Your God in heaven is your Papa." And this molded the direction of his life.

He was baptized by John, became a disciple, and he fortunately escaped arrest when John was stolen away by Herod Antipas and later was beheaded. As John's most promising disciple, and as a matter of fact he was a prodigy who surpassed John in popularity with the masses of people who came out to learn and be baptized, Jesus became leader of the group after John's demise.

He taught and lived as a man completely bound by the limitations of a man, but he had the personality and love of God.

During a Passover celebration in Jerusalem, Jesus ran headlong into the ruthless powers sent by Rome to suppress any sign of upheaval. Jesus died because of the political situation. Pilate was sent by the Emperor to make sure the Judeans would not rebel. If Pilate failed, he would have been executed by the Emperor. Pilate chose the High Priest each year with the specific command that the High Priest would keep the people under control, through the use of religion. Jesus threatened that.

As I wrote earlier, Jesus confronted the dreadful decision of whether to spare the lives of others by sacrificing his own life. He could have cut and run. He made his decision not knowing he was God, and this is one sign of his nobility. His greater nobility was yet to be revealed. He chose to die instead of the other people, most of whom he probably didn't even know, and he made the decision without knowing at all what awaited him after his death. All he knew was what he had learned from scripture and those who had taught him. He then knew no more about the afterlife than you do now. "My God! My God, why have you forsaken me?"

What a reunion it must have been, God meeting God, the merging of the two parts of his mind. Realize that this debriefing was God talking with God, Son with Father. Despite all he had been through in the world of time and space, all the rebuke and torture and shameful death, Jesus said to Father, "I love them. Truly they do not know what they do. They are limited by how I made them and they sin, but I love them. I will not myself go on without them." This was the greater nobility of Jesus. This time there was no doubt about death. By choice he would cease to exist unless humankind would become a part of his own eternal life.

Now the course of the story will become bizarre for some of you, because God decided to live again the life of Jesus, a second time and this time knowing he was God, this time able to perform miracles as revelation to his beloved and adopted creatures. This overlap of the Jesus-man with the Jesus-God is confusing to us, but given the existence of God outside the parameters of time and space, if you can invest in that cognitive leap, it's not at all farfetched. It is a reason why so many of us perceive Jesus as only man, and others perceive him as God; for whatever Jesus was and is, may be a function of our perception, consistent with the weirdness of quantum mechanics. Both perceptions are accurate. I told you this would be unbelievable.

To give us the eternal survival Jesus demanded of Father, God invested himself into every living soul. Because he was God living in eternity, beyond the confines of time and space, the advent of himself as the Holy Spirit into the living beings of creation was not for just those souls living in the Common Era after the life of Jesus. It was for all souls of all time. It was the same Holy Spirit who came to reside in King David as in Mother Teresa. The Holy Spirit is the resurrected God within us.

If you would like to play with concepts of physics, remember my piece in which I shared how physicists now are challenging the concept long held that time and space are a continuum. The theory has been that there is no break in time or space between any two points within it. Now evidence is mounting that time and space are particulate, and these tiniest particles actually flow around regions of tremendous gravity, such as black holes. I pondered that if time-space particles flow, what is it within which they flow? And one answer I offered was the possibility they flowed within eternity.

So maybe you will enjoy playing the mind game with me that before Jesus, time and space were indeed continuous, surrounded by but not invested with God-eternity. Because of Jesus the time-space continuum became particulate and God-eternity invested all of the time-space creation. He is around and within everything that exists. Now when we study time and space, they seem both like continuum and like flowing particles because what they are depends upon our perception. Both concepts are accurate.

The answer to why didn't God just save us? He did, and for only one reason. He loved us.

Why did Jesus have to die? He died because his convictions ran him into trouble with the governing riff-raff of his time, and given the chance to run or die, he chose to die for the sake of others. Then he confronted Father, and again he would have chosen to die rather than to abandon his beloved humans.

This is my Jesus. His behavior is what it means to be Christ.

139. JESUS PAST AND FUTURE

Stan the Rev wrote.

Even after the resurrection, up until the day of Pentecost when the Holy Spirit came upon the disciples and gave them new understanding, they thought Jesus was going to set up a heavenly kingdom on earth. Time and time again when asked, Jesus told people that his kingdom was not a physical one. His kingdom was "within." Revelation states that at the end of time both the old heaven and the old earth will be no more. How does that fit into your theological thought process?

As for Jesus not being bound by the confines of time, his soul isn't but the historical person Jesus of Nazareth was. Your soul and my soul are not bound by linear space and time, but our physical selves are. The writer of the gospel of John was careful not to name Jesus but rather stated that, *In the beginning the Word was with God and was God* .... St. Paul believed that Christ (notice I use the word Christ, not Jesus) was present in the Old Testament. If you read Old Testament scriptures carefully you will notice such things as, *the angel of the Lord God.* Mom identified those phrases as the presence of Christ with Abraham and Moses. The act of Jesus' ministry, crucifixion and resurrection fulfilled the covenant God made to the chosen people of Israel. They are saved too. And it began a new covenant of salvation for the rest of the world. So you are right that Jesus' act does extend in all directions of time as well as space.

I consider evil as the result of our delusion that we are individuals separate from each other and separate from Hashem(God). If we believe that all life is complete in Hashem, then evil has no power. From my point of view evil is an illness. Sin is symptomatic of the illness, and Hashem's plan of salvation is to heal those who are sick with evil. In the light of Hashem's love, evil melts away and ceases to exist.

140. EXTRAPOLATION

This short little piece may scare the bejesus out of some of you.

If it is true that we are one, then there are some scary experiences awaiting each and every one of us.

If, as is implied by Einstein's theory of special relativity, it is true that every moment is eternal, then there is plenty of room for every physical being to house every soul, and so when I look at another person I can see within him or her the Holy Spirit as well as the soul of every living creature who ever has existed or will exist, including myself.

When mystics meditate and astral project, when they leave their bodies and later return, sometimes they encounter another spirit trying to enter their body, or so it seems to them. And they struggle with this spirit until they themselves enter. Think about the possibility that these astral travelers return to a slightly erroneous point in the eternal character of that physical body, and so they struggle with the spirit that rightly belongs there. And the spirit that rightfully belongs there thinks that it has been invaded by a demon. But the struggle ends with the spirits finding their correct places and all is well.

I remember as a boy looking into the mirror and asking myself, *How do I know that the spirit inhabiting this body is the same spirit that inhabited it yesterday.* Ha!

Many of the very anxious among you will be fearful of the experience you must endure of being the small child thrown into boiling water, and you will say to yourself that you do not have the psychological make up to endure it. My answer to you is that, at that moment, your psychological make up will be as able as the psychological make up of the child who was boiled in this particular event of the world.

So this is instant karma. We all get the same. Pretty scary! Or maybe we experience all of this only if we, ourselves, choose to be the Christ. Was this the ultimate choice that Jesus made? Was this his gift to us all? "For even as you did it for the least of my brothers, you did it for me." It doesn't matter whether you believe it. Christ was, is and ever will be in each and every one of us. Believe it or not.

When I have said to enthusiasts of Gibson's *The Passion of Christ* that I think of the movie as little more than a horror flick, they frequently answer by saying it was meaningful to them because it showed how much he gave us. I think this answer is shallow, a meager concept at best. What if, at the moment of crisis, Christ is willing to become the conscious awareness of any one of us? What if he is willing instead of you to be the child thrown into boiling water, the baby shot in the face, the tortured prisoner, the beheaded hostage? What if Christ is the spiritual entity who frees us from our own karma? People have no fucking idea about the greatness of Christ's gift.

Could this be the hope of the world? When it is my turn to be Hitler, a man in need of spiritual rehabilitation, instead of murdering twelve million souls, maybe through tremendous effort of Christ within me and others, I will be able to kill only eleven million. And the Hitler after me will kill only ten million.

And right now, writing this book, maybe I can convince you that if you force yourself to do the right thing, despite the passions of your makeup, despite the genetics and environment that shaped you, maybe I can make a difference. Maybe right now, each of us by trying that little extra bit harder to love everyone as if they were ourselves, because they are, the world will change. Maybe this is the hope of God.

By the way, Stan the Rev asked me how the phrase in Revelation fits my theology. *At the end of time both the old heaven and the old earth will be no more.* And I already have answered that question. God looked at his creation from beginning to end and found it unsatisfactory. And through the experience of the Christ, he changed the heaven and the earth. It has been done already.

141. AGNOS HAS THE LAST WORD

I began, "Well my friend, have we learned anything from the experience of writing this book?"

Agnos answered, "There are a lot of maybes in this book, and we've learned that you are a boob, but personally I know that you will answer to other names."

"You may call me a dreamer."

"But you're not the only one."

"I hope one day you'll join us."

"Ha! So the world will be as one?" Agnos smiled almost to the point of laughing.

"Really," I asked, "What can we take away from this book?"

"Number one, a person can think and believe whatever they frickin' want, and it won't change the structure of the cosmos."

"So you agree that God will play fairly with his creation."

"If there is a God, and we don't know for sure that there is, then we also don't know whether this God is benevolent, wicked or indifferent."

"You're a tough one to crack, Agnos."

"Yes, well it's a matter of faith, isn't it? Not knowledge. And that means a faithful person satisfies an important prerequisite. All true spirituality begins with the admission that we don't know. If a person touts his beliefs without first admitting that in the end analysis we don't really know, then there is no honesty in him."

"True spirituality begins with agnosticism."

"Yes."

"But we can believe what we want."

"And the cosmos won't change regardless of what that is."

"We also know that we are here, and evidence points toward that being an extraordinary event. The odds are against it happening by accident alone."

"Through the ages humankind hasn't understood how it all happened, so it ascribed responsibility for this mystery to an unseen, unknowable entity and called it God."

"Do you believe in God?"

"By this definition almost everyone believes in God."

"Not everyone."

"Right. We can divide people into those who believe in at least a vaguely defined creator and those who don't. We can call that second group the accidentalists. And then there are the agnostics, but we all are agnostic whether we admit it or not. Admitting you're agnostic is quite comfortable and honest."

"Yes, but for many of us it is unsatisfying, so we reach for answers."

"Not me," Agnos countered. "At least it wasn't me before I met you. You roped me into this, remember. You've been searching for answers that cannot be answered because we, as participants within the universe, are precluded by logic from being able to reach by reason, an understanding of how forces outside the universe might have created us."

"Yes. So science will get us gradually closer to a constantly receding and unreachable knowledge, but it never will answer the ultimate question of why."

"Science is reliable."

"But incomplete. We can reach that knowledge only if we communicate with the creator."

"And we all know how well that has worked in the history of the world. We're fighting a disastrous war right now because of such a way of thinking. People talking with God are completely unreliable. They make God say whatever they want God to say. They can be a scourge."

"Hold on pardner. You're including me in that bunch."

"You're not a jerk."

"No. I'm a boob."

"Right."

"People choose the God they want."

"That's my point."

"So we have a variety of visions of God."

"Yes, and people fight each other about it."

"That's the scourge. So that is the value of choosing a benevolent God, one who chooses peace instead."

Agnos shook his head. "You take the cake; you know that. First you say God created you, and then you say that you choose which God will be your God. This is circular reasoning of grandiose proportion."

"Yes, Agnos. I'm agnostic about the creator of the world, but I'm firmly a believer in the benevolence of God. I choose a benevolent God. There is no other way for me."

"God may actually be a devil."

"And if he is I will defy him."

"Then your ass is in a sling."

"My friend Jesus was crucified for this."

"And you would choose that fate?"

"If I have courage enough."

He shook his head. "You need honesty. If you have enough honesty you will realize that if there is a God, there is nothing that proves he is either good or evil. He simply is who he is." Agnos paused, then he asked, "Earlier you wrote that a heretic sees himself as God's fist shaking at the here and now."

"Yes."

"That's arrogant."

"Admitted. It's arrogance of necessity, grown out of a recognition that we need to change."

"Only if we want the world to change."

"I want the world to change."

"That's ambitious."

"We must be the change we want to see in the world."

"Now you're pulling out the Gandhi."

"Stan the Rev always has told me adamantly that it matters to God what we believe, and until recently that never made a whole lot of sense to me. Finally it dawned on me. If we believe there is an eternity and each of us is part of it, and if we believe this physical world is not the whole of our existence, then we will not feel the urgent need to take from others in order to give to ourselves. We will be patient for luxury. The wealthy will be more willing to give to the poor."

"And the poor will be more willing to give to the rich."

"What?"

"Yes, because if spiritually we are each other as you have said, then some poor bastards, looking ahead at their stint as Donald Trump, will think *what if I could be just a little bit richer.*"

"You think you've got us pegged, don't you?"

"I don't know."

"Agnos!"

"Really, I don't know. Half the time I'm just talking, spouting off. Yes the other half of the time I'm trying to make sense out of what you say, but that's not such an easy thing."

"Agnos, let me ask you this. Is there a world of spirits?"

"Look at me please. Next question."

"Is there such a thing as reincarnation?"

"If there is reincarnation, then I think turtles would be happy to end up in a soup, because otherwise they'd have to live a long, boring, hundred year life. The destination of soup makes that go by faster. It's a good thing. They can move on to something else, hopefully more entertaining."

"What about war. Is there such a thing as a just war?"

"This is a crazy question, isn't it? Because all wars cause people pain and suffering. They bereave the world, and if there is a God who lives in each of us you say there is, then all wars cause God pain. This is an argument not so much for God's own benevolence as for God's desire that we be benevolent toward each other. It makes sense that he would want to stop being hurt. The way to answer this question then, is that given the personality of humanity as a whole, war is inevitable, and all the rules that people try to apply to it are only ways of assuaging their conscience while they thumb their noses indifferently at God's suffering."

"So we come back to that very first realization. If we are to have peace, then we must evolve."

"The justification, at least for a defensive war, is that we must not allow bullies to determine our evolutionary destiny."

Agnos suddenly became serious. "Listen. I have some sobering news for you. If your quantum trinity theology is true, then there never will be peace on earth. If God saw his creation from beginning to end and found it unsatisfactory, needing to be changed, then we're not going to evolve much between now and the end of time."

"Except that was the old earth, and in the new earth we have the Holy Spirit."

"So you now say that people actually do in fact have free will? Do you really think that people can break free of their chains to environment and genetics, and change? That's not consistent with science so far."

"We can try."

"I think you're absolutely frickin' lunatic nuts."

"But you only think I'm nuts. You don't really know that."

"Of course not, I'm Agnos. It's only that I believe deep down inside me that you are seriously crazy."

After a pause I said, "You do not."

He said, "If you ever do get your chance to play the role of Hitler, there's one thing maybe you shouldn't change. He had that nifty hand signal that changed forever the way conscientious people wave to each other. You may want to keep that."

I stared at him incredulously.

"Look, I'll tell you what you and others can do," he said. "You can smile. You can laugh. You can take life less seriously, and most of all you can help others to do the same thing. That's what this book is about; it's entertainment, and I know there are parts of it where you make points you think are profound, and you want to change the world and all of that. Some people will think, *Ooh*, and *Ah*, and *I never thought of that before.* And these same people will not change." Agnos smiled, "This is an entertaining book, Mr. T-the-splogger-boob-dreamer. Congratulations.

"There is one more thing though," he added, "and this needs to be said. If one imagines an alternative reality, then the imagining ought not to injure or to alienate anyone."

142. DAMN! I SHOULD HAVE

The man was standing outside of Starbucks at 5:30 in the morning, wearing an appearance of both chronic and acute worry. "Sir, could you give me a little change?" He stumbled over the words. "Just ten or fifteen cents."

I gave him a dollar, and as I drove away I thought about how this man seemed different than other beggars. I wished I had given him five.

Father said, "Actually I was quite pleased that you gave me the one dollar."

Damn! I should have given him twenty.

143. YOUR LIFE CHANGED MINE
Before I met you I was out of control.
Oh no! Yes, out of control.
Those years without you, oh they took their toll.
Oh no! Yes, they took their toll on me.

But then I found you, and your life changed mine.
Oh no! Yes, your life changed mine.
You hooked me like a fish upon a line.
Oh no! Yes, on a line to you.

I struggled and I fought, but it was no use.
Oh no! Yes, it wasn't any use.
I finally had to make a lover's truce.
Oh no! Yes, a lover's truce with you.

And now my life has gotten under control.
Oh no! Yes, it's under control.
I want you madly, and I give you my soul.
Oh no! Yes, I give my soul to you.

NINETEEN

Encore

144. WE'RE NOT DONE YET

Agnos commented, "We're not done yet; are we."

"No," I answered. "I think we'll never be done. Now you and I are wondering about the supposed finding of Jesus' tomb."

During the last week of February and the first days of March, 2007, the country conversed on the documentary drama by film maker Simcha Jacobovici about the finding 27 years earlier of a curious burial site. In Talpiyot, a suburb of Jerusalem, a construction crew was excavating in preparation for a new building, and the earth collapsed into a tomb wherein were found ten stone, 2000 year old ossuaries, small caskets for bones.

It is not clear to me why it took twenty years for experts to decipher the names on the caskets, but that's the case. My secret operatives have told me that the first deciphering led to the names Corky Ben Sanford, Mindy, Mindy Max, Mikhail, Mork, and Castro Ben Corky. Archeologists regarded these as unlikely names during the time of Roman occupied Judea, so they tried again. Somebody figured out that *ben* was actually *bar* and meant *son of.* So Corky was son of Sanford, and Castro was son of Corky. Then they brushed away a bit more dirt and changed their decoder rings, and after awhile they arrived at the names Jesua son of Joseph, Maria, Mariamne Mara (Mara meaning master), Matthew, Jose and Judah son of Jesua.

People, who were interested in making a big publicity splash and maybe in jolting the foundations of Christianity, claimed this was possibly the burial site of Jesus and his family. Hoopla ensued. It was entertaining.

There were bodily remains, bones, within the caskets, even Jesua's, and so this finding might challenge the theological position of Catholic and evangelical Christians who believe Jesus arose bodily from death. The rank and file weren't perturbed by this because already they were thinking it was Jesus' spirit that arose, and they might point out that when Mary Magdalene first met the risen Jesus, she didn't recognize him until he spoke to her. Up to that moment she thought he was the gardener. Well, in fact he might have been, and Jesus' spirit inhabited his body.

But leaders of the church are not supposed to go there. In the Apostle's Creed, Christians profess to believe in "the resurrection of the body." So leaders of the church need to adhere to this scientifically improbable event.

Unwittingly, Jacobovici now has provided an alternative, intermediate theology. Jesus' body might have arisen from the dead, only without his bones. Heaven knows he was able to walk on water, so as a master of bodily levitation Jesus really didn't need his bones to support himself. Mary Magdalene and later witnesses of his resurrection probably saw his boneless body hovering in the air with his feet just millimeters off the ground. When he moved from place to place he swung his legs to make it look like he was walking, but he really didn't need to, and to the close observer his feet sort of swung over the ground like a character in an inexpensive animated movie.

At that first meeting, Mary didn't recognize Jesus because without his bones, his face was misshapen. Mary was too polite to point or laugh or criticize, and so with social grace she said, "Oh I didn't recognize you at first. I thought you were the gardener."

Then she became obsessed with the gummi-like Jesus and started bending his arms into funny, unnatural positions. Jesus said, "Mary, stop doing that."

She responded, "This is weird. You don't have any bones."

Jesus answered, "Stop that now. I've not yet ascended to the Father, and you're going to make it hard for me to look my best. This is an important interview coming up, and I would think you'd want me to make a good impression."

Then Mary started laughing, and with pure joy she ran to tell the disciples. Between giggles she announced, "Wait until you see this. You're never going to believe it." But of course they did, and people have been twisting and turning Jesus ever since.

Printed in the United States
101954LV00002B/52/A

9 781596 635616